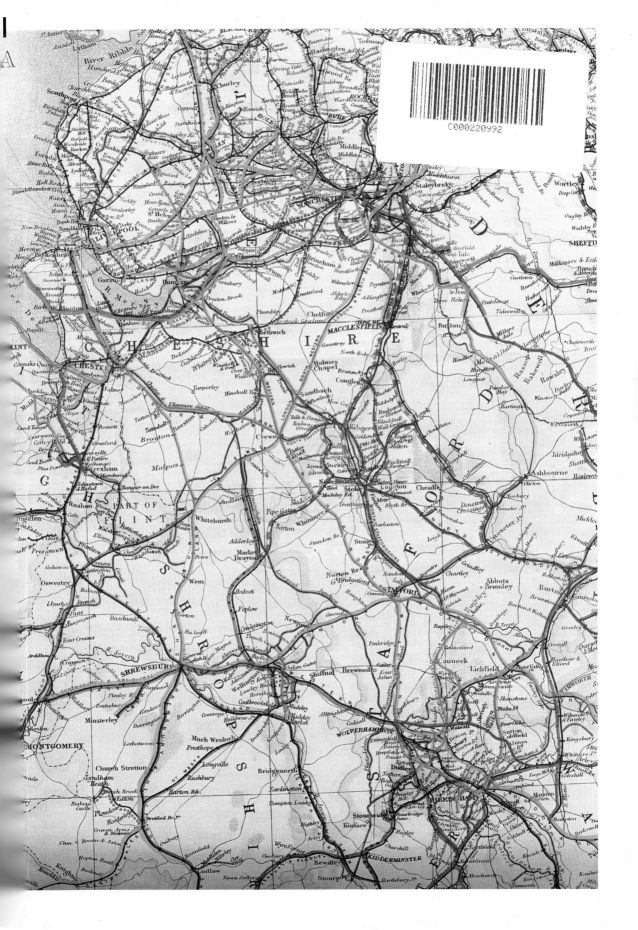

THE RAILWAYS OF WALES
circa 1900

Front and rear endpapers from
1899 Railway Map of Britain.
(*Courtesy Paul Gooderham*)

THE RAILWAYS OF WALES

circa 1900

GWYN BRIWNANT JONES

and

DENIS DUNSTONE

On the 31 December 1899, the last 'down' train of the nineteenth century from London to west Wales was recorded at Llanelli. The locomotive was a 2-4-0 of the '3232' Class.

Llanelli Library

First impression—2000

ISBN 1 85902 868 3

© Gwyn Briwnant Jones & Denis Dunstone

Gwyn Briwnant Jones & Denis Dunstone have asserted their right under the Copyright, Designs
and Patents Act, 1988, to be identified as Authors of this Work.

Printed in Wales by
Gomer Press, Llandysul, Ceredigion

CONTENTS

The overwhelming might of industry in the Ebbw valley where man-made slag-heaps rivalled the mountains.
WIMM/GW Coll.

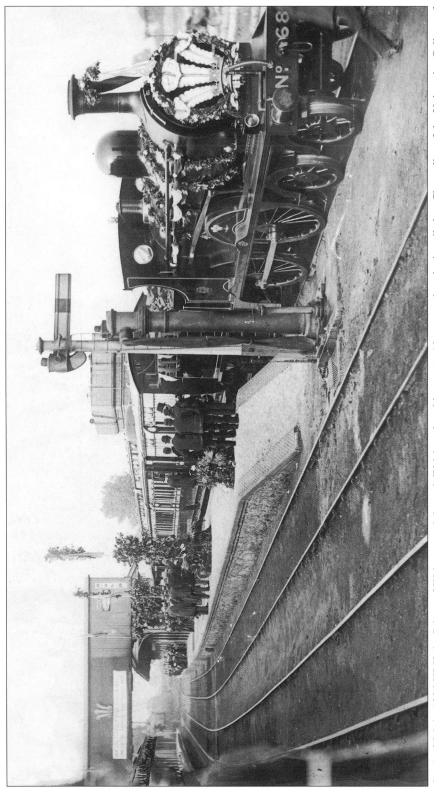

On the 25 July 1896 HRH the Prince of Wales passed through Welshpool on his way to Aberystwyth to be installed as Chancellor of the University College of Wales. The banner spanning the Cambrian tracks bears the message 'Our lost Llewelyn seems to come again for love of learning to his ancient home'. The GWR Royal Train in which he travelled contained at least two of the newly-constructed royal carriages destined for Queen Victoria's Diamond Jubilee train.

Courtesy Tudor Watkins

FOREWORD

The advent of a new millennium has acted as the stimulus for the publication of numerous books of a retrospective nature. It is salutary to remember that the history of railways is on a vastly shorter time-scale of barely two centuries, but there have nevertheless also been a number of books examining the changes in various railways in Britain through a then-and-now photographic approach. For those who search for former railway routes and structures such publications are admirable, but they convey little of the countless other changes which have taken place in the operation, infrastructure and evolution of the British railway system.

There is, in fact, a great dearth of such comparative accounts and the present authors have seized the opportunity presented by the turn of the century to examine a comprehensive range of aspects of railway operations and to place them in a unified context.

They have elected to study aspects of railways in Wales in 1899/1900 and have adopted an objective approach, unblinkered by the romance associated with the steam locomotive, to demonstrate both the positive and negative changes over the last century. Their choice of Wales is an apposite one, containing as it does rural and urban areas, commuter and tourist traffic, large-scale industrial and small-scale agricultural traffic, small marginally profitable and large wealthy railways. The choice also reflects the authors' extensive and detailed knowledge of, and life-long interest in, the railways of Wales. This rapport with their subject enables them to identify the interrelationship between changes in the railways and the relevant industrial, economic and social factors pertaining at the time.

This comprehensive approach considers such aspects as collaboration and competition between companies, changes in motive power, and the frequency and nature of passenger and freight services, including an illuminating examination of passenger travel between north and south Wales, a perennial problem which still exercises much thought today.

Of particular interest are the authors' comparative examination and analysis of some of the economic and financial aspects of freight and passenger operations in Wales. Such a quantitative consideration, albeit with data of limited availability in some instances, is of inestimable value in helping to dispel some of the myths and misconceptions relating to railway operations a century ago.

Although the authors have focussed on the years around the turn of the twentieth century, they have been careful to identify any anomalies in using data from such individual years and to place their conclusions in the relevant overall context.

The book represents a salient contribution to the history of railways in Wales and should encourage any future discussions on railway operations to take place on a more informed and accurate basis.

Stuart Owen-Jones

A characteristic period scene on the Mumbles Railway around 1900. The leading carriage of the train bears what appears to be a large smoke and sparks deflector. *PRO: RAIL 1014/53/42*

The colourful railway and a mountain of slate. A Blaenau Ffestiniog to Bala train at Manod, hauled by 0-4-2T No. 5811; August 1955. *J.B. Snell*

PREFACE

This book does not set out to be a detailed history of the Welsh railways over the past 100 years; its aim is to provide a description of the way they were at the turn of the century in 1899/1900. Inevitably, this leads to the pointing of some comparisons with today, and the intervening century is by no means ignored, particularly in the illustrations. However, the principal focus is the turn of the twentieth century. Examples are given of how the railways were operated and what they were like, both to see and to experience. This examination covers both freight trains and the more familiar passenger trains, together with wider aspects of railway operations and their relations with society. Accordingly, it includes some material which is closer to social and economic history than to the nuts and bolts of trains. It is inspired by the examination of the impact of the railways on social and economic life initiated by the late Professor Jack Simmons in *Victorian Railways* and in *The Railway in Town and Country* and pursues some of the topics covered there as they applied to Wales. Following the same lead, it looks at the Welsh railways as part of the economy, and examines their profitability, in comparison with one another and with those English companies which also operated in Wales. In the process, comparisons are made with the railways of today.

It is suggested that the dangers inherent in considering only a short period of time can be avoided if the historical context is kept in mind. Focussing on events which occurred at the turn of the twentieth century and identifying their part in the development of railway history may provide fresh illumination. Hopefully, evidence also emerges that is of relevance to a wider area of Britain.

In 1900 Wales had an almost unrivalled variety of railways. Not only variety of ownership, but of propulsion, gauge and function, as well as fast main lines, sleepy branches and bustling mineral lines. Along the north and west coasts the railway dodged the sea, and through the centre it struggled with contours, over Talerddig and Torpantau, under the Sugar Loaf and Blaenrhondda. There were operating extremes like the Pwllyrhebog branch in the Rhondda at a gradient of 1:13 and the Irish Mail route to Holyhead, the constant procession of trains through Pontypridd and the lonely ascent to the top of Snowdon, the summit at Waunavon at over 1,400 ft and the tunnel under the Severn.

The north end of the Blaenrhondda tunnel, nearly 2 miles long and completed in 1890. Photographed in 1960.

G.H. Platt

The engine shed at the top of the Pwllyrhebog incline on 6 June 1948. A severe incline was necessary to reach the Rhondda valley, partly visible in the right distance.

B. Roberts/courtesy J.A. Peden

The Severn tunnel carries the railway deeper than anywhere else in Britain but Wales has held other records. The first steam engine to run on rails was at Penydarren near Merthyr Tydfil in 1802. The first passenger trains in the world ran in 1807 on the Swansea & Mumbles. The first bogie carriages in Britain ran on the Ffestiniog. The last steam engines on British Rail were on the Vale of Rheidol and the last British Rail horse-drawn train was on the Nantlle. The highest tunnel in Britain was at Torpantau, and the Irish Mail was the first named train in the world. Swansea had more terminal stations than any other British city outside London, and on Anglesey there is still the longest station name in the world. Finally, and perhaps the most significant fact in 2000, it was in Wales on the Talyllyn that the world's enthusiasm for preserving steam railways was born.

In one sense the year 1900 is a numerical incident of no particular significance. However, it happened to be near the peak of Welsh railway activity, with coal production near its zenith, and railway route mileage almost at its maximum. It was a time when all trains were, for the lovers of such things, colourful and characterful, ornate and idiosyncratic. Major developments in locomotive technology and passenger comfort were being introduced, and it was an exciting time. The challenges to be faced from electric trams and motor buses were localised, and the private car was merely an expensive play-thing of the wealthy. Two world wars and the immense demands they were to place upon the railway, not least in Wales, were beyond contemplation. Queen Victoria reigned and the British Empire would seemingly go on forever.

The railway in the sublime Welsh landscape. *En route* for Talerddig, No. 75033 with the last 'up' Cambrian Coast Express on 4 March 1966.

J.B. Snell

A picturesque juxtaposition of road, railway and canal at Talybont-on-Usk with No. 9618 and a short train making for Torpantau; 1 September 1963.

B.J. Ashworth

A poster from 1948 celebrating one hundred years of the world's first named train, the Irish Mail.

WIMM

CHAPTER 1

ECONOMIC AND SOCIAL BACKGROUND

The years 1899 and 1900 are not immediately associated with any great or important events. The Boer War was being fought, Queen Victoria was near the end of her reign and Lord Salisbury was Prime Minister. In 1900 the first Labour Member of Parliament appeared on the scene, Keir Hardie, MP for Merthyr Tydfil. In that year too, the first wireless transmission across the Atlantic was made. At a political level, it was a period when relations with Germany were continuing to deteriorate and, economically, British business enterprise and wealth creation were beginning to show signs of slowing down.

In attempting to picture the railways in Wales at that time it is necessary not only to conjure up images and describe relevant events that happened, but it is also helpful to remember what was not known and did not exist but which is now taken for granted. The effect on human lifestyles of air travel, the telephone, wireless, cars and computers was still to be experienced. The railway set the pace of communication, whether by post or in person. Even the telegraph followed the path of the railway. The railway was also a dominant activity in the economy, on the stock market, as employer, as manufacturer and as exporter. Distribution in an increasingly sophisticated consumer market was based on the railway, with only local delivery by horse and cart (though even these were often owned by the railway companies). The steam engine, in particular, impressed and stirred the imagination,

and the railways were an inspiration to artists, architects and writers.

Except for a few, the hours of work were long and travel beyond the immediate vicinity was unusual. The pace of life at the time was slower, especially on Sundays, and perhaps this contributed to the peak attendance at places of Christian worship. By the middle of the nineteenth century there was seating capacity in Welsh churches and chapels for 75% of the entire population of Wales, and 74% of the population of Monmouthshire were said to be regular attenders. In 1906 as many as 549,000 people, a quarter of the total population, were said to be chapel members. The railway reflected this: no freight trains operated on Sundays; the Taff Vale Railway provided a Bible at every station and its 1856 rule book linked regular attendance at Sunday worship with prospects for promotion. Society was probably more law-abiding than at any time within 100 years before or after. Conscience was no doubt influenced by the fear of losing a job or, more importantly, status, and work on the railway carried both prestige and stability. At the turn of the century, although the hours were long, work on the railway was respected as being important and of social significance. Every station had its hierarchy of stationmaster, inspectors, superintendants, booking-clerks, porters and signalmen. There was, at all levels, a sense of pride in providing the service.

Railway, colliery winding gear and houses – the components of the archetypal south Wales valley scene at the height of coal production. Tonypandy & Trealaw station in the Rhondda valley early in the twentieth century.

Lens of Sutton

Typical coal tip at Hirwaun in July 1962.   *GBJ*

However, as will be demonstrated later, the period witnessed signs of change on the railways of Britain and inevitably also on those in Wales. In 1900 the first electric tram arrived in Cardiff and, in spite of major technical developments, a decline in the profitability and efficiency of the railways was continuing. Handsome locomotives were hauling faster and more comfortable trains, but average ticket prices were falling, freight rates were fixed by government, and industrial relations were deteriorating. Coal movement, the biggest single justification for the Welsh railways, was near a peak, and the first 'toot' of the motor horn could be heard.

Any attempt to describe the railways of Wales as they were 100 years ago leads to a comparison in the mind of the reader with the

Coal production alongside the former Cardiff Railway at Nantgarw in 1978.   *GBJ*

Primitive winding-gear at the Minera lead mine, *ca.* 1905. *Clwyd Record Office*

concentrated railway network in the world. Wales has long been characterised by its mineral wealth; gold, lead, slate, iron and coal have been produced for centuries. But only during the last 100 years did these activities reach such enormous proportions, peaking in the case of coal in 1913 at 57 million tons, with one third of world traded coal being shipped from Welsh ports.

Now, at the close of the twentieth century, the extractive industries of north and south Wales have virtually ceased to exist. They have been replaced by modern manufacturing industries, by service industries and by tourism. At the same time the nature of transport has itself seen a massive shift towards the road. At the end of the eighteenth century, the builders of the new roads had hoped to be able to provide the links to the canals, but their turn did not come until the end of the nineteenth century when the arrival of the internal combustion engine and the pneumatic tyre enabled the inherent flexibility of the road to become a practical alternative to the railway.

way they are now. Since transport is the life-blood of the economy and directly reflects the industrial, agricultural and social activities around it, the mind is instantly drawn towards a comparison of Wales itself, at the one time at the peak of its industrialisation, and at the other in the post-industrial age. At the peak, the railway was the principal means of transport for both freight and people. By the end of the nineteenth century, south Wales had acquired what was probably the most densely

The GWR feeder bus service, which also carried parcels and mailbags to the railway at Abergavenny, seen at Crickhowell at about the time of the First World War. *M. Scott Archer Collection*

The ubiquitous motor car amidst the sand-dunes of Cardigan Bay, at Dyffryn-on-Sea, August 1938.

WIMM/GW Coll.

The effect of these changes on the railway system has been profound. Gone are the massive movements of coal to the ports and to England, and the pounding of coal trains down and across the valleys; gone too are the little slate trains in the north. The labouring oil, chemical and iron-ore trains alone remain as a reminder of the massive weight of freight once carried by rail. The changes in general transportation have been no less striking; gone is the local goods train serving small communities throughout the country, and the charming but infrequent branch line passenger train. The lorry, the bus and then later the private car have taken their place. Over longer distances the railway is still able to serve tourists, business and administrators. Over short distances the passenger train survives only where there are commuters. As a freight system, only block trains of raw materials and mass-produced goods compete with the road, but the railway continues to provide what was the first stimulus to trunk railway construction in Wales, namely two routes to Ireland for both passengers and goods.

Farming, the one economic activity which has somehow survived the changes of the twentieth century, demonstrates the advantage

A rare instance of a rail-served farm, at Brynglas on the Talyllyn Railway in April 1952.

Geoff Charles/NLW

of the road, which conveniently reaches right up to the farm gate. At its peak, the railway offered certain opportunities to the farming community; movement of sheep and stock on the hoof, faster movement of packed farm produce and the delivery of fresh milk to the big cities, but even then most farmers relied upon the horse and cart for more local transport, sometimes to the railway but mainly to market. D. Parry Jones in his book *Welsh Country Up-bringing* describes life on a Carmarthenshire farm, 14 miles north of Carmarthen in the Teifi valley, at the turn of the century. In 1900, the journey once a week to Carmarthen market, with two horses to haul the loaded *gambo* (a narrow, two-wheeled cart), started in the dark shortly after two in the morning. Once on the turnpike, one of the horses was sent back. The whole exercise took most of the day. Market-day and the chapel on Sunday were the social centres of an isolated and tough existence. The journey to market has changed qualitatively, but existence on a remote Welsh farm has been facilitated not hindered by developments. Ironically, although Parry Jones does not admit it, he was one of the many Welsh farmers who, at that time, lived within five miles of a railway station (probably Henllan on the Newcastle Emlyn branch), but the only occasion he refers to the railway is when he makes the journey to college at Lampeter. By 1999 the railway has become a complete irrelevance to farmers. In 1900 there were more than 65,000 farms in Wales and although today there are less than half as many as there were, the area under some kind of cultivation or rough grazing has increased from about 3 million acres to over 3.5 million. Over half the farms are still engaged in keeping cattle and sheep, and the proportion of acreage under grass has risen. But now every small farm is within reach of the bulk milk truck and most have at least one four-wheel drive vehicle.

Day and night, the milk lorry now reaches the remotest farms, here on the coast of Cardigan Bay in July 1999.
Shelagh Collingwood

In 1900 the greatest concentrations of people lived along the Bristol Channel and in the terraced houses of the mining and quarrying areas; the men were engaged in mainly manual work while their wives kept house. Across the rest of the country they lived on farms or in small towns and villages. Travel from the area of the home was limited, whether they were town dwellers or countrymen. The railway existed primarily to carry minerals and general goods traffic.

A hundred years later, travel has become common-place as living standards have risen and the nature of work has changed. As will be demonstrated in a later chapter, although the mileage of the railway has been reduced to something less than 40%, the volume of passenger traffic has been broadly sustained.

Travel has become a widespread social habit and, while rail travel has lost market share, it has managed to keep a place in the more densely populated areas and is gradually increasing.

A good illustration of how the peace of once tranquil valleys was disturbed in the quest for minerals, in this case at Blaengarw around 1900.
John Ryan Coll./ courtesy J.A. Peden

Industry's invasion of the valleys created stark contrasts between the domesticity of the lower slopes and the open splendour of the mountain tops; this example showing the Rhondda & Swansea Bay main line at Blaengwynfi was photographed from the GWR's Abergwynfi branch on 2 July 1960.
G.H. Platt

The contrast between Wales in 1900 and in 2000 seems great enough, but the greatest structural change in the history of Wales had occurred in the one hundred years immediately before 1900. During that time coal-mining and iron production stimulated a nearly four-fold increase in population. At the time of the 1801 census the population was 587,000, split 43% north, 57% south. By the time of the 1901 census the total stood at 2,019,000: half were in urban areas and more than one half lived in Glamorgan alone. During the twentieth century the population has continued to grow. In the first decade it grew by 20%, mainly by immigration from southern England into south Wales. In the second decade the population declined, but began to grow again slowly after 1950. It had reached 2.9 million by 1996 but at the cost of a rise in the average age, due to the immigration of English people for retirement and an exodus of the young. This has resulted in Gwynedd, the county with the highest proportion of Welsh speakers, having a population of which 25% are not of Welsh origin. The split of overall population between north and south has become 20% north, 80% south, with a concentration in the coastal conurbations of Swansea, Neath, Cardiff and Newport.

But in the last one hundred years, although the tendency towards urban living has continued and the balance continues to shift from the north to the south, the process has slowed down, such that the main changes during the period have not been so much in numbers as in the nature and quality of life and work. Admittedly, the number engaged in agriculture has halved, but this is from a low base. And although the countryside has lost numbers, the numerical effect is in total slight; most of the small country towns, with a population of 2,000 to 5,000, dotted all over Wales, have managed at least to maintain their numbers, if not increase them. As a result, only Anglesey, of the rural counties, has lost numbers in the last two decades of the twentieth century; others have gained, mainly by immigration from England. Elsewhere population decline has been confined to the old industrial areas, such as Merthyr Tydfil and Neath, and the old iron towns of Monmouthshire.

The biggest changes have been brought about by two things. The first is the decline and virtual disappearance of extractive industries, and their replacement by modern manufacturing. This process has coincided with an explosive growth in the service sector and the employment of women. The second is the advent of the private car which has stemmed the decline in numbers in the more remote areas. The private car, together with the lorry, have simultaneously altered and preserved rural economic activity. Yet, despite the fact that the route mileage of the railway has been more than halved, and large areas of the country are now more than 5 miles from a railway station, the railway still reaches some 80% of the population. This is partly because of the shift to the towns and partly because most of the lines which have been closed served relatively small numbers of people. Many of the 20% who no longer have a railway station nearby have been liberated by the car and enabled to live in relatively remote locations without being isolated.

Abergwynfi station in its mountain setting, terminus of a GWR branch from Bridgend and Tondu. 2 July 1960.
G.H. Platt

The narrow confines of the valley squeezed the railway, houses and industry together at Abertillery, seen in the early days of the twentieth century.
GBJ Coll.

Near the heads of the valleys the railway was often forced out onto the open moorland. Locomotive No. 5652, banked by No. 5660, heads a train for Dowlais out of the Taff Bargoed valley .

Steam & Sail/
courtesy E.S. Owen Jones

Another mountain scene with the railway pushing up the valley, at Cymer Afan, *ca.* 1960.

A. Jarvis

A comparison of employment over the last 100 years reveals the immense shift in economic activity which has occurred. In 1900 a quarter of the entire population were coal-miners. In 1939, after the appalling slump in the early '30s, one third of all Welsh male employment was still in coal-mining, but by 1948 this had dropped to 18%, though it was still the largest single employment category. By 1974 the decline in mining was dramatic and only 6% of the male labour force were still thus employed. By 2000 the number is insignificant. The pattern has been repeated in the case of slate. In the late 1880s as many as 16,000 men

Houses originally erected for miners in the Rhondda Fach bear silent testimony to another age; 10 November 1999.

A. Jarvis

By 1984 greenery was returning to the valleys. The mighty tip overlooking Bargoed had by 2000 been removed.   *John Davies/ courtesy Ian L. Wright*

were employed in the slate quarries of north-west Wales. By the turn of the century this number was in decline, and by 1914 had fallen by half. This was caused by a combination of American competition, labour disputes, and conversion to the use of tiles.

The precarious working conditions of slate quarrymen are well portrayed in this view of part of the Penrhyn Quarry in 1913.

NLW

A smartly turned out *Blanche* with a typical slate truck on the Penrhyn Railway at Port Penrhyn, June 1961.

NLW/G. Charles Coll.

In 1948, the second largest employment sector was 'transport and communications' which accounted for 12% of male employees. By 1996 the cut-back on the railways had led to a drop to only 4%.

The big growth has been in the number of women in employment; their numbers equalled half the male total by 1966 and have since had an important influence upon the numbers employed. Women have contributed significantly to the 50% increase in total employment since 1948. (Like the rest of Britain, Wales has more women than men; at the 1991 census only Creigiau in Glamorgan had more men than women, though Magor in Monmouthshire had exactly equal numbers.)

There has also been a big shift in the nature of work, away from physical outdoor labour, in favour of indoor, mainly sedentary occupations. By 1996 two-thirds of all employees were in 'distribution' (mainly in warehousing, shops and delivery), 'financial services' or 'public administration' (which includes teaching and health).

Closely associated as it is with the changes in work and lifestyle, transport has seen dramatic evolution during the century. Road transport has been the agent of change. In Wales in 1926 there were 26,000 private cars, i.e. one car for every 100 people. This figure had increased tenfold by 1961; it was then doubled in the next 10 years and reached 1 million by 1992. By that time nearly every other adult ran a car.

Crosville and GWR buses meet at the Feathers Hotel, Aberaeron, July 1928.   *WIMM/GW Coll.*

Commercial vehicles have stabilised at about 100,000, having increased from only 13,000 in 1926. Public transport vehicles, mainly buses, developed as a feeder service to the railways in the years following the First World War. Numbers dropped from a 1926 peak of 8,000 to half that number by the end of the 1930s. This was mainly due to an increase in capacity. With this increased capacity came improved performance and buses began to compete with the railway. They then had something of a golden age in the 1940s and '50s when cars were scarce and again reached 8,000 once again in 1988. Since then de-regulation, a more rigorous attitude to operating economics, and the continued popularity and availability of the car have caused another decline to about 5,000.

Crosville Leyland, KA 51, at Llysfaen, late 1930s. By this time bus routes were competing with the railways.

GBJ Coll.

The bus could cut distances in mountainous country, as here by the Western Welsh between the Rhondda and Cynon valleys; 1950s

A. Jarvis

During the First World War the use of road vehicles was immensely stimulated; consequently, at the end of the war, a large number became available for civilian use. The GW took advantage of an ex-army lorry and adapted it for off-road excursions to the top of Plynlimon (*sic*). July 1928.

WIMM/GW Coll.

The growth in civil aviation has had a less obvious effect on the railways, but reflects increasing travel overseas for both holidays and business. The Costa Brava has undermined the holiday market of Cardigan Bay. Even as early as 1938, there were 7,380 aircraft movements in Wales, equivalent to 21 a day. This number was not equalled again until 1964. However, aircraft had been growing in capacity and the 1938 passenger numbers of 26,315 were exceeded as early as 1956. By 1974 a quarter of a million passengers were carried into and out of Wales, over half in charter flights. In 1994 over 1 million took to the air, 80% of whom were on charter flights, and nearly all from Cardiff.

The dramatic growth in foreign tourism set in motion by the airlines in the second half of the twentieth century was preceded by a similar

Prior to the First World War horse-drawn coaches were used for excursions from the railway. This one operated from Prestatyn station.

NLW

In the early 1900s the railway companies promoted Wales as a tourist destination, with even the Neath & Brecon exploiting the image of the lady with the tall hat.
PRO: RAIL1014/2

The LNWR operated its own tourist charabancs in north Wales. An immaculate restoration of this one, a Leyland 'Torpedo' of 1914, was recently completed by the photographer.

Mike Sutcliffe

The first purpose-built tourist railway in Wales was the Snowdon Mountain Railway. Here a train is seen at Llanberis terminus in the period before the First World War.

NLW

The official GW photographer followed the railway into the remotest areas in search of picturesque material for publicity purposes. This is the justification for including this delightful scene at Llan Ffestiniog, devoid as it is of transport content.

WIMM/GW Coll.

growth in inland tourism, prompted by the railways in the first half of the century. The turn of the century marked a big increase in promotional activity by the railways, aimed at stimulating a demand for transport to the north Wales coast, to Cardigan Bay and later to Pembrokeshire. It was, in fact, the railways which had created Llandudno, Rhyl and Colwyn Bay, and they caused a rapid expansion at Aberystwyth, Barmouth, Pwllheli and Tenby. As early as 1889 the LNWR took 21,000 people to Llandudno for the August Bank Holiday in over 50 extra trains. By the time of the Second World War, 40,000 people a week were arriving at

This picture captures the restrained period gentility of Station Road in Colwyn Bay. It appeared on a postcard posted in 1908.

DD Coll.

Llandudno by train. Inland, the LNWR did much to promote the attractions of the spa towns. Llandrindod, Builth, Llanwrtyd and Llangammarch were all on or near the Central Wales Line. By the early years of the twentieth century Llandrindod was receiving over 100,000 holiday-makers a year.

In the second half of the twentieth century the railways remained a key component in Welsh tourism but now in a different role; they had themselves become the object of the journey. Since the start of railway preservation in Wales in 1950, first narrow gauge and later standard gauge railways have become important tourist attractions. The action of a band of railway enthusiasts led by L.T.C. Rolt, who kept the Talyllyn Railway running after the death of its owner, was to lead to railway preservation becoming a leisure business, not only in Wales but eventually all over the world. The 'Great Little Trains of Wales' have been marketed as a major part of the appeal of Wales for holidays.

As early as 1952 the Talyllyn Railway had acquired two locomotives from the Corris Railway; No.3 ex-Corris was photographed at Tywyn Pendre Shed.

R. Wood

A postcard showing a Ffestiniog Railway train at Minffordd, probably during the 1960s, when only 10 years previously such sights were believed to have gone forever. *J. Arthur Dixon*

That this world-wide trend started in Wales is perhaps accidental, but as will be demonstrated later, there was such variety, character and interest in Welsh railways that there was fertile ground in which the idea could flourish. The idea of the railway itself as a tourist attraction, which was initiated by the Snowdon Mountain Railway at the turn of the twentieth century, was picked up again in 1950 and by 2000 has become big business.

Another area of contrast between 1900 and 2000 lies in the cargo handled at Welsh ports.

Oil, chemicals and iron products have failed to compensate for the decline in coal exports, so Cardiff and Barry, the two largest coal exporting ports, which both reached 11 million tons in 1913, have lost nearly all, as have Swansea and Neath, each with 6 million and Newport and Penarth with 4 million. Swansea remained a significant importing and exporting port into the 1970s, partly because of oil refining at Llandarcy. But only two ports have seen growth since then. Milford Haven imported 34 million tons of crude oil in 1994, and Port Talbot was

Holyhead harbour before the arrival of the railway, *ca*. 1830. *DD Coll.*

Holyhead harbour with the LNWR owned SS *Cambria*, *ca*. 1920.
GBJ Coll.

A busy Penarth Dock, probably photographed between the wars.

PRO: RAIL 253/418/8

The rail approach to King's Dock, Swansea, 1962.

G.H. Platt

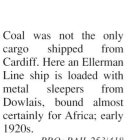

Coal was not the only cargo shipped from Cardiff. Here an Ellerman Line ship is loaded with metal sleepers from Dowlais, bound almost certainly for Africa; early 1920s.

PRO: RAIL 253/418

still importing as much as 11 million tons of iron ore in 1995. Petroleum now accounts for some 65% of all cargo shipped at Welsh ports. There is a residual ferry activity at Swansea, Pembroke Dock, Fishguard and Holyhead in connection with Ireland, but Milford Haven has become the largest port both in tonnage and in ship movements. Holyhead is close behind in ship movements, while Fishguard has only one third of Holyhead's level of activity. In tonnage terms, Cardiff and Newport have dropped to the same level as Holyhead.

Heavy industry has been concentrated in the Swansea valley for more than 300 years, with successively the world's greatest manufacture of copper, tin-plate, nickel and zinc. In 1900 copper, zinc and nickel were near their peak. It happens that tin-plate was suffering a temporary drop at the turn of the century due to the imposition of protective tariffs by the USA, the largest market. This recovered during the Edwardian era and reached a peak of over 800,000 tons a year by 1913. After the Second World War, this heavy industrial activity went into terminal decline and has almost totally disappeared. Consequently, Swansea and the Tawe valley have seen a dramatic environmental clean-up. During the century, oil refining has both entered and left the Swansea area. Only a residual activity remains. At Milford Haven the industry arrived late and continues, though one refinery out of the three built has already been closed. The oil industry is a relatively small employer, and much of the product movement is by pipeline or ship. Accordingly, the demand for inland transport associated with refining is relatively small.

At the turn of the twentieth century north Wales, too, had its concentration of heavy industry. This was based on the coal reserves in the area of Denbighshire and Flintshire to the north-west of Wrexham. Here a complex network of railways brought coal to steelworks at Brymbo and Shotton. The GWR, the LNWR and, from 1901, the Great Central competed to gain access to the coal, though the scale was small compared with the south. There the bottom of every valley was filled with pit-head gear, factory chimneys

The smoke of locomotive and industry merge at Brymbo; 7 April 1960.   *NLW/G. Charles Coll.*

Brymbo, Vron (*sic*) Junction; on the 11 July 1959 it was still a busy place.   *C.A. Appleton/courtesy J.A. Peden*

The site of Vron Junction; by the 16 June 1984 the industrial activity had ceased and the whole environment had deteriorated.   *J.A. Peden*

and railway lines, while the rows of houses rose up the valley sides, and sometimes out onto the top of the mountains. A hundred years later only the terrace houses remain as a reminder of that past frenetic activity.

With such overwhelming changes in industry, employment and transport, there is little wonder that the railways have been transformed in the past 100 years.

CHAPTER 2

THE STRUCTURE OF THE RAILWAY SYSTEM

Most of the railway lines in operation in Wales at the turn of the twentieth century had been constructed in the thirty years between 1840 and 1870. Before that time there were scattered mineral lines, often successors of early tramroads, and there was initially no sense of cohesion; the purpose of each railway was to convey coal, slate or iron to a canal or the sea. Then came the trunk lines along the north and south coasts, stimulated by the demand for a fast route from London to Ireland. Eventually, in the 1850s and '60s, came the cross-country lines and branches, winding their way across most of Wales, and establishing something of a network, though with a strong east-west rather than a north-south bias. A glance at a map of the railways in 1899 (see endpapers) immediately reveals how much of Wales was reached. It also shows an extremely dense and complex network of lines in the valleys of the south, and a great variety of ownership relative to area. Here the railways ran approximately north-south down to the Bristol Channel ports. Every valley had a railway, some such as the Afan, Cynon, Taff, Rhymney and Llwyd had two.

Much of the best of the railway landscape remains; the north coast line clinging to the cliffs at Penmaen-mawr, and running down to the Menai Strait; the Cambrian coast line with its wonderful seascapes and wild skies; the pastoral Tywi valley below Llandovery, and the estuary of the same river between Carmarthen and Cydweli; the picturesque LNWR line to Blaenau Ffestiniog winding its way up the Conwy valley. These are compensation for the loss of lines such as the dramatic climb up the Clydach gorge from Abergavenny to Brynmawr. Sadly, it is no longer possible to follow the upper Wye on the Mid Wales or cross the Brecon Beacons on the Brecon & Merthyr.

The picturesque setting of Barmouth with a 'down' train entering the tunnel behind a '4575' Class locomotive; June 1960. *J.B. Snell*

A GWR publicity photograph showing the Vale of Rheidol Railway winding its way up the picturesque valley; July 1928.   *WIMM/GW Coll.*

An unidentified 'Manor' Class 4-6-0 leaves Frongoch tunnel on the Dyfi estuary with a Birmingham to Pwllheli train; August 1964.   *J.B. Snell*

The physical grandeur of the Port Talbot line to Maesteg and the Rhondda & Swansea Bay line through the Blaenrhondda tunnel to Treherbert can now only be imagined by the walker or the motorist. A sad slip in timing lost us the Mumbles tram, and the construction of a reservoir precipitated the premature closing of perhaps Wales' most beautiful railway of all, the line from Bala to Ffestiniog. But it is cause for celebration that parts at least of the Dee valley can be enjoyed on preserved railways and the narrow gauge can still take us to the top of Snowdon, to Blaenau Ffestiniog, and to Devil's Bridge.

As elsewhere, the motor car and the lorry have had a devastating effect on what was, a hundred years ago, the most important means of transport, and indeed, apart from the horse, the only means available for general visiting, holidays and business, and for the carriage of all kinds of merchandise. The movement of coal to England and to the south Wales ports has virtually ceased, as has the coal traffic in the north around Wrexham and the slate traffic to Porthmadog and Caernarfon. Gone too are the general goods trains, calling at nearly every station to shunt waggons in the yard. The two accompanying maps illustrate how the railway has been cut back so that it no longer reaches so many points across the country. The black areas are those beyond 5 miles from a railway station. The 1999 map is based on some generous assumptions about the operations of tourist railways, without which the black area, particularly in the north, would be even greater. Only if the radius on the 1999 map were extended to 10 miles, would the shaded area compare with that shown in 1899.

A map drawn today showing places more than 5 miles from a petrol station would not be dissimilar to the 1899 railway map. A quarter of Wales lies above 1,000 ft and the black spaces on the 1899 railway map are only found on remote coastal headlands or at a height well above 1,000 ft. Not that this height was enough to exclude the railway altogether. Brynmawr had a busy station at 1,200 ft and, as already noted, the top of Snowdon has a station even today. Waunavon at 1,400 ft was one of the highest stations in Britain.

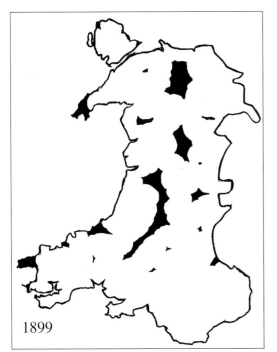

1899

1999

Two maps of Wales showing in the shaded area those parts of the country in 1899 and 1999 more than 5 miles from a railway station.

DD

34 *The Railways of Wales circa 1900*

Brynmawr station viewed from the east in its bleak mountain-top setting, 1,200 ft above sea level. The line in the foreground is from Blaenafon while the main line from Abergavenny approaches on the right, behind the water tower. It was photographed on 4 January 1958, the day before the last passenger train ran between Abergavenny and Brynmawr.
C.H.A. Townley/ courtesy J.A. Peden

In 1899 every county had a railway network. Today, although there is no county without some railway, Cardiganshire has retained some 60% and a third of its stations, mainly, it has to be said, because of the Vale of Rheidol narrow gauge tourist railway. Pembrokeshire has retained 70% of its mileage. Surprisingly, Carmarthenshire still has about 60% and even remote Anglesey has retained 50%. Merioneth lost 60% of its extensive mileage with the closure of the railways to Bala, but Brecknock has suffered worse with only about 15% left and only two stations out of 30. Neighbouring Monmouthshire has also seen its railways drastically cut back; in 1899 it had a dense network of which less than 30% remains. Of the 52 railway stations in existence in Monmouthshire in 1961, only 7 remained in 1994. By chance, the most fortunate county overall is Montgomery where some 80% of route miles

The branch train at Cardigan station headed by 0-6-0ST No. 1982, before the First World War.
Lens of Sutton

The handsome station building at Llanidloes when still in use by the railway; 6 May 1954.
T.J. Edgington

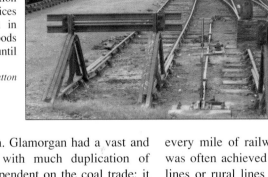

Newcastle Emlyn station after passenger services had been withdrawn in September 1952. Goods traffic continued until 1973.
Lens of Sutton

remain in operation. Glamorgan had a vast and complex network with much duplication of competing lines dependent on the coal trade; it has, accordingly, lost two-thirds of its railways though it retains what is still a respectable network of passenger services.

This reduction in the network results in a route mileage only some 40% of that 100 years ago. The effect of this on each railway company is examined in Chapter 3. In 1899 there were no more than 1,100 people for every mile of Welsh railway whereas in Britain as a whole there were 1,600. The effect of closures has been to increase the intensity in Wales to some 4,000, whereas in the whole of Britain it has increased to over 5,000 (cf. India with 200,000 people for

every mile of railway). Across Britain closure was often achieved by shutting down duplicate lines or rural lines serving a small population, but in Wales a significant proportion of closures involved lines built to move coal and minerals. Of the 1,800 miles operating in 1899, over one third had been built primarily for this purpose.

Associated with the cut-back in the railway is the closure of stations for both passengers and goods. Out of nearly 600 passenger and goods stations operating in 1900, only about 160 remain. Over 70 of those which have been closed were on lines which are still open to passengers. Such was the penetration initially achieved by the railway that Beaumaris, Llangurig and St Davids were the only significant settlements without a

Ruthin (*sic*) station in 1959. This handsome building has now been demolished; a craft centre occupies the site.
Mowat Coll.

station. In 2000 they are joined by many, some of great local importance such as Amlwch, Abertillery, Bala, Brecon, Brynmawr, Cardigan, Caernarfon, Corwen, Denbigh, Dolgellau, Ebbw Vale, Lampeter, Llandysul, Llanfyllin, Llangefni, Llanidloes, Mold, Monmouth, Newcastle Emlyn, Rhayader, Risca, Rhuthun, Tredegar and Usk. In 1900 Brecon was served by four different railway companies; its nearest station in 2000 is Builth Road, some 18 miles distant. Monmouth, Ebbw Vale and Blaenafon each had two stations and now have none. Merthyr was served by five companies, the GW, LNW, Taff Vale, Rhymney

and Brecon & Merthyr, all at the same station. In contrast, Swansea which was served by three of the English companies, the GW, LNW and Midland, had six terminals and now has one. Wrexham was served at three stations by three companies, the GW, GCR and the Cambrian; it still has two of its stations. But Pontypool, like Abergavenny, had three and now has only one. On the other hand, Blaenau Ffestiniog still has the benefit of two railway companies and two stations out of three present in 1900, while Porthmadog still has three stations served by three companies.

A view at Holyhead in LNWR days showing the large hotel, now destroyed, and a 'Problem' Class locomotive.
F. Moore/S. Reid Coll.

Another view of the hotel at Holyhead with the LNWR Royal Train in the foreground – locomotive No. 1915 of the 'Jubilee' Class – probably in July 1911 on the occasion of George V's tour. The royal party arrived on the 12 July from Dublin in the Royal Yacht and joined the train at Holyhead. The Prince of Wales' Investiture took place at Caernarfon on the 13 July and the party spent that night on board the Royal Yacht before proceeding on their tour by train the following day.   *LNWR Soc.*

In spite of the railway closures, a passenger familiar with the railway network in Wales in 1900 would find 100 years later much that was superficially unchanged. From Ireland, Holyhead still functions as a ferry terminal for the railway, though it has lost its large hotel; on the other hand, Fishguard was not built until 1906. Entry into Wales over the remaining routes is frequently marked by noteable structures and engineering. On the border with England, the point of entry on the Chester & Holyhead at Saltney is unremarkable since the crossing of the Dee is entirely in England. This was once the scene of a noteable failure by Robert Stephenson when his bridge collapsed, an event which could have destroyed a lesser man. Further south, the Shrewsbury to Wrexham line enters Wales over the Chirk viaduct across the Ceiriog river; 846 ft long, it was built by Henry Robertson, engineer to the Shrewsbury & Chester Railway. To Robertson fell the honour of building the replacement over the Dee at Chester and near Llangollen he built a long and elegant viaduct, also over the Dee. Elsewhere, the Shropshire

Former LMS 2-8-0 No. 48255 crosses the border at Saltney, 10 March 1958.   *J.A. Peden/courtesy W.G. Rear*

Henry Robertson's masterpiece, the Cefn viaduct with 'Hall' Class No. 6980 *Llanrumney Hall* and an 'up' passenger train.   *V.R. Webster*

Robertson's second viaduct at nearby Chirk overshadows Telford's aquaduct in the background.   *GBJ Coll.*

border crossings were unspectacular and the lines from Whitchurch to Welshpool and Ellesmere to Wrexham are now closed; only the former joint GW/LNW line from Shrewsbury to Welshpool survives and, shortly after an insignificant border crossing, is carried over the Severn at Buttington.

To the south, the Central Wales line enters Wales just before Knighton and, shortly after, crosses the Knucklas viaduct – thirteen arches carrying the line over the river Teme – yet another Robertson masterpiece. The branch lines to Presteigne and New Radnor wandered into Wales in unspectacular fashion and are now closed. The old Newport, Abergavenny & Hereford Railway still enters Wales by way of a three-arched stone bridge over the Monnow at Llangua. As the line then follows the course of the winding river for several miles it does, in fact, re-enter England by

The triple-arch bridge over the Monnow at Llangua, built by the Newport, Abergavenny & Hereford Railway in 1853. At this point the Monnow marks the border between England and Wales; January 2000. *GBJ*

a cast-iron girder bridge and enters Wales a second time over a simple concrete beam structure. The lines to Monmouth from Ross and Chepstow are both closed. They followed the course of the Wye in very picturesque scenery. The Ross line entered Wales near Monmouth. The line from Chepstow left the Gloucester line in England and crossed the Wye to re-enter Wales at Tintern.

At Chepstow the old South Wales Railway from Gloucester originally crossed the Wye on a suspension bridge designed by Brunel, but this was replaced in 1962 by a lattice girder structure. Finally, the Severn tunnel remains, uniquely identifying the border, even in the days of the high-speed train.

Elsewhere the railway still uses the Penrhyndeudraeth, Porthkerry, Landore, Loughor and Cynghordy viaducts. On the line to Blaenau Ffestiniog the Lledr viaduct, also known as Cethyn's Bridge, designed by Williams Smith, manages to blend with its wild surroundings.

About 100 years ago, when this photograph was probably taken, the Lledr viaduct blended well with the bare and rocky terrain. Today, as in many other parts of Wales, trees have grown and softened the landscape.

NLW

A BR Class 4 4-6-0 hauls a 'down' train over Pont Briwet at Penrhyndeudraeth, August 1965.   *J.B. Snell*

The Dyfi and Barmouth viaducts have both been partly replaced since 1900; in fact, work on rebuilding the latter began in 1899. The tubular bridge at Conwy, built by Robert Stephenson in 1849, with its mock-medieval stonework and massive iron tubes slung only 20 ft above the river, still stands, but sadly its rather higher and grander successor over the Menai Strait had to be rebuilt after a fire in 1970. The unique bascule bridge over the Tywi at Carmarthen survives but it replaced the Brunel original in 1911. It no longer lifts a section for the passage of ships. One of the most distinguished relics still in use, but largely disregarded, is Brunel's massive single span at Pontypridd. Further up the Taff valley at Quakers Yard is a Brunel viaduct, again seldom recognised as it is largely unseen, being in a particularly secluded spot well screened by trees.

The original bridge at Barmouth about 1900, with Cambrian 2-4-0 No. 54 on a 'down' train.   *LGRP*

Barmouth bridge with a southbound train in June 1960. *J.B. Snell*

An early engraving of Robert Stephenson's tubular bridge at Conwy, *ca*. 1850. *DD Coll.*

An LNWR east-bound train leaves Conwy bridge and castle hauled by one of the ubiquitous and versatile 0-6-0 engines.

LNWR Soc.

Brunel's daringly wide skew arch at Pontypridd was built in 1840 to carry the then single track Taff Vale Railway on its way to Merthyr. When his successors doubled the track they lacked his audacity and inserted an additional support under the new track; this is visible in the centre of the picture. The viaduct in the distance carries the Rhondda Valley line; September 1999.   *GBJ*

The former Port Talbot Railway viaduct at Pontrhydyfen surviving as part of a tourist trail; February 1984. This imposing brick structure carried the PTR branch line to Tonmawr.

GBJ

Crumlin viaduct looking east, with the Vale of Neath line in the foreground and the former Monmouthshire Railway in the valley below; probably *ca.* 1960.   *Steam & Sail/courtesy E.S. Owen Jones*

Other viaducts survive even though the railway has long gone; such are the Blaen-y-cwm viaduct near Nantybwch, Pontrhydyfen near Port Talbot, Cefn Coed and Pontsarn near Merthyr, Hengoed over the Rhymney, and Cwm Prysor in north Wales. Possibly the most spectacular of all, the Crumlin viaduct, 200 ft high and nearly a mile long, was pulled down in 1965. Like the much sturdier Walnut Tree, Llanbradach and Penyrheol

viaducts on the former Barry Railway, which all suffered a similar fate, it was built to carry coal.

Sadly, unless the line was sharply curved, most railway passengers were unaware of these wonderful structures. They tended to be more familiar with station buildings. Generally, Wales has not been blessed with the quality of railway architecture of other parts of Britain. Among the surviving stations there has been much change

Carmarthen station, looking north, the best surviving example of a station of the turn of the century; *ca.* 1914.
Lens of Sutton

during the twentieth century, especially in the case of the larger stations. Thus Cardiff (which received a flattering face-lift in 1999), Newport, Aberystwyth and Swansea all received new buildings during the 1920s or '30s. Although Bangor received some new building in the '30s, the original Francis Thompson building on the 'up' platform survives; unfortunately, its handsome profile is partly obscured by heavy canopies. Regrettably, Neath was rebuilt in the '60s. However, Carmarthen is little altered since it was built new on the present site in 1902, and as such is possibly the best surviving example of a station of the turn of the century. Like

Wrexham General of 1909, it is a typical larger GWR station of the period. Other examples were at Neath, and in England at Ealing Broadway and Ross-on-Wye.

Generally speaking, the stations which have survived in a state that would cause them to be recognisable to a passenger from 1900 are in intermediate-sized towns on main routes, large enough to continue to have a service, and fortunate enough to have some architectural merit and pressure to preserve them. Among those with buildings still in use by the railway are Abergavenny by Charles Liddell, Bridgend and Pantyffynnon by Brunel, Caersws and

The main entrance of Charles Liddell's station at Abergavenny, built in about 1853 and the last survivor of three which existed in the town in 1900; September 1999.

GBJ

A northbound mail train passing Abergavenny station in September 1999.

GBJ

Brunel's Pantyffynnon station on the former Llanelly Railway line from Llanelli to Llandeilo. The station stands at the junction of the branch to Ammanford and Brynaman; September 1951.
H.C. Casserley

By 1998 only the Brunel building survived at Pantyffynnon.
DD

The street frontage of Machynlleth station, *ca.* 1900, immediately recognisable 100 years later. *R.C. Riley*

Machynlleth by T.M. Penson, Llandudno by Mellard Reade et al. (though now without most of its overall roof), Llandrindod and Knighton on the Central Wales, Barmouth, Llandudno Junction, Rhyl and Tenby. The station which would be most familiar to a passenger of 100 years ago is possibly Llanelli, which has retained its massive canopies and covered footbridge. He or she might feel equally at home at, of all places, Dinas Junction on the

long-closed Caernarvonshire Railway; here the narrow gauge has recently taken over and the old buildings in the extensive yard are humming with activity. At Pontypridd the site would be substantially familiar, though the station was considerably extended in the early years of the twentieth century. By contrast, although the buildings are intact, Llandrindod would be almost unrecognisable, stripped as it is of its original canopies.

Llandudno station in October 1999. The removal of the overall roof has left this station looking bare, even though reasonably intact.   *GBJ*

Tenby station, looking west, *ca.* 1910, and little changed in 2000.   *Lens of Sutton*

At other stations interesting buildings survive but not in railway use. These include: the fine buildings at Llanidloes and Newtown; the Victorian vicarage-style at Montgomery; the Regency at Cardiff Bute Road; country house Gothic at Ruabon by Henry Robertson; the classical Flint by Francis Thompson, and Holywell Junction, one of his most successful; Brunel's Chepstow; and the unexpectedly charming little gem at Pembroke Dock.

Welshpool has experienced an elaborate and sensitive rebirth, while Aberdovey has survived twice, having been the original station building at Pwllheli, whence it was moved brick by brick and stone by stone in 1908. The Cambrian coast line has been fortunate with Porthmadog, Criccieth and a truncated Pwllheli still standing; Tywyn can be said to be standing but in a sadly bricked-up state. At Penhelig, Aberdovey's second station, a GWR 'pagoda' waiting-room is still in use. Aberdare High Level, on the other hand, is a particularly unhappy example of a Grade 2 listed building being 75% restored by the local authority but abandoned by Railtrack in favour of a bus shelter. Elsewhere, architectural merit alone has not always been sufficient to preserve a station as the fate of Cardiff Queen Street, Brunel's Merthyr and later, in a supposedly more enlightened age, Penson's Chirk testify.

A rather dreary corner of south-west Wales is brightened by the charm of the surviving Pembroke Dock station; October 1999.

DD

Bereft of its railway, Llanidloes station stands alone, ignored by the usurping main road; September 1998.

GBJ

Montgomery station in its heyday, *ca.* 1900. The building still stands in 2000 though it is no longer a station.

GBJ Coll.

One of the few remaining landmarks in the major re-development of Cardiff Bay, the once busy Taff Vale station at Bute Road survives in 2000 but without a use. Photographed in August 1960.
G.H. Platt

The exterior of Welsh-pool station which has been sympathetically adapted for a new purpose; October 1999.
DD

Aberdyfi station, looking north, during the 1950s.
GBJ Coll.

Porthmadog station building in good shape and with a new use, looking west, in October 1999. *GBJ*

Pwllheli's second station as it was in Cambrian days, about 1910. The half-timbered buildings survive in 2000 though obscured by later GWR extensions. GWR optimism in the 1920s led to elaborate extensions both here and at Aberystwyth. *NLW*

By 1991 the GW extensions at Pwllheli had been cut back and a supermarket built on part of the platform; 2 August 1991. *J.C. Hillmer*

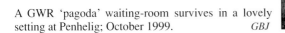

A GWR 'pagoda' waiting-room survives in a lovely setting at Penhelig; October 1999. *GBJ*

Sometimes, on preserved lines, it has been possible to revive the character of the stations before they were allowed to deteriorate too far. Such are Bronwydd Arms on the Gwili, Barry Island on the Vale of Glamorgan, Minffordd on the Ffestiniog, Carrog and Llangollen. On the other hand, a total transformation is achieved where stations have been modernised and reduced to the bare essentials of a bus-stop. Examples of this trend are to be seen at Pontypool Road, Penmaen-mawr and Port Talbot on main lines, and at the recently reopened Maesteg. There are instances, such as Aberystwyth, where even though the station building survives, the much reduced activity creates a somewhat ghostly air, hinting at past glories, as the wind whips the litter across a massively wide platform, built for holiday crowds of another age.

The partially restored High Level station at Aberdare on the former Vale of Neath line. The bus shelter, which serves as a station in 2000, can be made out in the right distance; 1996.
DD

The fine façade of the Taff Vale's Queen Street Station in Cardiff, built flamboyantly and with confidence in 1887 to house the TVR offices. When these became redundant in the 1970s the site was too valuable for the building to survive, though the station still functions in 2000.
NLW

Brunel's train shed at Merthyr was still surviving on the 31 August 1951 when this photograph was taken and was destined to last for another 20 years.

Ian L. Wright

Grade 2 listing was not enough to save the station building at Chirk from demolition; 30 June 1984.

N.D. Mundy

Roath station in Cardiff on the main line was closed in 1917. These buildings have by 2000 totally disappeared, although the site can still be identified by the tall boundary fencing and the now superfluous bend in the track, originally at the start of the platform. A 'Duke' Class locomotive heads a passenger train in the Newport direction; *ca*. 1905. *GBJ Coll.*

Nantyderry station, south of Pontypool Road, on the main line of the old Newport, Abergavenny & Hereford Railway. It had become a private dwelling when this photograph was taken in 1964 and survives as such in 2000.

G.H. Platt

The multitude of smaller stations has suffered more. Many have simply disappeared, such as once important town stations like Brecon, Builth Wells, Denbigh, Ruthin and Caernarfon, branch line termini such as Cardigan, Newcastle Emlyn or Aberayron, and a multitude of minor stations on closed lines. The site of Brynmawr, once a hive of activity, is now totally unrecognisable. Closed stations standing beside surviving running track have frequently been completely obliterated with not a shred of surviving evidence of past glories; such are Moat Lane Junction, Afon Wen, Roath and Abergavenny Junction. Some have survived by finding alternative uses, often as a residence, like Nantyderry, with trains hurtling past the sitting-room. Others on closed lines, like Erwood on the Mid Wales, have the space to preserve something of the past in a small museum. Many, like Govilon, Penrhyndeudraeth and Talsarnau, are private houses, while others like Eyarth in Denbighshire and Rosebush in Pembrokeshire make the most of their railway associations as guest houses or pubs.

The exterior of the former LNWR station at Builth Road on the Central Wales line, called the Heart of Wales Line in 2000. The station building survives as apartments; 1994.

GBJ

The 'interior' of Builth Road station; 1994.

GBJ

The most enduring part of a station tends to be the platform, the edge of which is often the only remaining clue to a station's former existence; that and, if it were a GWR station, a row of pine trees. Abercrave on the Neath & Brecon was closed in 1932 but the site can still be identified. Among the rosebay willow-herb and dandelions at the former Nelson & Llancaiach on the Taff Vale Extension, it is the platform edges which give a clue to the station's lay-out. In other cases it is a gatepost, perhaps of cast-iron, or old Barlow and bridge rail as at Neyland, or a surviving goods yard crane as at Ruthin, or its mere foundations as at Ystradgynlais. At Pontypool Clarence Street the former approach road provides the only clue.

Apart from the station, it is often the engine shed or goods depot which manages to survive. These were almost always built with good materials and attention to detail, and in 1900 would still have been well maintained and cared for. In 2000 a large shed with a good roof and an open floor area can be adapted to many uses and many of them have survived as bus depots, workshops, offices and garages; in some cases they have survived long enough to revert to their original use. The Corris Railway shed served as a workshop before returning to railway use for preservationists; similarly at Barry a former Barry Railway goods shed has been acquired for use as a preserved railway workshop. At Panteg & Griffithstown near Pontypool the goods shed is being made into a railway museum by a few devoted and determined individuals.

The earlier GWR goods shed at Cardiff seen towards the end of the nineteenth century. The photograph illustrates the high quality of construction employed at the time on even the most functional of railway buildings.

PRO: RAIL 253/442

The former goods shed at Panteg & Griffithstown under reconstruction as a private railway museum; September 1999.

GBJ

The 1960s style BR box controlled an attractive group of semaphore signals at Radyr on the former TVR, north of Cardiff; May 1963.   *A. Jarvis*

The biggest single change in the appearance of the railway is possibly in the signalling arrangements. Modernisation of signalling, with electric switches replacing mechanical levers, has rendered most boxes redundant and has replaced the colourful and sometimes statuesque signal gantry with a row of traffic lights. In the whole of Wales in 2000 there are no more than 40 boxes left in operation whereas in 1900 every station had at least one, and there was one for nearly every junction. An extreme case was the Vale of Neath line between Neath and Pontypool Road where in the span of 41 miles there were 20 junctions and at one time as many as 64 signal-boxes. Sometimes signal-boxes were located in remote countryside. But wherever they were, the average passenger paid them little attention. They were, however, the heart of the railway system. The signalman still performs a key task and his box often reflects

An array of semaphore signals at the approach to Rhondda Fach North Junction, looking down the grade from the Maerdy branch; 1964.
G.H. Platt

The Taff Vale signal-box at Walnut Tree Junction, Taff's Well, was a typical example of this railway's use of brick, timber and elaborate barge-boarding; 1978.

GBJ

The former LNWR box at Llandudno, a typical plain and functional North Western design and still in operation in 2000; October 1999.

DD

A GWR box in the picturesque setting of Usk station. Passenger services here ceased in 1955 not long before this photograph was taken.

Rev. R.W.A. Jones/ Ian L. Wright Coll.

the importance of the role. The Taff Vale had a particularly attractive style of box with ornate barge-boarding, while those on the LNWR tended to be plain and functional. The Midland built nearly all its boxes of timber with a hipped roof and finials and particularly large, deep windows. The GWR had a standard pattern, normally with a brick base and timber accommodation. At Porth, in the busy junction between the two Rhondda valleys, the Taff Vale built a stretched version in a strange semi-detached format. The Barry devoted attention to the quality of all its infrastructure and its signal-boxes were built as though to last for ever. By contrast, many of the boxes on the Manchester & Milford were of a makeshift pattern with an almost agricultural flavour. In 2000, mechanical signalling survives in a few places other than on preserved railways, notably on Anglesey, on the old Rhymney line and on the Vale of Glamorgan line. In contrast, the whole of the Cambrian line from Sutton Bridge Junction, Shrewsbury, to Aberystwyth and Pwllheli is controlled from one box at Machynlleth.

The unique 'semi-detached' box at Porth which served Rhondda North Junction; 1964.   *G.H. Platt*

This GWR station building at Cwmgorse near Gwauncaegurwen (GCG) was never used, as completion of the railway to Pontardawe was prevented by the First World War; 10 October 1923.   *WIMM/GW Coll.*

The third side of the triangular junction planned at GCG was never needed and so this viaduct, which still stands in 2000, has never borne a train. Diesel locomotive No. D6889 is hauling a freight train up to Gwauncaegurwen; 20 February 1973.   *J.A. Sommerfield/Courtesy J.A. Peden*

In many cases where the railway has closed since 1900 some traces of it remain, and often the course of the line can be followed on the ground. This is because many of the closed lines are in sparsely populated countryside with relatively low land values. Bridge abutments, cuttings and embankments are often easy to see. An experienced eye will recognise GWR post-and-wire fencing even if covered in undergrowth in a thick wood. Where lines have been closed in heavily populated areas, such as the Taff Vale Extension, and the LNWR and Midland lines in

Delapidation and decay at the Boston Lodge Works of the Ffestiniog Railway give no hint of the revival shortly to occur; 1952.   *R. Wood*

Swansea, road improvements and new housing tend to obscure completely the evidence of the railway's existence. An exception was the Merthyr, Tredegar & Abergavenny which fell victim to a new road, in spite of its route lying across open mountains. Here, only the viaducts survive to tease the imagination. On the other hand, in the Clydach gorge the MTA track-bed can be clearly followed, while the Mid Wales line can be traced for nearly its entire route; even the short spur to Llangurig, which was intended to be the core of the Manchester & Milford and which only ever carried one goods train in 1864, is still discernible. Even more extreme is the

This 1960s postcard view of Llangurig shows quite clearly in the foreground the surviving embankment and (now demolished) single-arch road bridge constructed 100 years previously as part of the ambitious Manchester & Milford Railway. This part of the line is reputed to have carried just one goods train and that was in connection with the works.   *GBJ Coll.*

Railway archaeology 20 years after closure. The southern end of the Morlais tunnel on the former LNWR line from Merthyr to Abergavenny can be seen bricked-up in the centre of the picture. To the right is the remaining brickwork of the signal-box. In the thicket to the left is the track-bed of the former Brecon & Merthyr line to Pontsticill Junction; August 1982.

GBJ

The track-bed of the former Brecon & Merthyr Railway high up in the Brecon Beacons at Torpantau; January 1983. Steam trains may well reappear at this spot early in the twenty-first century if the plans of the narrow gauge Brecon Mountain Railway materialise.

GBJ

case of the line which was to link the Neath & Brecon with Llangammarch on the Central Wales; no track was ever laid but earthworks can still be traced near Defynnog. In the north, a few rather obscure traces remain of the erstwhile Vale of Clwyd or Denbigh, Ruthin & Corwen lines but, to the west, cuttings, embankments and the Cwm Prysor viaduct provide dramatic reminders of the fortitude of earlier generations in building a railway between Ffestiniog and Bala. Elsewhere, part of the route lies submerged beneath the waters of Llyn Tryweryn, emerging from time to time during periods of drought.

Drought conditions at Tryweryn reveal the inclined track-bed of the former Bala to Blaenau Ffestiniog branch; August 1989. This line was sacrificed in 1960 to provide water for Liverpool Corporation. *GBJ*

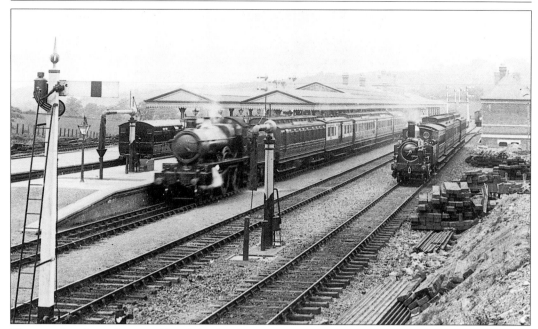

The second station at Pontypool Road shortly after completion in 1909. One of Churchward's 'County' Class
locomotives heads a southbound express while 'Metro Tank' No. 975 stands in the siding near the station
building.   *NLW*

But where the railway is still in operation, besides the loss of semaphore signals, the most striking visible difference is the general untidiness of the modern railway. In 1900 there were no problems with leaves on the line as the surrounding cuttings and embankments were all kept shorn. The track was impeccably maintained without the aid of weed-killer, and around it there was none of the general mess created by old bits of equipment so often left lying about by the modern railways. Nor was there any graffiti with that weird cartoon script and spikey incomprehensible scribble. As can be seen from contemporary photographs, railway buildings were in good condition and often bore favourable comparison with those around them. They were soundly built of good materials and proudly maintained.

Besides the good order and general tidiness, the traveller from 1900 would miss the air of bustle associated with all but the sleepiest of country goods yards. Perhaps Pontypool Road, of all stations left on the operating railway, would present a passenger from 1900 with the greatest shock and contrast. Gone are the sidings full of waggons and reserve stocks of carriages. No longer is there a massive locomotive shed surrounded with simmering steam engines. The surviving line runs isolated and bare as it passes the long grass, ragwort and young trees where formerly locomotives hissed, waggons rattled and milk churns clanged. Gone are most of the people – railway workers as well as passengers – and gone most of all is that air of importance associated with the fact that everyone used or depended upon the railway.

The station entrance and main building, looking south, at Pontypool Road; 17 February 1973. By this time the large platform canopies and buildings had been replaced by a small bus shelter.

J.A. Sommerfield/courtesy J.A. Peden

A view from almost the same spot twenty years later shows the station building under demolition; 1993.

DD

THE RAILWAY OPERATIONS

The large number of companies was perhaps the most remarkable characteristic of the Welsh railways in 1900, but they also operated to a wide variety of gauges (twelve, including standard) and with a diverse choice of locomotives and vehicles. By far the largest companies operating in Wales were the two English companies, the GWR and the LNWR. Together they reached most of the country. But considerable distances were also covered by the independent companies whose freight operations achieved a rare intensity.

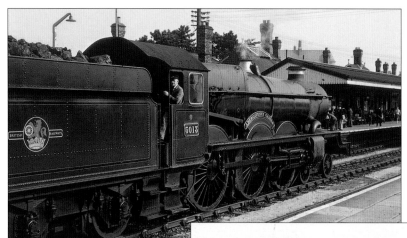

Locomotive No. 5013 *Abergavenny Castle* at Carmarthen. In 1900 this the most south-westerly outpost of the LNWR; 20 August 1959.
Ian L. Wright

LMS Locomotive No. 6691 (LNWR No. 1143) stands in the bay at Llandeilo station with a local train for Carmarthen; 31 May 1947.
S. Reid Coll.

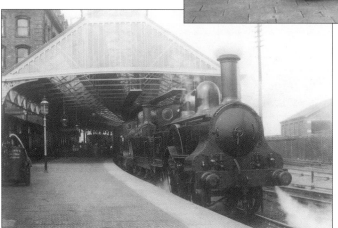

Holyhead, the north-western extreme of the LNWR in Wales, with a 'Problem' Class locomotive at the main departure platform, probably about the turn of the century.
H.C. Casserley/S. Reid Coll.

THE COMPANIES

Unlike Scotland, whose railways at the turn of the twentieth century were almost exclusively Scottish-based, the railways in Wales were dominated by the GWR, mainly in the south, and the LNWR, mainly in the north. A third, the Great Central, acquired the Wrexham, Mold & Connah's Quay Railway in 1906, having operated it from 1901. This tangled with the GW and the LNWR in the Wrexham area where a complex network of lines served the coal and mineral mines of Flintshire and south-east Denbighshire. This acquisition enabled the adventurous Great Central to penetrate mid-

An unexpected sight in Wales, an LNER train at Wrexham Central; 8 April 1939. The locomotive is a former Great Central 4-4-2T.

C.A. Appleton/courtesy J.A. Peden

The LNWR's route along the north Wales coast contended with a number of natural obstacles. A westbound LNWR train is seen at Conwy around the turn of the century, hauled by one of the 4 cylinder compound 4-4-0s.

GBJ Coll.

Wales by courtesy of the Cambrian. The GWR had a long and straggling line across the north, to Dolgellau, almost on the coast of Cardigan Bay, and from Bala into the mountains at Blaenau Ffestiniog. The LNW reached mid-Wales and the south as well as the north, and, like the fourth English company, the Midland, focussed its attention on gaining access to Swansea. All achieved their positions by the acquisition of smaller companies, which in some cases they had promoted, or by obtaining running powers.

One of the challenges to the railway in the Welsh landscape was altitude; LNWR locomotives snow-bound 1,200 ft up at Dowlais Top; *ca.*1922.   *S. Reid Coll.*

Snow on the line on the Brecon & Merthyr Railway, also at Dowlais Top; 1947.   *WIMM/GW Coll.*

The remaining Welsh railways were primarily mineral lines, built to convey raw materials from mines to the ports; those in the north were narrow gauge for carrying slate and tended to be isolated from one another, while those in the south were standard gauge and often competed with one another in an intense jungle of lines down and across the valleys. They were mainly confined to the area south of the Tywi and Usk valleys. The Cambrian was the only Welsh railway which could be described as a trunk line and, in operating long

In August 1965 'Manor' Class No. 7827 *Lydham Manor* skirts the rugged coast of Cardigan Bay near Llangelynin with a through Pwllheli to Paddington train.   *J.B. Snell*

distances over mainly single track, it resembled the Highland Railway of Scotland. Its main purpose was to link England to the shore of Cardigan Bay. The Brecon & Merthyr and the Neath & Brecon were similar but much shorter and both had two personalities; north of the watershed they were country railways, while to the south they became primarily mineral lines.

The existence of so many independent railways as late as the turn of the century was unusual. There were two reasons for this. Those like the Taff Vale which were successful, with high dividends and a high share price, offered little to the predator. Those which were still independent but less successful, with an uncertain financial position, were likely to be a drain on resources rather than an opportunity to grow value. Furthermore, by 1900 the main English companies with an interest in Wales had already penetrated to the most important industrial area at Swansea. Accordingly, most of the companies which were operating at the turn of the century remained independent, until Parliament forced them together in the grouping.

The main surviving monument to the Barry Railway is its former head office building at Barry Docks, now the offices of the Vale of Glamorgan Council.
GBJ

By 1900 the pattern of the network and of ownership was set. Most of the lines ever to be built were already operating a system that had been in existence since before 1870 and was to remain largely intact until after 1960. The Barry alone was a turbulent newcomer. Ruthlessly exploiting its competitive port facilities, and having control of both dock and railway, it sought by all means available to exploit its competitive advantage to gain access to additional collieries and to divert trade from the ports of Cardiff and Swansea. It was thus a company with a different motive. In the early days of the twentieth century it was still building new connections to the Rhymney valley and seeking imaginative ways into the neighbouring Sirhowy and even across to the Western Valleys.

The Barry was ultimately responsible for two take-overs after the turn of the century. In both cases take-over meant an operating agreement rather than a purchase or transfer of shares. In the first, in 1906, the GWR took-over the operation of the Rhondda & Swansea Bay Railway, guaranteeing a 5% dividend to the shareholders, hungry for any dividend at all. This was to foil the move by the Barry to gain control over lines with access to Swansea and was prompted by

powers obtained in 1902 to subscribe to the Neath, Pontardawe & Brynamman Railway. The second case arose in 1907 and involved the Port Talbot Railway, which was itself in the process of absorbing the South Wales Mineral Railway. The Port Talbot had been approached by the Barry Railway as part of its attempt to control access to competing ports. The GWR put a stop to this by agreeing to operate the railway against an agreed guaranteed dividend.

Pressure on margins and the Barry's aggressive tactics led to an attempt by the Taff Vale to take over the Rhymney and the Cardiff Railway in 1909 and again in 1910. This was prevented by opposition from the Barry, which had grown rapidly by playing one company off against another; it was therefore determined to prevent the creation of such a large and powerful bloc. Its iconoclastic activity had earned the Barry friends in influential places, and Parliament, encouraged by the coal owners and shippers, accepted the Barry's argument.

The only other take-over before the grouping of a standard gauge line that was independent at the turn of the century was the GWR's acquisition in 1911 of the Manchester & Milford Railway. This line, which linked Aberystwyth to the Carmarthen & Cardigan

At Aberystwyth two 'Duke' Class locomotives depart with a train for the Machynlleth line, *ca.* 1925. The railway has enabled what was a small settlement to become both a holiday resort and the unofficial cultural capital of Wales.   *NLW/A.J. Lewis Coll.*

Railway at Pencader, was the rump of a dream, never fulfilled, to link Manchester with what was hoped would become a rival to Liverpool for the American trade. The GWR was motivated to acquire it as a means of gaining its own access to Aberystwyth. In so doing it prevented the Cambrian from extending any further south from there, along the shore of Cardigan Bay. This position was reinforced by the opening of the Aberayron branch in 1906.

The exterior of Aberystwyth station decorated to celebrate the Royal National Eisteddfod of Wales, August 1952. The GWR added this imposing street frontage in 1924/5. *WIMM/GW Coll.*

Interior of Aberystwyth station on the same occasion, 5 August 1952. *WIMM/GW Coll.*

Cambrian Railways No. 34 heads a train at Aberystwyth station in Cambrian days, before the GW additions had been made. This locomotive was bought from the Metropolitan Railway as a 4-4-0T and was converted into a tender engine by Beyer Peacock in 1915. On the left stands a Manchester & Milford line train; 5 June 1920.   *LCGB/Ken Nunn Coll.*

By the 1970s the Vale of Rheidol Railway had replaced the Manchester & Milford in the bay platform at Aberystwyth and the extensions to the canopies put up by the GWR in 1925 had been cut back to the Cambrian original.   *Lens of Sutton*

The railway companies were the first commercial organisations large enough to create a distinction between ownership and management. Most were publicly owned by independent shareholders, though the Cardiff, the Barry and the Port Talbot were owned by dock interests. By the turn of the century, the entrepreneurs and adventurers who created the railways had largely given way to a more serious and professional class of railwayman. The colourful draper Thomas Savin; the dynamic contractor David Davies of Llandinam; the brilliant organiser of men, Thomas Brassey; the entrepreneurial engineer Henry Robertson; the enthusiastic solicitor William Banks; the tough and capable captain of industry Crawshay Bailey; the admirable local politician Starling Benson of Swansea, all gave way to a new generation. They were succeeded by men, who with no less strength of character, quietly and doggedly, with persistence and determination, drove their enterprise forward, often devoting their whole lives to it. Big landowners, like the Butes around Cardiff, the Morgans at Newport, and the Beauforts at Swansea, continued to be a powerful influence, but the coal owners had become pre-eminent. Boards of directors which had been dominated by landed and political interests were tending to become more the place for businessmen.

At the turn of the century there was still a tendency for shareholders' meetings to be held in London where the capital market was located. This applied particularly to those companies whose financial state was more fragile and was the case with the B & M, the N & B, and the Cardiff. The registered office of even the Snowdon Mountain Railway was in Grosvenor Place, London. The Cambrian used Manchester, while the Taff Vale used Bristol out of respect for a long connection; this stemmed from the original investment by Bristol businessmen seeking to control competition with the Port of Bristol. The Rhymney was very much a Cardiff company, and the Rhondda & Swansea Bay held its rowdy meetings in Swansea.

By comparison with companies operating at the end of the twentieth century, 100 years ago it was common for company managements to be in position for long periods. Cornelius Lundie was general manager of the Rhymney Railway from 1862 to 1904, at which point he became a director, a so-called consultant director, which meant that he continued largely as before, controlling in detail every operation of the company. He died at the age of 93 in 1908. He claimed to be the oldest railway director in the world and the last person alive to have known Sir Walter Scott personally. The first chairman of the company was John Boyle who remained in office from 1858 until the beginning of 1899. He was succeeded by William Austin who had been deputy chairman since 1880.

James Inskip was a respected chairman of the Taff Vale. He was a Bristol solicitor and lay-preacher. When Eamon Beasley was appointed general manager in 1891, Inskip resigned. It was Beasley's hard and reactionary policies which contributed to the strike in 1900, and it was a letter from Inskip to *The Times* which harnessed the general opinion which forced the Taff to agree to negotiate with the strikers.

The Cambrian had the benefit of capable management at the turn of the century thanks to the chairmanship of the much liked and respected J.F. Buckley and his energetic general manager, C. S. Denniss. The upgrading of permanent way to accommodate heavier trains was an important contribution towards effectively promoting the coast of Cardigan Bay as a new tourist area in competition with north Wales and Devon and Cornwall.

Long service and strong local connections were not confined to the managers of the Welsh railways. Joseph Bishop, who had joined the Shrewsbury & Hereford Railway under George Findlay in 1856, was the first LNWR district manager at Abergavenny, appointed in 1864. He became the first mayor of the new corporation of Abergavenny when the charter was restored in 1899. (The original charter had been confiscated as a result of active opposition to the succession of William and Mary.) To celebrate the event he was presented with 'a scarlet Cassimere robe with fur points and trimmings, corded silk cocked hat, robe bag, and air-tight case'.

Today, the ownership and control of the main line railways in Wales are largely outside Wales. The first exception is Cardiff Railways, based in Cardiff. The second, Wales & West, although also based in Cardiff is responsible for trains in south-west England as well as in south Wales. Great Western is run from an office in Swindon, North West from Manchester, and Central from Birmingham. Virgin is run from London. Railtrack manages its Welsh affairs from offices in Swindon, Birmingham and Manchester. The English, Welsh & Scottish Railway, the freight company, is based in London but has a Cardiff-based marketing manager. Freightliner is involved in establishing a major new freight terminal at Wentloog, east of Cardiff. Perhaps greater autonomy in Wales will put pressure on changing this, but the Welsh railways remain dominated by movements into and out of England and are much less cohesive than those of Scotland.

In 2000 the narrow gauge remains locally managed, though most of the employees, management as well as workers, are volunteers rather than employees, and they travel from all over England and Wales to be guards, drivers, porters and platelayers. Many of the shareholders are now English preservation enthusiasts, whereas in 1900 the Talyllyn, the Padarn and the Penrhyn were locally and privately owned. Since 1900, only the Welshpool and the Vale of Rheidol became part of a larger railway undertaking, in both cases first the Cambrian, and then the GWR, and so BR. By 2000 all the narrow gauge railways in Wales are privately owned, though some receive grants from time to time from the public purse.

ROUTE MILEAGE

Reference has already been made to the major overall cut-back in route mileage between 1900 and 2000 but before any discussion of railway statistics, it is desirable to clarify what is meant by the term 'railway'. In the knowledge that opinions differ, it can only be stated that here it refers to lines which were for the public carriage of passengers and freight with trains hauled at some time by steam engines on segregated track. Somewhat illogically part of

the Croesor tramway is included on the grounds that it subsequently became part of a railway. The Penrhyn and Padarn were not available to the public but they did convey workers in steam trains; they are included. On the other hand, only that part of the Corris which carried passengers is included. The Glyn Valley and Mumbles are both included, in spite of the fact that much of their track was not segregated from the roadway, since they operated steam trains and carried passengers and thus resembled a railway more than a tramway. On the other hand, the Great Orme and the Llandudno & Colwyn Bay are excluded as they were all electric, even though their track is or was partly segregated. The accompanying table is included in the knowledge that calculations of railway mileage are beset with pitfalls and there will, no doubt, be varying opinions on some of these figures. Notwithstanding potential discrepancies, the broad picture is clear and the table shows a comparison of the approximate route mileage of the railway companies operating on 31 December 1899, with the position for passenger route miles on the same date in 1999. Dock railways and sidings have generally been excluded though definitions are coarse. In the 1999 figures, lines which are for freight only have been excluded due to the short term fluctuations in their status.

There are a number of interesting conclusions to be drawn from these figures. The first is the sad confirmation that Welsh railways have been cut back by nearly two-thirds between 1899 and 1999. This is worse than the average for the whole of Britain (23,000 to 11,000). Of the Welsh-owned railways the Cambrian was by far the largest in respect of route miles, and over half its Welsh mileage survives. The Taff Vale was over half its size, in spite of being confined to a limited area. The similarity in the mileage of the Manchester & Milford, the Brecon & Merthyr, the Rhymney and the Barry is of interest considering the difference in their character and profitability. The Midland had a similar owned mileage to that which was to become, in 1906, owned by the Great Central. The GWR was the largest by a considerable margin, yet its survival rate is

RAILWAY COMPANIES IN WALES ROUTE MILEAGE			
	GAUGE	ROUTE MILES	
		1899	1999
SWANSEA & MUMBLES	4'	5	–
PADARN	4'	7	–
	1' 11½"	–	2
SNOWDON MOUNTAIN	2' 7½"	5	5
WELSHPOOL & LLANFAIR	2' 6"	–	8
GLYN VALLEY	2' 4½"	9	–
CORRIS	2' 3"	6	1
TALYLLYN	2' 3"	6	6
BRECON MOUNTAIN	2' 0"	–	3
TEIFI VALLEY (HENLLAN)	1' 11¾"	–	3
CROESOR/WELSH HIGHLAND	1' 11½"	4	1
NORTH WALES NARROW GAUGE	,,	12	–
WELSH HIGHLAND (CAERNARFON)	,,	–	3
FFESTINIOG	,,	13	14
VALE of RHEIDOL	,,	–	11
BALA LAKE	,,	–	4
PENRHYN	1' 10¾"	6	–
FAIRBOURNE	1' 0¼"	2	2
TOTAL NARROW GAUGE.		**75**	**63**
NEATH & BRECON		32	–
BRECON & MERTHYR		48	–
CAMBRIAN (in Wales)		223	122
MAWDDWY		7	–
CARDIFF		7	3
BARRY		48	7
VALE OF GLAMORGAN		20	20
RHYMNEY		50	23
TAFF VALE		124	50
MANCHESTER & MILFORD		41	2
BURRY PORT & GWENDRAETH VALLEY		21	–
GWENDRAETH VALLEY		3	–
LLANELLY & MYNYDD MAWR		13	–
ALEXANDRA (NEWPORT & SOUTH WALES) DOCKS		9	–
RHONDDA & SWANSEA BAY		29	–
PORT TALBOT		33	–
SOUTH WALES MINERAL		13	–
WREXHAM, MOLD & CONNAH'S QUAY		22	22
TOTAL WELSH STANDARD GAUGE		**743**	**249**
MIDLAND		29	–
LNWR		359	167
GWR		641	297
TOTAL ENGLISH STANDARD GAUGE IN WALES		**1,029**	**464**
GRAND TOTAL		**1,847**	**776**

In the heart of Snowdonia former LNWR 2-4-2T engine No. 835 brings the 1.00 p.m. train from Caernarfon to a halt at Llanberis on the 30 August 1936. This branch was finally closed in 1964, though regular passenger trains had ceased in 1932. Thereafter summer excursion trains were run until 1939 and again from 1946 until 1962.   *H.C. Casserley*

A general view of the locomotive and goods sheds at Llanberis. The station was behind the camera; 2 May 1937.
W.A. Camwell/ courtesy S. Reid

similar to that of the LNWR. It may be a matter of surprise that the Welsh-owned standard gauge railways had in total a route mileage greater than that of the GWR in Wales. It is also noteworthy that the highest survival rate is among narrow gauge railways.

As has already been mentioned in the context of tourism, it was on the Welsh narrow gauge railways that the railway preservation movement was started. L.T.C. Rolt had led the continuation of Talyllyn Railway operations by volunteers immediately after its closure in 1950,

and this became an inspiration and role model for the whole of the British Isles and, later, the rest of the world. Within 50 years the Talyllyn has been transformed from a shambles, with ancient locomotives struggling over uneven and unstable track, to being a safe and efficient organisation attracting crowds from all over the world. But it was its very decrepitude which in the first instance captured the imagination of those volunteers who first set about restoring the line. At the time it was doubted whether the Ffestiniog would ever be revived, but the success of the adventurers who restored the Talyllyn gave courage to others who set about overcoming even greater obstacles. And still it goes on. The Welsh Highland project now under way is perhaps the most daring of all.

Snowdon Mountain Railway locomotive No. 3 *Wyddfa* stands at Llanberis station with a train of waggons. The distant hillside is deeply scarred by the Dinorwig slate quarries; *ca.* 1900.
NLW

A view up the Snowdon railway near Llanberis in 1898.
NLW

The approach to the summit of Snowdon by the only rack railway in Britain.
GBJ Coll.

The original Talyllyn Railway No.1 resting in a barn at Tywyn before restoration work began; 1954.   *R. Wood*

Hand shunting by sports-jacketed volunteers at Quarry Siding on the Talyllyn Railway in the early days of railway preservation; 1954.   *R. Wood*

The fact that the survival rate on the narrow gauge is greater than on the standard gauge is due to the originally limited economic purpose being offset by cheaper operation; these lines are therefore easier to preserve as a museum, enthusiast or tourist railway and their smaller size appeals to the public. The conversion in Wales of some 12 miles of standard gauge track to narrow gauge supports this argument. Part is operated successfully by the Brecon Mountain Railway on the track-bed of the Brecon & Merthyr just north of Merthyr. A short stretch of the Ruabon to Dolgellau line has been laid as narrow gauge in the vicinity of Bala Junction, and the Newcastle Emlyn branch has had a similar revival at Henllan. The surviving part of the Padarn in north Wales has changed from 4' to 1' 11½". A Heritage Lottery Fund grant of £4 million and much determination, which are helping to restore the ill-fated and short-lived Welsh Highland between Dinas Junction and Porthmadog, have already facilitated the restoration of three miles of the former standard gauge LNWR line from Caernarfon to Dinas Junction as a narrow gauge line.

Within five years coach tours were being arranged to the Talyllyn Railway. Locomotive No. 4, which had also been No. 4 on the Corris Railway, stands at Tywyn Wharf. *GBJ Coll.*

By July 1978 the Talyllyn's rolling stock and infrastructure had received major attention. This view shows No. 3 outside the shed at Pendre. *GBJ*

A Talyllyn Railway Preservation Society Special hauled by No. 7827 *Lydham Manor* and No. 4555 approaches Penmaenpool; September 1964. This society set a pattern for the supporting organisations of preserved railways.   *J.B. Snell*

Changes of gauge to standard have occurred in some instances. Apart from the major change from broad gauge to standard on the GWR made in 1872, the Nantlle changed in part from 3' 6" to standard gauge. Later, the 4 miles from Ffestiniog to Blaenau Ffestiniog, which had originally been laid to the same 1' 11½" gauge as the Ffestiniog Railway, were converted to standard gauge. This was caused by the arrival in 1883 of the GWR with its branch from Bala to Ffestiniog.

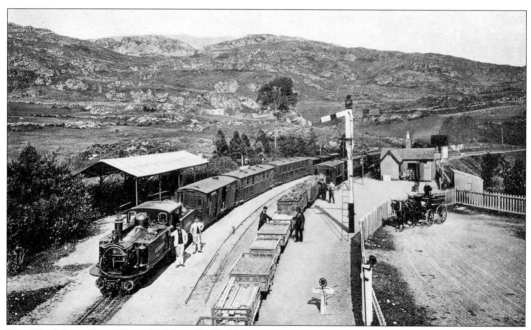

Two Ffestiniog trains at Tan-y-bwlch station in 1898.   *DD Coll.*

The Ffestiniog locomotive *Palmerston* was loaned to the Vale of Rheidol Railway during the First World War and is seen here departing from Aberystwyth; 13 August 1913.

LCGB/Ken Nunn Coll.

Vale of Rheidol locomotive No. 1 and the former Plynlimon & Hafan 2-4-0T, *Talybont*, renamed *Rheidol* by its new owners, at Devil's Bridge; July 1921.

W. Leslie Good/IAH Coll.

Vale of Rheidol 2-6-2T No. 8 outside the former GW main line shed at Aberystwyth, with the station visible in the distance; July 1972.

GBJ

The two gauges at Dinas Junction shortly after 1900.   *LNWR Soc.*

Much remains at Dinas Junction in spite of being out of use for 30 years; in 2000 it is the bridgehead for the Welsh Highland advance into Snowdonia; October 1999.   *GBJ*

Whereas the survival of both the GWR and LNWR lines has been helped by their competing routes to Ireland, both have suffered from having other lines with a poor basic economy, with no specialised function and therefore dependent on passengers and general goods traffic. The trade for which they were built has been insufficient to keep them economic. In most cases their creation was beset with financial difficulties, and their very construction required abnormal risk-taking by Welsh entrepreneurs optimistic about potential traffic growth and, in some cases, fired with a vision of developing the Welsh tourist industry. The Red Wharf Bay and Amlwch branches, half the Brecon & Merthyr, half the Neath & Brecon, the Mid Wales, most of the former Midland Railway, the Caernarvonshire Railway, the Vale of Clwyd line, the Carmarthen to Aberystwyth, the Ruabon to Dolgellau, the Bala

Horses were still engaged on slate trains on the Nantlle Railway in 1959. *NLW/G. Charles Coll.*

The busy yard at Talysarn where slate was transferred from the narrow gauge Nantlle to the LNWR. From a postcard posted in Talysarn on 27 May 1907.
DD Coll.

Penygroes station between Caernarfon and Afon Wen was the junction for the Nantlle branch. The branch train stands in the bay platform; probably early 1900s.
LNWR Soc.

Afon Wen station, looking south, in 1965 soon after closure of the line from Caernarfon.
GBJ Coll.

Torpantau station, looking south, with the 11.15 a.m. Newport to Brecon train hauled by No. 46524 in May 1953.
D. Chaplin

A Ruabon train progresses along the Mawddach estuary between Arthog and Penmaenpool headed by a 2-6-0 locomotive; June 1952. This beautiful line has been a victim of economics.
J.B. Snell

The 'up' Cambrian Coast Express leaving Dyfi Junction behind No. 7819; August 1964.   *J.B. Snell*

to Ffestiniog, and the Maenclochog were all in this category. If they developed a strategic role, it was in competition with other more robust lines. The bus, the car and the lorry dealt the knock-out blow. Remarkable, therefore, is the survival of the Cambrian lines which are stretched over lightly populated country. The coast line, in particular, was spared on political rather than economic grounds, but the decision has been justified by steady increases in passenger numbers, amounting in 1998 to 15% on the Pwllheli section and over 12% between Shrewsbury and Aberystwyth. Additional services were promised for 2000. The former LNWR Central Wales line has been similarly blessed though increases are less.

A 'down' Cambrian Coast Express approaches Llanbrynmair behind 'Manor' Class No. 7819 *Hinton Manor*; August 1964. Such a scene has been enjoyed since the official demise of steam, thanks to the activities of preservationists and the subsidised railway.   *J.B. Snell*

A BR Standard Class 3 2-6-2T emerges from the Abertafol tunnel between Aberdyfi and Dyfi Junction with an 'up' train; August 1964.   *J.B. Snell*

Alternatively, if prosperity was dependent upon one type of trade, usually mineral extraction, exhaustion of the minerals has removed the justification for the railway. Narrow economic purpose applied to many GWR and LNWR lines in Monmouthshire and Glamorgan, as well as to many of the smaller companies whose lines have disappeared altogether, such as those around Llanelli, and the Port Talbot and Rhondda & Swansea Bay. In the case of the Midland, the extended route from Hereford to Swansea suffered from being both a mineral line and covering an area of low population.

The survival of much of the system in the valleys of Glamorgan, the ultimate in specialist mineral lines, is attributable to the density of population. In an area of confined access, relatively low incomes, high population density and much commuting to work, the railway has some advantages over the car. As a result, the Taff Vale lines from Penarth to Treherbert and Merthyr and much of the Rhymney have maintained their passenger services without disruption following the Beeching report. The lines from Bridgend through Tondu to Maesteg and from Abercynon to Aberdare have actually been reopened after closure. There is now some support for reopening the line from Newport to Ebbw Vale and also for an attempt to restore passenger service on the Anglesey branch to Amlwch.

Another characteristic of the survivors is age. In Wales the rule 'first in, last out', seems to apply. The Ffestiniog, the Llanelly and the Taff Vale were the first railways in Wales, and among the first in Britain. Their original lines survive. The Chester & Holyhead, the Shrewsbury & Chester, the Shrewsbury & Hereford, the Newport, Abergavenny & Hereford, the Monmouthshire Railway's main line, and the South Wales were in the second

This view of the station at Pontardulais illustrates the principle of 'first in, last out'. The line to the right, through the short tunnel, was built as early as 1839 by the former Llanelly Railway and survives in use in 2000. The later arrival, on the left, the LNWR line from Swansea, lasted less than 100 years and was closed to passengers in 1964; 8 September 1951.   *H.C. Casserley*

round, but they have continued to perform a strategic role. The Barry, starting as late as 1889, was among the first to go. Once again, the Cambrian and the Central Wales seem to be the exception to the rule, and the Vale of Glamorgan has held on as a coal carrier and as an alternative main line.

The most remarkable rule breakers of all are the three youngsters from the final years of the nineteenth century, the Vale of Rheidol, the Snowdon Mountain and the Welshpool & Llanfair, all of which are narrow gauge and have focussed on tourist income. These and the narrow gauge lines of the north-west have become major tourist attractions.

The most successful of the standard gauge preserved Welsh railways is the Vale of Llangollen, pushing its way steadily up the Dee

A train of narrow gauge waggons, carried 'piggy-back' on the 4 ft gauge Padarn Railway, approaches the head of the incline down which the narrow gauge waggons were lowered to Port Dinorwig; August 1961.   *GBJ*

4-4-2 locomotive *Count Louis* setting off for Penrhyn Point with a Fairbourne Railway train; Summer 1966.
Ian L. Wright

The Mumbles tram near the southern terminus in the 1950s. This historic line was closed in 1960, just too soon for the wave of preservation enthusiasm which might have saved it.   *Ian L. Wright*

Brecon Mountain Railway locomotive *Graf Schwerin-Lowitz* at Pant station; June 1983. This railway, run with prudence and commercial good sense, is gradually creeping up the old Brecon & Merthyr track-bed towards Torpantau. *GBJ*

valley. Possibly the most ambitious is the Vale of Glamorgan with local government support and a role in an emerging major transport museum. Perhaps the most strategic is the Gwili on the line from Carmarthen to Aberystwyth, for the case for reopening the whole of this line as part of a north-south link through the unofficial cultural capital of Wales is aired periodically.

More might have survived had there been a determined effort to make a direct link between north and south Wales. A later chapter will demonstrate that a rail journey from north to south through Wales was not easy, even in 1899; in 1999 it required a diversion into England. The Glacier Express in Switzerland is a reminder of what might have been possible from Llandudno to Cardiff through Ffestiniog, Bala, Dolgellau, Llanidloes and Merthyr.

PROFITABILITY

The turn of the century witnessed something of a golden age in railway operations. On 6 January 1900, *Railway News* said, 'Never before has the history of the railways of the UK shown so much activity as in the year just passed'. Wage levels had risen, but moderately, and the economy was still expanding. In Wales the coal trade was fundamental to the railways and was not due to peak until 1913, and the passenger traffic was still growing. The only competition to which the railway was exposed came from coastal shipping and the electric tram. However, in 1888 and 1894, Parliament had introduced controls on the freight rates the railways could charge, operating costs, especially wages, were rising and competition was pushing the companies into upgrading passenger trains in comfort and speed. As a result, the basic determinant of profitability, the proportion of expenses in relation to total receipts, called the Operating Result, was continuing the slow deterioration which had begun in the 1870s.

This can be readily seen from the accompanying tables which reveal a number of yardsticks for determining efficiency. Detailed comparative statistics are only available from 1903 and, for the sake of identifying trends evident at the time, comparison with 1912 has been made. In 1903 the Barry was arguably the most efficient Welsh railway with expenditure at 51.5% of total receipts; the least efficient was the N & B at 70%, but, unlike most of the rest, it was able to improve by 1912, to 54%. The Cambrian result reflected extended rural lines but there was a small improvement against the trend over the period; the TVR and the RR were similar at 56.7% and 58.8%, respectively. The three English companies with a significant activity in Wales are included for the sake of comparison. Their figures are global as their Welsh activities are not separately identifiable. In 1900, 65% was the average across the whole of Britain.

There was no immediate correlation between the operating result and dividends, due to variations in financial structure; so, in 1899, the Rhymney yielded the most at 10%, the Barry was next at 9%, while the TVR, in a trough of abnormally low profitability, yielded only 3⅜% (a tough management lifted this to 8⅛% in 1900). The N & B, the B & M and the Cambrian had no ordinary shareholders; their shakey financial histories had left them with only priority backers.

The number of passengers carried in a year enables some assessment of relative size to be made. In 1900, across the whole of Britain, 1.1 billion passenger journeys were made. (In the financial year 1998/99 it was 892 million.) Of the Welsh companies, the Taff was by far the largest with over 9 million, representing over 10% of the GW's 83 million. Remarkably, three very different companies, the Rhymney, the Cambrian and the Barry all carried about 2.5 million. The Barry had done well to catch up with the Rhymney after only 10 years' operation, but the Rhymney was fighting a very successful rearguard action and showing exceptional growth in passenger numbers, seemingly at the expense of the Taff; indeed, this was the only Welsh railway showing a decline in total numbers carried

An examination of train miles operated by the companies introduces another indicator. Taking passenger train miles, it is not surprising that the Cambrian, with its route mileage, heads the list. More surprising, perhaps, is that the Taff, with only some 124 miles, was so close behind. The rate at which this indicator was growing varied but in all cases, except that of the Rhymney, it was

COMPANY	OPERATING RESULT % 1903	OPERATING RESULT % 1912	% ORD. DIVI- DEND 1899
BARRY	51.54	58.81	9
CAMBRIAN	63.15	62.02	–
NEATH & BRECON	70.2	54.25	–
RHYMNEY	58.76	59.7	10
TAFF VALE	56.69	56.96	3⅜
BRECON & MERTHYR	63.63	63.93	–
GREAT WESTERN	61.49	63.92	5½
LONDON & NORTH WESTERN	63.08	65.05	7⅛
MIDLAND	61.41	61.57	5⅜

PASSENGERS (1903 and 1912)						
COMPANY	000's	% CHANGE 1903/1912	TRAIN MILES 000's	% CHANGE TR. MLS (1903/12)	RECEIPTS % CHANGE	RECEIPTS/ TRAIN MILE % CHANGE
BARRY	2,486	11.64	430	23.06	12.04	(8.96)
CAMBRIAN	2,554	2.5	1,062	6.65	1.29	(5.02)
N & B	N/A	–	32	41.56	30.05	(8.13)
RHYMNEY	2,553	40.8	312	32.41	36.24	2.85
TAFF V.	9,332	(1.75)	903	8.94	0.85	(7.44)
B & M	745	34.51	198	29.52	17.02	(9.66)
GWR	83,450	18.14	25,401	12.72	23.01	9.14
LNWR	85,962	(8.00)	27,225	7.60	13.60	5.56
MID.	50,667	(11.61)	21,688	(3.70)	11.67	15.97

growing faster than the rate of growth in receipts. The receipts per train mile were nearly all decreasing, whereas the three English railways were all showing an increase. Only the Rhymney saw an increase in receipts per passenger train mile, though by only 2.8%. It is hard to understand why its performance should differ so markedly from that of the Taff Vale and the Barry but, as we have seen, it had an unusually strong growth in passenger numbers. To take the Cambrian as an example, its passenger train miles increased by 6.6%, yet this coincided with a fall in receipts per train mile of 5%; how much this was due to lower pricing or too many trains requires further study.

% CHANGE PASSENGER NUMBERS BY CLASS 1903/1912			
	1ST	2ND	3RD
GWR	6.15	(98.28)	29.43
LNWR	(23.87)	(94.55)	(1.13)
MID.	(37.61)	–	(10.9)

There was a national trend towards Third Class, stimulated by the Midland's abolition of Second Class travel in 1875 and, on top of that, a tendency to undercut the standard rate with excursion, workmen's and other discounted fares. In spite of this, the three big national companies all saw increases in receipts per passenger train mile over the period, 9% in the case of the GWR. The GWR was also increasing passenger numbers, no doubt in

response to the investment in route shortening and in the promotion of holiday traffic. The improved receipts per train mile were probably due to the introduction of longer trains of larger carriages with restaurant cars and, in the case of the GWR, an unusually healthy First Class. The Midland must have weeded out some unprofitable passenger trains, as they alone dropped train miles, yet made an impressive improvement in receipts per passenger train. Moving against the trend, in 1899, C.S. Denniss, the energetic general manager of the Cambrian restored Second Class on through trains, and in 1900 on local trains as well.

The ratio of passengers carried to passenger train miles is an indicator, though imperfect, of how well occupied the trains were. Assuming trains of equal capacity, it would seem that there was more than twice the chance of a seat on the Cambrian (2.5 passengers per train mile) as on the Barry (5.7) and, more surprisingly, that there was nearly twice as much on the Barry as on the Taff (10.3). The B & M (3.7) and GWR (3.0) were comparable. As a demonstration of how statistics can be used to prove anything, the Corris Railway with 110,000 passengers and 20,000 train miles had an average of 5.3 passengers per train mile, though one would hesitate to compare its profitability with that of the Barry.

Goods train miles, on the other hand, presented a very different picture and for most companies there was a decline over the next ten years.

GOODS TRAINS				
COMPANY	TRAIN MILES 000's	%CHANGE TR. MLS. (1903/12)	% CHANGE RECEIPTS	% CHANGE RECEIPTS/TR. ML.
BARRY	1,078	12.67	14.56	1.68
CAMBRIAN	577	(17.06)	(7.51)	11.51
N & B	57	58.72	52.91	(3.65)
RHYMNEY	1,736	18.64	20.08	5.99
TAFF V.	3,090	(2.85)	9.89	9.89
B & M	304	(1.10)	18.65	19.98
GWR	21,046	(6.68)	23.08	31.90
LNWR	18,176	(5.57)	19.66	26.71
MID.	25,111	(0.71)	13.40	14.22

Only the Rhymney, the Neath & Brecon and the Barry saw growth, in the case of the Rhymney by as much as 18.6%. In all three cases this was no doubt stimulated by new collieries happening to be within their reach, but the figures coincide with the Barry's determined and successful efforts to go out of its way to tap new sources. This drive appears to have had the greatest impact on the performance of the Taff Vale. The Cambrian's train miles dropped by as much as 17% and even the GWR lost 6.7% but, in spite of the drop, in both cases there was an improvement in receipts per train mile. On the Cambrian this was achieved despite a drop in total receipts, presumably by increasing train sizes. Indeed, receipts per goods train mile rose generally; the only exception was the N & B where the enormous growth in goods train miles of 58.7% resulted in a drop of 3.6% in receipts per goods train mile. Whether this was due to competitive rate cutting or discounting for increased volume remains to be investigated. The increases on the other Welsh railways ranged from nearly 20% on the Brecon & Merthyr, to a mere 1.7% on the Barry. Large increases by the big companies of 32% for the GW and 27% for the LNW illustrate the powerful economic effect produced by the longer trains, made possible by the introduction of larger locomotives. On the GWR, in particular, the turn of the twentieth century witnessed important developments in locomotive design which will be dealt with in a later chapter.

% CHANGE TOTAL WAGES 1903-1912

BARRY	24.3
CAMBRIAN	(3.92)
N & B	24.87
RHYMNEY	31.00
TAFF V.	8.92
B & M	14.78
GWR	28.03
LNWR	16.62
MID.	8.93

On all except the Cambrian, the total wages bill increased, in some cases, such as the Barry, the Rhymney and the GWR, by large amounts.

The Midland and the Taff saw noteably low rates of increase, the latter possibly reflecting a continuation of the management policy which led to the strike in 1900. It is not clear from these figures what proportion of the increases was due to rates of pay rising or shorter working hours and the extent to which they were influenced by increases in numbers of employees. Although business was increasing, so was train capacity, and there were few significant new activities like new lines or stations to account for more employees. For the previous ten years there had been mounting criticism of the long hours required of railwaymen, which had been given as the cause of accidents. This and the general atmosphere of industrial unrest across the country would suggest that a good proportion of these increases was due to a combination of higher wages and shorter working hours. If this was so, it makes it more difficult to understand what was happening on the Cambrian. A clue may lie in the fall in goods train miles and the unique decline in total receipts from goods trade. This and the relatively small increase in passenger train miles and passenger receipts may have prompted a determined drive for improved efficiency. In an operating area largely rural in nature it may also have been easier to hold down wage increases and maintain the hours worked.

The profitability of the smaller companies is not recorded in the official statistics. All that can be said with certainty is that, at the turn of the century, all were earning enough to keep running in an adequate state of maintenance, except for the North Wales Narrow Gauge and the Talyllyn. The former closed its passenger train service in 1916 and the latter only survived beyond 1911 due to the determination and generosity of its owner, Sir Henry Haydn Jones.

It is hard to find the equivalent figures for today. The train operating companies, not altogether unreasonably, treat their profitability as commercially sensitive. It is, however, possible to make some assessments and in this respect John Davies has been of great help. He believes the total 1999 proceeds from Welsh operations to be in the region of £120 million, of which as much as £78 million could be in the form of government support, which is set to decline. The £42 million derived from passenger business is thought to be split roughly as follows :

North coast (NW)	£10 m.
Mid-Wales (Central Trains)	3
South and west (Wales and West)	10
Great Western	10
Valleys	7
Virgin	2

In addition, there is an unquantified income from freight. The Central Wales Line provides a sobering example of railway economics:

Income	£500,000
Operating costs	£1,000,000
Maintenance	£1,000,000
Overheads	£4,000,000 (This includes

administration overheads and a provision for major maintenance, such as bridge and tunnel repairs. However, even if the railway were closed much of this would remain as an on-going obligation.)

With no figures identified separately for the English companies' operations in Wales, it is hard to compare figures over the 100 year period. In 1899, income from carrying freight, especially coal, must have been a major contributor to profit, as the results of the Rhymney, Taff Vale and Barry testify. How far it was possible to make some level of profit from rural passenger and goods traffic can only be guessed at on the basis of the results of those companies which were still independent. The Cambrian scraped a modest living, while the Golden Valley and the Manchester & Milford were clearly struggling. Those lines whose profitability was obscured by being part of something larger only became exposed when the overall profitability of railways was questioned after nationalisation. By then the carriage of coal was declining, investment was insufficient to maintain efficiency following the asset-exhaustion caused by the Second World War, the motor car was increasing its penetration, and we entered the era of public subsidies. It has been impossible for the railways to meet the continuous reduction in the cost of motoring,

The ultimate general purpose locomotive for the country railway, Ivatt 2MT No. 46421 near Llangelynin Halt; August 1965. *J.B. Snell*

A Pwllheli to Birmingham train, headed by Standard Class 4 No. 75014, passes along the Dyfi estuary at Frongoch between Aberdyfi and Dyfi Junction; August 1964.   *J.B. Snell*

The rust encrusted footbridge on the former Barry Railway at Wenvoe still had a further two years in use when photographed in 1960. It was the abandonment of redundant railway infrastructure during the 1960s which encouraged a fever of collecting. As a result, back gardens and spare bedrooms across the country now accommodate a multitude of small railway relics and artefacts which would otherwise have been lost.   *Ian L. Wright*

even with the very high fuel taxes. The improvements in rolling stock and propulsion efficiency have been inadequate, and when the immense cost of maintaining the infrastructure is added, the railways cannot compete on equal terms. Arguably, track technology has lagged behind but demands for greater speed and safety make it unlikely that great economies can be made there. If at any time the railways are left entirely to their own financial resources, it is open to speculation how many places in Wales will be within even 50 miles of a station.

CHAPTER 4

FREIGHT TRAINS

In 1900 the sea was still the principal means of moving bulk cargoes around the British Isles. The railways fed the ports and served bulk markets up to about 200 miles distant, especially where the other end of the chain was an inland location, such as Northamptonshire with its iron ore. Over longer distances coastal freight persisted and indeed has survived until 2000. Only during wartime was it necessary to use the railway for moving coal for the Royal Navy as far as the north of Scotland.

Military traffic was important in Wales before and during both world wars. LNWR 4-6-0 No. 1558, one of the '19 in. Goods', hauling a westbound military train along the north Wales coast around the time of the First World War. This class, introduced in 1906, was the mixed traffic version of the 'Experiment' express passenger class of 1905. *S. Reid Coll.*

The Royal Field Artillery en-training at the special military station at Trawsfynydd in the early 1900s.
GBJ Coll.

A double-headed army special passes Llanbedr & Pensarn, hauled by No. 9021 and another unidentified 4-4-0; April 1951.   *J.B. Snell*

It was for general cargo, packed goods, perishables and livestock that the railway was paramount, though the tonnages carried were small compared with bulk minerals. On the independent Welsh railways at the turn of the twentieth century general merchandise was only 10% of mineral trade, 4 million tons as opposed to 42 million. On the GWR and LNWR across the whole of Britain it was as much as 20%. It was an important business and the railways offered reasonable speed, security and nation-wide coverage. Livestock was still moved on the hoof, continuing the practice of the drovers, though with the help of the railway;

refrigeration was in its infancy and Londoners were still getting much of their milk from local farms. Initially, agricultural areas like Wales used the railway for supplying milk products such as butter and cheese to the towns. By the turn of the century trains were conveying milk in 10 gallon churns, though the dedicated bulk express from such places as Whitland and Carmarthen was not yet known. For fish the railway was ideal and dedicated fish trains to London and the major cities were among the fastest of the day, from Milford Haven and Swansea as much as from Grimsby and Peterhead.

Rebuilt 'Royal Scot' No. 46152 *The King's Dragoon Guardsman*, demoted to hauling a Holyhead to Rugby freight train, passes Connah's Quay, 28 April 1964.   *J. Hobbs/courtesy J.A. Peden*

The most striking feature of railway freight operations in Wales at the turn of the century was the contrast between the leisurely pattern on the rural lines in thinly populated areas and the intensity of traffic, mainly bulk, in the industrial areas. An examination of some examples will demonstrate the extent of the contrast.

PRO: RAIL 937/71

A page from the GW Working Timetable of 1899 covering the 45 miles from Ruabon to Dolgellau.

If we look at a day's activity over the 45 mile GW line from Ruabon to Dolgellau across the whole of northern Wales, it is clear that the absence of double track can have presented no serious problems in operating the fairly leisurely schedule. There was no heavy industry on the line so no bulk traffic. Demand for general cargo was also light as there were no large centres of population, so that at this time no daily goods trains travelled from end to end. Five goods trains ran each way between Corwen and Ruabon, and three from Llangollen; two ran between Llangollen and Corwen, all averaging about 10 m.p.h. There was only one in each direction between Dolgellau and Corwen which trundled along at an average speed of 7 m.p.h.

Eastbound goods from Machynlleth, No. 7807 *Compton Manor* approaches Bell's Bridge on the final section towards the summit of the line at Talerddig; August 1964.   *J.B. Snell*

BR Standard 4-6-0 No. 75014 curves away from Comins Coch towards Llanbrynmair and Talerddig with an 'up' freight train; August 1965. Such trains have been replaced in 2000 by lorries on crowded roads.

J.B. Snell

'Dean Goods' 0-6-0 No. 2315 pilots a Cambrian 0-6-0 on an 'up' J Class Goods at Moat Lane, *ca.* 1935.

GBJ Coll.

'Dean Goods' 0-6-0 No. 2452 approaching Pant-y-dŵr with the 9.45 a.m. Talyllyn Junction to Moat Lane freight train; 24 May 1952. In 1900 such a train was a familiar sight and formed the principal business of many country railway lines.

Ifor Higgon

The Cambrian main line was more active. Looking at 'down' trains only, there were two morning goods trains all the way from Oswestry to Aberystwyth and one in the afternoon, two from Welshpool to Machynlleth, and one from Oswestry to Moat Lane. Whereas the overnight mail train covered the 77 miles from Oswestry to Aberystwyth in just over three hours at 25 m.p.h., the early morning stopping goods took eight and a half hours, averaging 9 m.p.h. However, this included seven stops for goods handling, one of which at Machynlleth was for an hour and twenty minutes, and another was for half an hour at Moat Lane Junction. From Machynlleth, which served as a transit point, there were two daily trains as far as Pwllheli, and one to Dolgellau. From Moat Lane one train made for Brecon and another for Merthyr.

The Midland's strategic 78 mile route between Hereford and Swansea was a little more stretched, partly because it had to cope with altitude and bad weather, but the influence of Swansea and Birmingham at either end was apparent. Goods trains were not run through between Hereford and Swansea but were shunted at Brecon, approximately half way. Between Brecon and Hereford there were seven freight trains each way, four all the way to and from Birmingham which were operated during the night. The other three which ran during the day between Hereford and Brecon took some two and a half hours for the so-called 'Express Goods' and as much as six hours for the slow, an average speed of only 6 m.p.h.

Between Swansea and Brecon there were six trains each way, three during the night.

The fastest was a mineral train which took only two hours due to its limited need to stop, whereas the slowest goods took eleven. An example of the need to juggle with trains over a lengthy single line is provided by No. 9, the 5.20 a.m. mineral train from Brecon for Neath, conveying empty waggons for Swansea as required. These were to be detached at Penwyllt. The rest of the train ran on to Colbren Junction, which it was due to reach at 6.45 a.m. There a Neath & Brecon locomotive would have taken the train down to Neath. The Midland locomotive was then required to run extra trips as necessary down to Ystradgynlais, five miles down the Tawe valley, and then to be available to haul train No. 22, the 11.05 a.m. minerals train from Colbren, down to Ynysygeinon, the junction for the Brynamman branch. It had to be at Ystradgynlais at 11.48 a.m. to pass an 'up' train, No. 20, and then be available to haul 'up' train No. 22 from Ynysygeinon returning in front of the 10.30 a.m. 'up' from Swansea. If it could not hold this schedule, then 'down' train No. 22 was not to be run and No. 22 'up' was only to run between Colbren Junction and Brecon. Something of the flavour of this high and lonely line is obtained

from the instructions concerning the 6.30 a.m. goods train from Brecon which was to stop at the summit point called Bwlch to pick up the signalman and take him to the next inhabited place down the line, Penwyllt. After a lonely night at 1,200 ft this was no doubt welcome.

By 1911, there was some speeding up and the fastest train of the day was a 'Fish and Perishables' train from Swansea to Worcester which covered the 78 miles from Swansea to Hereford in just over three hours at 25 m.p.h. The 'Class A' goods to Birmingham was taking over five hours, but no longer were such through goods trains between Birmingham or Worcester and Swansea being shunted at Brecon.

The south Wales main line along the south coast was busy. Looking only at eastbound traffic, which would have been duplicated by balancing movements in the opposite direction, only three trains covered the whole distance from New Milford, the 'Irish Express Goods', the 'Second Irish Express Goods' and the 'Bristol Goods', but there was the 'Trawl Fish Train' from Old Milford to Paddington, the 'Haverfordwest Cattle' as far as Neath, the 'Carmarthen Junction and Pontypool Road Express Goods' and another general goods train

At Strata Florida 4-4-0 No. 9022 assisting 2-6-0 No. 5395 with a Carmarthen to Aberystwyth freight is coupled 'inside' for this leg of the journey as it is a returning banker; 30 April 1955.   *Ifor Higgon*

2-8-0T No. 4296 takes a westbound freight on the south Wales main line at Cardiff; 6 July 1947.

H.C. Casserley

between Haverfordwest and Neath at the end of the day. The 'Llanelly and London Minerals' was directed via Gloucester, and there were the 'Landore and Gloucester Goods', the 'Gloucester Goods' from Carmarthen Junction to Gloucester, and the 'Neath and Gloucester Goods'. Three trains of locomotive coal were directed through the Severn tunnel for Swindon, one from Neath and two from Llantrisant. There were about 20 coal trains from mid-Glamorgan which joined the main line at or near Llantrisant for Cardiff, and another 20 trains operating past Swansea within the area bounded by Llanelli and Neath. In parts, the line was therefore carrying something over 10 million tons of coal a year.

Dusk falls on two milk trains crossing at Cardiff Canton. 'County' Class 4-6-0 No. 1015 *County of Gloucester* approaches with the 'up' train; September 1962.

GBJ

'King' Class No. 6014 *King Henry VII* takes over an 'up' milk special at Cardiff Canton; 1962.   *GBJ*

Something of the complexity of managing this traffic can be gained from the instructions accompanying the Working Timetable. With no computers, but every type of merchandise from perishable food, livestock and fish, to minerals and parcels of all sizes consigned to points all over the country, the administration must have required discipline, diligence and a pedantic attention to detail. For example, at 3.00 a.m. a train left Llanelly for Gloster (*sic*) limited to 22 trucks from Llanelly, but to make up a load of not more than 26 at Landore and Neath: 'If there is not sufficient for beyond Gloster the train can take on trucks for via Severn Tunnel and also pick up at Cardiff. When necessary the 3.00 a.m. will be extended from Gloster as far as required. Guard to hand particulars of the loading of train to the Inspector at Cardiff who will immediately wire this information, together with the departure time to Mr Bridger, Gloster,

A train-spotter at the east end of Newport station with the GW version of the versatile 0-6-2T type frequently found in the south Wales valleys, in this case an early member of the class, No. 5602; August 1955.

G.H. Platt

in order that an engine and guard may be in readiness to take the train forward from there when required. On Sunday the train to be limited to a single engine load for Pyle Bank as bank engine is not available after 5.0 p.m.'

The 11.30 a.m. 'First Irish Goods' was supposed to take full loads of Irish goods, perishables and cattle only, from New Milford to London. However, the management were clearly keen to optimise. As a result, it was also to take trucks of pigs for Birmingham as far as Cardiff to catch the 8.20 p.m. from there to Birmingham, and traffic for Birkenhead and Manchester as far as Newport to catch the 7.40 p.m. for Pontypool Road. It was to take trucks of hides, when required, from Swansea to Cardiff and to

call, when required, at Port Talbot passenger station for consignments of copper and yellow metal for stations beyond Manchester. Mr Hargrave was to wire Mr Martin, Neath, when this was required and the engineman and guard were to be informed at Neath. The train was to be brought to a stand at Cardiff with the 'station truck' opposite the 'up' platform (station trucks were for the carriage of parcels to be unloaded at passenger stations). From Cardiff to Gloucester the load was not to exceed 30 trucks. And, almost an afterthought, there was to be a stop at Marshfield, when required, to put off cattle.

The 'Second Irish Goods' left New Milford at 3.35 p.m. 'to be started punctually on

A page of detailed instructions from the GW Working Timetable for 1899.
PRO: RAIL 937/71

to Neath Junction as early as possible each night of the number of Trucks and destination on this Train, so that it may be loaded sufficiently light to clear Port Talbot. Any Trucks for Stations which can be served by the 10.0 p.m. ex Llanelly Dock, or 3.0 a.m. ex Neath to be kept for these Trains when the 8.5 p.m. is so loaded as to necessitate its reducing the load to take on traffic at Port Talbot. Stations sending Birmingham and South Staffordshire traffic on the 3.35 p.m. New Milford must wire Port Talbot so that this Train may be kept for it.

8.30 p.m., Ely to Cardiff, to clear Ely of Paper Traffic for London to go forward by the 9.40 p.m. ex Cardiff.

9. 0 p.m., Llanelly Dock to Pontypool Road, to take Trucks for Stations at which it calls, and for beyond Pontypool Road. Trucks for North and South Docks to be put off at High Street Storage Sidings unless required for immediate shipment. Traffic to go on by this Train from Eastern Depot to be marshalled by Pilot Engine. Train to have one Goods Brake Van in front and one in rear. One Van to be put off at Neath Junction to return from there by 7.25 p.m. Pontypool Road to Llanelly Dock. To call at Cockett to set down Brakes only. Journal rendered to Mr. REES, Swansea, must show Cattle Trucks on Train giving numbers and Stations from and to.

9.30 p.m., New Milford to Tondu to take Trucks for Llantrisant, L. and O. Line, Port Talbot and Briton Ferry, and make up with local traffic. To clear Johnston of Up Line traffic and put trucks except cattle for 11.0 a.m. ex New Milford off at Haverfordwest for that Train to take on. To take on at Pembrey Empties for L. and O. Line only These Trucks to be shunted in readiness for 9.30 p.m. to pick up. Neath, Briton Ferry and Llantrisant trucks to be put off at Dynevor Sidings to go forward by the 5.45 a.m. Landore and Gloucester Train.

10.15 p.m., Carmarthen Junction to Gloucester, S. T. Nos. 434 and 435. Trucks for Llanelly, Llanelly Dock, and Llanelly Line to be kept together and put off at one shunt at Llanelly. Traffic for the Train to take on to be shunted out by Pilot Engine at Llanelly, and placed in readiness for the Train. To call at Gowerton when required for London traffic only. To call at Cockett to put down Brakes only. Traffic from Swansea to be worked to Landore by 9.50 p.m. North Dock to go on from there by this Train. Neath to wire Llantrisant nightly what traffic on Train when leaving for Taff Vale Line. When required urgent traffic for Pontypool Road from Stations where timed to call. Traffic from West of Landore (except cattle) for Port Talbot, Bridgend, and Llantrisant to be put off at Neath to go forward by subsequent trains. To pick up important paper traffic, when required at Cardiff for West of England, to go forward from Severn Tunnel Junction by the 7.5 p.m. ex Pontypool Road.

10.30 p.m., Neath Junction to Swindon and London, to take Coal for Stations east of Swindon, also take tin-plate traffic from Swansea for London.

10.45 p.m. Tondu to Exeter, Tuesdays, Thursdays, and Saturdays, to convey Loco. Coal.'

10.55 p.m., Llanelly Dock to Gloucester and Paddington. Train to be limited to 22 Trucks of Goods and Minerals from Llanelly Dock for Swindon and beyond, and to make up a load of not more than 24 at Landore or Neath. The time of departure of this Train to be wired daily from Severn Tunnel Junction to Messrs. Bridger and Williams, Gloucester, immediately the Train leaves. The Engines and Guard to be changed at Gloucester.

11. 0 p.m., New Milford to Neath, to work local traffic. On week-days, Empties for Cae Duke to be put off at Loughor. To run on to Briton Ferry when required, leaving Neath with Briton Ferry Trade only. To call at Swansea Valley Junction when required to put off traffic. To call when required at Dynevor Sidings to take Crippled Wagons for Repairing Shops, and other Traffic for Neath. Train and Engine to be relieved as soon as possible on arrival at Neath, and Crippled Wagons to be taken to Shed by Shed Pilot. On Sundays, CR at Llandilo Junction to put off Cae Duke and Loughor Colliery Empties. When running late every effort must be made to get this Train to Neath to connect with 10.50 a.m. thence to Tredegar Junction, and, if necessary, Trucks must be picked up unmarshalled, but Guards must give full particulars of such cases on their journals.

11.20 p.m. Pwllcarne to Cardiff, to convey shipment traffic.

11.25 p.m., Nantymoel to Cardiff, to convey Coal for shipment.

11.30 p.m., Tondu to Pontypool Road, to convey Loco. Coal, &c., and Station Trucks from Cardiff

Station Truck Traffic to be limited, as far as possible, to the Station Truck Trains.

The foregoing Regulations are intended for the guidance of the Company's Servants in forming Trains, but it must be understood that a Truck of Perishable or Market Traffic may be sent in preference to any other traffic

Thursdays whether the traffic is ready or not', an unpunctual departure on other days of the week being by implication acceptable. But if traffic had to be left behind on a Thursday, it was to be put on a special which was to overtake the main train at Neath. To enable the special to achieve this remarkable feat, locomotive, van and guard had to be provided, and if they were not in the event needed, they were to assist the main train as far as Carmarthen Junction and then work their way back to New Milford. On Tuesdays, Thursdays and Saturdays, when the Irish traffic was particularly heavy, there was a relief train at 12.25 p.m. as far as Carmarthen Junction. The locomotive was to be available to assist the 'Second Irish Goods' 'as far as required', and the guard and van were to accompany it, so that they could together work a train back. The 'Second Irish Goods' had a complex task. Its main role was to convey traffic for Didcot and beyond but it was also to pick up from stations west of Landore. At Landore it was to pick up goods for Birmingham and south Staffordshire, which was to be put off at Port Talbot in time to catch the 8.45 p.m. from Neath to Worcester. At Port Talbot, only London traffic was to be loaded. It was important that the train arrived at Neath at its booked time as it had to make connection with a Vale of Neath train, which was kept at Neath until 9.00 p.m. in order to load cattle for Merthyr.

Another important train was the 3.05 p.m. 'Trawl Fish Train' from Old Milford (Milford Haven) to Paddington. This was limited to 20 waggons for one engine. Assistance was required as far as Carmarthen Junction for up to 35 waggons and, if there were more, a relief train was to be run at 3.35 p.m., just when the 'Second Irish Goods' was leaving New Milford (on Thursdays). Bristol fish was to be put off at Cardiff. From New Milford, no fish was to be carried in any other train. On the other hand, it seems that horseboxes and carriage trucks could be added, presumably as they were light and required a fast train. Fish for London was 'to be formed together' and was to be loaded as far as possible in vacuum brake vehicles. Every effort was to be made to run this train punctually.

At 2.00 p.m. a train left New Milford for Bristol Temple Meads with a particularly complicated set of tasks. On Tuesdays, Thursdays and Saturdays, it was to consist of no more than six waggons on departure so that it could pick up at stations to Carmarthen Junction. On other days the load was not to exceed 16 waggons and at stations (only as far as St. Clears) it was to pick up livestock, perishables, Bristol traffic and GW empties (to be put off at Carmarthen Junction), and to make up a load with trucks for the Vale of Neath line. At Clarbeston Road it was to place trucks in the 'up' line siding to be picked up by the 11.00 p.m. goods and it was to be prepared to take cattle for Ferryside and Kidwelly. From Carmarthen Junction it was to pick up trucks for destinations beyond Pyle only, but it was not to take on trucks for main line destinations beyond Severn Tunnel Junction. It was to call at Gowerton for cockles and Bristol Temple Meads traffic only. It was also to call at Pembrey for cockles for the Vale of Neath line. Then came the real test. Traffic for Bristol East from west of Landore was to be put off at Neath 'to go forward' by the 12.50 a.m. Landore to Bristol East, with the exception of livestock for stations served by the 8.25 a.m. from Bristol Temple Meads to Didcot. If the train was running to time, this was to be taken to Bristol. Instructions in the event of the train not running to time were not given. Finally, the train was to call at Briton Ferry and Port Talbot for Bristol Temple Meads traffic only.

Every day at 8.10 a.m. there was a catch-all so-called 'Station truck goods' which contained parcels traffic for stations between Neath and Gloucester. It was not to do any shunting at stations and on Mondays and Thursdays took a gunpowder van. It was to take on traffic which could not be worked by other trains up to a limit of 20 trucks, and guards were to marshal trucks for beyond Gloucester together, in order to 'reduce the amount of transfer to be done at Gloucester'.

In summary, the main 'up' GWR freight trains over the whole distance between New Milford and the Severn tunnel were:

12.30 a.m.	'Goods' Alexandra Docks to Pontypool Rd
12.35 a.m.	'Pick-up goods' Pembrey to Cardiff
12.35 a.m.	'Goods' for Merthyr, Cardiff to Aberdare via Nine Mile Point
12.45 a.m.	'Coal' Cardiff to Exeter (alternate days)
12.50 a.m.	'Fast goods' Landore to Bristol
1.00 a.m.	'Coal' Rogerstone to Exeter (alternate days)
1.35 a.m.	'Empties' Cardiff to Rogerstone
2.15 a.m.	'Empty waggons' Carmarthen Junction to Bristol
2.30 a.m.	'Coke for South Staffordshire' Bridgend to Pontypool Road
2.35 a.m.	'Coal' for London. Rogerstone sidings to Swindon
2.55 a.m.	'Goods' Cardiff to Bridgewater
3.00 a.m.	'Goods' Llanelly to Gloster (*sic*) and excess from the 10.55 p.m.
3.10 a.m.	'Empties' Penarth Jc. to Ebbw Vale
4.00 a.m.	'Empties' Llanelly to Landore
4.30 a.m.	'Empties' Penarth Jc. to Branches Fork (Eastern Valley)
4.40 a.m.	'Coal' Tondu to Cardiff
4.40 a.m.	'Coal' Rogerstone to Bristol
5.45 a.m.	'Goods' Landore to Gloucester
6.05 a.m.	'Empties' Cardiff to Cwmtillery (Western Valleys)
6.20 a.m.	'Coal' Llantrisant to Swindon
6.25 a.m.	'Goods' Pontypool Rd to Bristol from Manchester etc.
7.00 a.m.	'Coal' Llantrisant to Bristol
7.00 a.m.	'Goods' Stormy to Alexandra Docks
7.00 a.m.	'Goods' Newport to Pontypool Rd via Llantarnam
7.05 a.m.	'Goods' Pontypool Rd to Exeter
7.05 a.m.	'Empties' Penarth Jc. to Rogerstone
7.40 a.m.	'Goods' Penarth Jc. to Swindon
8.00 a.m.	'Empties' Llanelly to Briton Ferry
8.10 a.m.	'Station Truck Goods' Neath to Gloucester
8.50 a.m.	'Bricks and tiles' Pontypool Rd to Portskewett
9.30 a.m.	'Coal' Tondu to Severn Tunnel Junction
10.30 a.m.	'Minerals' Landore to Swindon
11.00 a.m.	'Empties' Penarth Jc. to Ebbw Vale
11.30 a.m.	'First Irish Goods' New Milford to London
11.40 a.m.	'Goods' Alexandra Docks to Pontypool Rd
12.25 p.m.	'Relief Irish Goods' New Milford to Carmarthen Jc.
12.25 p.m.	'Empties' Llanelly to Neath
12.30 p.m.	'Coal' Tondu to Cardiff
12.30 p.m.	'Coal' Gilfach to Cardiff
1.15 p.m.	'Mixed traffic' Whitland to Pembrey
1.35 p.m.	'Coal' Nantymoel to Cardiff
1.45 p.m.	Landore to Tondu
2.00 p.m.	'Goods' New Milford to Bristol
2.00 p.m.	'Empties' Penarth Jc. to Rogerstone
2.10 p.m.	'Empties' Penarth Jc. to Nantyglo
2.50 p.m.	'Coal Empties' Swansea to Tondu
3.05 p.m.	'Trawl Fish' Old Milford to London
3.30 p.m.	'Empties' Neath to Llantrisant
3.30 p.m.	'Empties' Penarth Jc. to Pontnewynydd (Eastern Valley)
3.35 p.m.	'Second Irish Goods' New Milford to London
4.00 p.m.	'Coal' Pwllcarn to Cardiff

4.25 p.m.	'Express Goods' Carmarthen Jc. to Pontypool Rd
5.00 p.m.	'Goods' Llantrisant to Cardiff
5.05 p.m.	'Goods' New Milford to Neath
5.10 p.m.	'Coal' Cymmer to Cardiff
5.30 p.m.	'Coal' Tondu to Cardiff
5.35 p.m.	'Coal' Gilfach to Cardiff
5.45 p.m.	'Coal' Nantymoel to Cardiff
5.55 p.m.	'Coal' Llantrisant to Swindon
6.00 p.m.	'Express Minerals (tin)' Swansea to Worcester
7.05 p.m.	'Empties' Penarth Jc. to Rogerstone
7.20 p.m.	'Goods' Cardiff to Exeter
7.40 p.m.	'Coal' Branches Fork (Eastern Valley) to Bristol
7.40 p.m.	'Goods' Newport to Pontypool Rd
7.50 p.m.	'Coal' Llantrisant to Swindon
8.05 p.m.	'Express Goods' Swansea to Worcester via Pontypool Rd
8.20 p.m.	'Important Goods' Cardiff to Birmingham
8.50 p.m.	'Goods' Cardiff to Newport Dock St
9.00 p.m.	'Goods' Llanelly to Pontypool Rd
9.00 p.m.	'Goods' Cardiff to Salisbury for LSWR
9.30 p.m.	'Empties' New Milford to Tondu
9.40 p.m.	'Coal' Rogerstone to Swindon
9.40 p.m.	'Express Goods' Cardiff to Paddington via Gloucester
10.15 p.m.	'Goods' Carmarthen Jc. to Gloucester
10.15 p.m.	'Goods' from Eastern Valley Pontypool Rd to Bristol
10.30 p.m.	'Coal' Neath to London
10.45 p.m.	'Coal' Tondu to Exeter
10.50 p.m.	'Goods and Minerals' Cardiff to Wolverhampton
10.55 p.m.	'Coal and Goods' Llanelly to London
11.00 p.m.	'Goods and Empties' New Milford to Neath
11.00 p.m.	'Empties' Penarth Jc. to Rogerstone
11.10 p.m.	'Goods' Cardiff to Pontypool Rd
11.20 p.m.	'Coal' Pwllcarn to Cardiff
11.25 p.m.	'Coal' Nantymoel to Cardiff
11.30 p.m.	'Coal' Tondu to Pontypool Rd
11.45 p.m.	'Coal' Rogerstone to Swindon

This rather exhausting list of 84 trains appears at first sight to be somewhat impenetrable. It does, however, reward study. The traffic in empties is immediately apparent, also the activity around Pontypool Road. Some interesting movements are revealed, as for instance the number of trains at Penarth Junction for the Monmouthshire lines, indicating that the Taff Vale monopoly at Penarth did not prevent the sourcing of coal from collieries not served by the Taff Vale. Indeed, the number of 'empties' suggests as much as half a million tons a year. The 12.35 a.m. train from Cardiff to Aberdare with general goods for Merthyr is channelled over what at first sight appears an odd route, requiring use of

LNWR metals from Nine Mile Point to the Taff Vale Extension at Tredegar Junction, but in 1899 the only alternative for the GWR was by way of Neath and the Vale of Neath line. The Taff Vale had the most direct route to Merthyr, and the Rhymney was also advantageously placed by way of Ystrad Mynach and Quakers Yard.

When considering the human activity behind these movements, it is worth a moment to speculate on the rivalry in Swansea between the Midland and GW traffic managers for the trade with Worcester and Birmingham. The GW train left East Dock at 8.05 p.m. and the Midland had an equivalent five minutes earlier at 8.00 p.m. from St Thomas. The GW train reached

Hereford by way of Cardiff at 4.15 a.m., left there at 4.40 and reached Worcester at 6.30. The Midland train reached Hereford at 2.10 a.m.

and, in spite of waiting there until 3.50 a.m., reached Worcester at 5.40 a.m.

Coed Talon station and a local goods train with locomotive No. 44065, an ex LMS Class 4 0-6-0. This former LNWR station lay on the branch from Mold to Brymbo. The suspicious-looking characters in the foreground are almost certainly railway enthusiasts as the second brake van was providing accommodation for a Branch Line Society tour; 18 April 1959. *C.A. Appleton/courtesy J.A. Peden*

In June 1964 a general goods train heads west from Usk behind 0-6-0PT No. 8495. *J.B. Snell*

Cilgerran, although only a small country station, generated considerable commercial activity at this time, especially timber; *ca.* 1910.

NLW

An early 1960s photograph showing the porter at Llandysul coping with a large consignment of Lyons cakes.

Lens of Sutton

The list also reveals the intensity of activity in only one direction, with an average of between three and four trains starting every hour of the day, nearly every train requiring attention at intermediate stations to have trucks removed or added, and the activity spread fairly evenly around the clock. At Severn Tunnel Junction, for instance, there were 26 'up' trains through the night between 9.00 p.m. and 7.00 a.m. It must have been extremely difficult to keep control of the locomotives and brake vans, let alone the waggons and their contents, and there is evidence from 'Special Notices' of quite a number of parcels and even rolling stock going missing. For example, even in August 1944 a corridor brake composite (No. 7370) was 'missing, and all concerned to keep a sharp look-out'.

Punctuality seems to have been a low priority. The instructions concerning a 'Cattle Special' from New Milford to Acton reveal both the pessimistic assumptions about punctuality

and the tendency to deal with priority movements on an *ad hoc* basis. The train was only to be run if there were more than 10 trucks for Acton and beyond, so it was not part of the timetable: 'It is important that the train be got through without delay and Station Masters . . . must take steps to ascertain the actual running of the train on receipt of advice from New Milford, and personally see the train through their respective stations.' For the cattle herded into the rattling trucks it must have been a rough ride but no doubt it delivered them in Acton in better shape than in the days when they had to walk all the way.

The difficulties created by unpunctual operating must have been enormous, yet it seems to have been policy to seek to optimise, on the day, the trains, the cargoes and line occupation. The timetable was subject to the proviso that the regulations were for the guidance of staff forming trains and it was to be

A short freight train passes the Penarth
Lime Works siding; 1958.   *Ian L. Wright*

understood that, 'a truck of
perishable or market traffic may be
sent in preference to any other
traffic named'. One can only admire
the effort and attention to detail, and
question whether a stricter
adherence to the timetable and a
movements plan could have
achieved profits greater than those
assumed by being flexible. It might
certainly have made it easier to run
passenger trains to time. There has
to be a balance in all things, and it
was no doubt an over-rigid
adherence to the timetable and
keeping it simple that destroyed
much of the railway freight business
in the second half of the twentieth
century. That much was lost due to
an unwillingness to care is proved
by the achievements of the
privatised freight companies whose
'can do' attitude is restoring some
of the freight previously given up to
road and coastal shipping.

This memorandum contains the story of just one parcel and
provides an example of the careful administration and attention to
detail required in the railway general goods business at the turn of
the century. In December 1893 it was sent by the Cambrian
Railways' parcels depot at Newtown to Shipley on the Great
Northern concerning a parcel destined ultimately for Baildon on
the Midland. In red ink the GN confirm having passed it on to the
Midland.   *GBJ Coll.*

A heavy freight, hauled by No. 4688, waits to proceed north through the busy sidings at Aberbeeg in the Ebbw valley, an indication of the scale of infrastructure needed to handle the immense coal traffic and, in this case, iron as well; April 1962.
Steam & Sail/ E.S. Owen Jones

A view up the Afan valley towards Blaengwynfi, a beautiful setting plundered for its coal; 1960s.
A. Jarvis

The teeming activity associated with a large coalmine and the close dependence upon the railway is displayed in this fine study of Lewis Merthyr Colliery in the Rhondda valley.
WIMM/GW Coll.

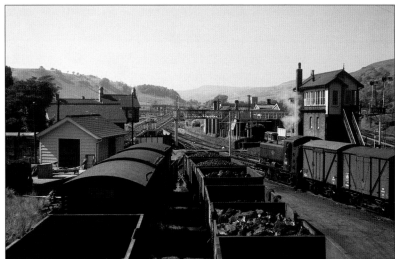

In June 1962 what is possibly locomotive No. 3415 shunts the coal yard at Taffs Well.

GBJ

A 'down' Taff Vale train at Mountain Ash hauled by TVR 'K' Class No. 158; *ca.* 1920.

G.H. Platt Coll.

The administration of the movement of coal was a major undertaking. These coal sidings are at Cardiff Canton; 27 September 1933.

WIMM/GW Coll.

In the authors' earlier book *The Vale of Neath Line* the movement of coal to England between Neath and Pontypool over this complex cross-country line is traced in some detail. In the 1880s 40 trains a day were moving coal from the Cynon valley, 28 to England and 12 down the Rhymney Railway line to Cardiff. By 1899 this activity had declined to about 30, due mainly to the exhaustion of some of the older pits. Before long, the increasing size of locomotives would start to make it possible to assemble longer trains. This development coincided with the continuing rise in total Welsh coal production up to the peak of 57 million tons in 1913. Through 1899 and for many years thereafter, some 1.5 million tons of coal a year were carried over the Vale of Neath line to England, with some dramatic peaks of activity during the two world wars. An impression of the activity can be gained by listing the 'up' English coal trains:

1.45 a.m.	Gelli Tarw (Jc. for Merthyr) to Swindon
2.30 a.m.	Aberdare to Bristol
4.00 a.m.	Aberdare to Swindon for London
5.05 a.m.	Aberdare to Swindon for West London line
12.05 p.m.	Gelli Tarw to Pontypool Road for Oxford
2.05 p.m.	Aberdare to Salisbury for Southampton
3.45 p.m.	Aberdare to Pontypool Road
4.20 p.m.	Aberdare to Swindon
5.00 p.m.	Aberdare to Swindon for west London
5.40 p.m.	Aberdare to Salisbury for Southampton
6.50 p.m.	Aberdare to Pontypool Road for Oxford
7.45 p.m.	Aberdare to Swindon for Brentford and Chelsea
8.30 p.m.	Aberdare to Swindon for west London
9.15 p.m.	Aberdare to Swindon for London
10.10 p.m.	Aberdare to Salisbury for Southampton
10.30 p.m.	Gelli Tarw to Swindon for Basingstoke
11.55 p.m.	Gelli Tarw to Pontypool Road for Oxford

These had to share a busy line with general goods and passenger trains, many of which joined and left the line at one or more of the 20 junctions which existed between Neath and Pontypool Road. In the middle there was the single track section through the 703 yard Cefn Glas tunnel, inclined at 1:100 against the load, and the approach to Pontypool Road involved a descent at 1:45 for four miles. However, trains due for Bristol or Swindon avoided this particular obstacle by taking the LNWR line at Tredegar Junction, though they then had to plough their way through the Severn tunnel.

Westbound on the Vale of Neath line, a heavy train of empty waggons is hauled from Hafodyrynys towards the Glyn tunnel by 2-8-2T No. 7230 and a 2-6-2T; June 1964.

J.B. Snell

Quakers Yard Low Level on the TVR main line with, on the left, at a higher level, the single line section of the Vale of Neath line from Cefn Glas tunnel to Quakers Yard High Level; 1964.

G.H. Platt

An illuminating example of the complexity and detail associated with the handling of general traffic on a line already busy with both passenger and coal trains is provided by these instructions concerning the 5.50 p.m. train from Merthyr to Pontypool Road. This train ran down the GW/RR joint line to Quakers Yard and then along the Vale of Neath line. 'To take Merthyr goods and iron from Cyfarthfa and coal from Merthyr Vale sidings. When it has "on traffic" for London and at the same time a full through load for Pontypool Road, it must stop at Rhymney Junction to put off the London traffic. When however it has to go into the yard at Quakers Yard to make up a load for Pontypool Road, the London traffic must be put off at

The once important goods yard at Pontypool Road, looking north; 30 July 1939. At one time 100 locomotives were allocated here. *J.A. Peden*

Tondu Junction near the turn of the century. This important junction for coal trains was dominated by a signal some 40 ft high.

John Ryan Coll./
courtesy J.A. Peden

An atmospheric picture of No. 4237 on Hall's Road in the Ebbw valley near Cwmcarn; 22 March 1962. This line was the successor to an old tramway built in 1805 to link the Ebbw valley with coalmines in the Sirhowy valley. It survived as an alternative route for the GWR between the Vale of Neath line and Newport.
C.H.A. Townley/J.A. Peden

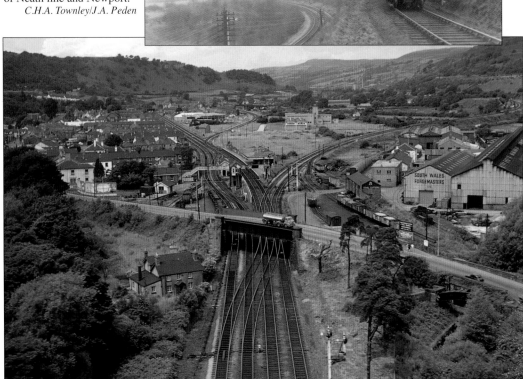

The view from the Barry's Walnut Tree viaduct looking up the Taff towards Pontypridd; 11 June 1959. The first line bearing away to the right (from near Taffs Well station) was the original main line of the Rhymney Railway to Aber Junction, Caerphilly. The second line was the 1953 spur, constructed by the Western Region to connect with the former Cardiff Railway line into the (then) new colliery at Nantgarw.   *Ian L. Wright*

Quakers Yard. Whenever skin traffic is sent from Merthyr by this train, Merthyr must advise Quakers Yard by wire that such traffic is being sent, and special efforts must be made to keep a clear line for the train, so that it may get to Pontypool Road in time to connect with the 10.00 or 10.30 train thence to Manchester.' It can safely be assumed that no one concerned would have wanted to keep a load of skins from a Merthyr tanning plant hanging about.

Running up and down the valleys, the activity was even more frenetic and a focal point was Pontypridd. At the turn of the twentieth century, the Taff Vale decided that they would have to expand the area occupied by the station as its traffic had grown fast and it had become one of the busiest places in Wales. About 150 trains a day in each direction made their way through it. Of these, as many as 50 movements were passenger trains, passing,

The approach to Pontypridd station from the south with the Pontypridd, Caerphilly and Newport line (PCN) entering on the right; 1959. This cross-country line was built to enable Newport Docks to tap Rhondda coal.
G.H. Platt

originating or terminating. The remainder were nearly all coal trains in one direction and empties back. Pontypridd is just below the point where the Cynon and Rhondda valleys join the Taff and, consequently, coal trains from these three major sources were concentrated here. Some 70% were destined for Cardiff, while Penarth received 20% and Barry 10%.

An elevated view of Pontypridd station looking north; *ca.* 1910.
John Ryan Coll./J.A. Peden

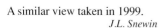

A similar view taken in 1999.
J.L. Snewin

The rebuilding of Pontypridd station, looking north, *ca.* 1906.   *PRO: RAIL 1057/2827*

The view southward during the rebuilding of Pontypridd Station, *ca.* 1906.   *PRO: RAIL 1057/2827*

A '5600' Class 0-6-2T stands at the northern end of Pontypridd station; 1964.

GBJ

There were movements all round the clock on weekdays. Only on Sundays was there a respite, when there were just six passenger departures each way and no freight moved at all. On weekdays, in its busiest hour between 2.00 and 3.00 p.m., ten loaded coal trains were moved down the valley through Pontypridd; another seven trains were scheduled in the opposite direction. At 2.00 p.m. a passenger train for Cowbridge departed. At the same time, an Aberdare coal train was due on its way to Penarth. At 2.02 p.m. a train of empties for

The northern junction at Pontypridd with the Rhondda line to Treherbert curving away left and the main line towards Merthyr to the right; September 1964.

G.H. Platt

The northern junction at Pontypridd, looking south; 2 July 1950.

WIMM/GW Coll.

Ynysybwl preceded an 'up' goods train due at 2.05 p.m. At 2.08 p.m. came a coal train from Merthyr for the Cathays Van Sidings in Cardiff. Only two minutes later another coal train was due, this time from the Rhondda valley, also bound for Cardiff. A 'Pentre Minerals' train for Cardiff was due at 2.15 p.m., passing empties for Maerdy, and then at 2.20 p.m. there was a goods train from Treherbert, also for Cardiff. At 2.27 p.m. came a train of empties for Aberdare. At 2.30 p.m. some more Rhondda coal for Cardiff preceded a Saturday workmen's train, also from the Rhondda. Simultaneously, a train of coal from Mountain Ash in the Cynon valley headed

for Penarth. At 2.33 p.m. there was a train of empties for Treherbert which passed a 'Treherbert Minerals' due at 2.40 p.m., followed by a 'Hafod Minerals' at 2.45 p.m., all for Cardiff. At 2.41 p.m. a Treherbert-bound passenger train had to be fitted into the schedule and at 2.50 p.m. coal from the Dare valley was due, bound for Cardiff, and at the same time there was a train of empties for the Eirw branch. At 2.55 p.m. came more 'Treherbert Minerals'. Assuming trains consisted of an average of twenty 12 ton waggons, something like 7 million tons was being moved in a year through Pontypridd. By 1913 this volume had nearly doubled.

Porth Junction with the line up the Rhondda Fawr to Treherbert on the left and the Rhondda Fach line to Maerdy on the right; 1964. The unusual signal-box illustrated on page 56 is located in the fork of the junction.

G.H. Platt

Porth station, looking south, viewed from the Rhondda Fawr line; 1960.

G.H. Platt

Another busy line was that up the border from Newport towards Shrewsbury. Pontypool Road has already been mentioned. It was a busy goods interchange as well as being a transit point for coal trains. In 1899, about one GWR train an hour left for the midlands and the north, throughout the day and night. From Abergavenny Junction they were joined by nearly as many from the LNWR. One of the authors living in sight of the line recalls the even more intense traffic during the Second World War. The activity was almost constant as a wide variety of both goods and passenger trains, LMS and GWR, ran down from Llanfihangel, over the embankment across the Llanthony valley, or pounded their way south.

A train of empties proceeds east through Cockett station on the south Wales main line, a familiar sight at this location for 100 years. Photographed *ca.* 1910.
Lens of Sutton

In the authors' earlier book, *The Origins of the LMS in South Wales*, an attempt is made to assess the volume of traffic carried by the LNWR and the Midland in south Wales. In round figures, it would appear that by the beginning of the First World War the Midland was moving nearly 5 million tons of coal and minerals, mainly to Swansea, but of that about 10% inland into England, while the LNWR was handling a similar total volume with a rather higher proportion to England by way of Abergavenny or the Central Wales line.

The movement of coal down the valleys to the Welsh ports was a massive operation involving an enormous army of waggons. Each of these would have borne the name of the colliery whence it came in large white letters, as it was the practice for the owners to provide their own waggons. Further west, the anthracite waggons often advertised the burning qualities of the fuel, as a higher proportion of this product went to the inland market. The waggons were normally leased to the colliery owners by finance houses such as North Central Finance and Lombard, and by today's standards they were kept remarkably clean.

The following table is an attempt to analyse how Welsh coal production was probably distributed at the turn of the century. The figures in the table are in millions of tons per annum but rounded to the nearest million, as anything more precise would suggest an impossible level of accuracy. They are based on a combination of recorded fact, deduction and elimination, but an overall picture is obtained which is probably sufficiently close to the truth to be of interest. Totals for each railway may not coincide with recorded totals for total tonnage carried due to the tonnages which were transferred between companies on the way between colliery and port.

1899/1900 WELSH COAL BY DESTINATION AND ROUTE. Mill. tons p.a.								
	TOTAL	LNW	MID	GW	TVR	RR	BARRY	OTHERS
EXPORT via CDF	8	1	–	1	4	2	–	–
P'ARTH	2	–	–	–	2	–	–	–
NPT	4	1	–	2	–	–	–	1
S'SEA	2	–	2	–	–	–	–	–
BARRY	7	–	–	–	–	–	7	–
OTHERS	1	–	–	–	–	–	–	1
TOTAL	24	2	2	3	6	2	7	2
INLAND	15	3	1	4	2	2	1	2
S.WALES TOTAL	39	5	3	7	8	4	8	4
N. WALES	3	1	–	2	–	–	–	–
TOTAL	42	6	3	9	8	4	8	4

The GWR had a diversified spread, its position boosted by its stronghold in the area of Tondu, whence as much as one million tons a year was exported through Cardiff. Another million tons was moved into England from Tondu and the Western and Eastern Valleys of Monmouthshire. With its reliance on Welsh coal for its locomotives in England and its access to Aberdare over the Vale of Neath line, whence perhaps one and a half million tons a year was taken to England, it was the largest supplier into England. As already noted, the LNWR was moving coal northward through Abergavenny, but also over the Central Wales line. Its movements to Cardiff south of the GW's Vale of Neath line were, it is thought, hauled by Rhymney locomotives. The Midland was dependent on Swansea, but there it was very strong. The 'other' railways include those feeding Llanelli, and the Neath & Brecon, Rhondda & Swansea Bay, Port Talbot, and Brecon & Merthyr. The 'other' ports include Port Talbot, Llanelli and Saundersfoot. 'Inland others' includes coastal movements.

In 1901, for the first time, Barry drew ahead of Cardiff as an exporter of coal though it dropped back temporarily in 1911. In that intermediate 10 years exports increased by 50% as the following table shows:

1911 MILLION TONS p.a.

CARDIFF	10
PENARTH	4
SWANSEA	5
NEWPORT	5
BARRY	9
PORT TALBOT	2
OTHERS	1
TOTAL	36

Meanwhile, in the north-west, little trains were crawling down the steep and winding tracks from the quarries, loaded with slate. The peak year for slate production was 1898 when some 500,000 tons were shifted. Most was loaded into ships at Port Dinorwic, Porthmadog, Degannwy and Caernarfon for both domestic and foreign consumption, but some was taken by rail from Blaenau Ffestiniog and there was also transfer to the standard gauge at Minffordd and Tywyn. It was, however, a less mechanised operation than the movement of coal and involved much physical handling by men.

By the 1950s the sidings and wharves at Port Dinorwic were reflecting the decline of the industry.

R. Wood

In 2000 the movement of freight is conducted in fewer and much heavier trains and is confined to bulk products such as oil, chemicals, coal, iron ore, steel products, stone and aggregates. With waggons of 25 tons axle loading marshalled in trains of, for example, 3,000 tons of iron ore, movements though regular are less frequent. As we shall see in the next chapter, this is in contrast to the trend in passenger traffic, where train carrying capacity is little changed but train frequency over the surviving track is much increased. However, freight traffic shares one feature with passenger traffic in that the movement of both is now concentrated over the core main lines along the north coast, along the south coast, and from Newport northward into England. The volumes over other lines from surviving coal production or of specialist loads like nuclear waste and waste material for land in-fill are relatively small and tend to be short-term.

A typical bulk freight train of 2000; an EW & S train of ore waggons hauled by No. 66073 heading west through Cardiff, with the new Millennium Stadium in the background; 12 May 1999.

A. Jarvis

CHAPTER 5

PASSENGER TRAINS

In 1900 railways penetrated nearly every valley in Wales and, in several instances, even managed to climb above them. But in spite of ready access to the railway, rail travel was not general. In some cases miners used the railway to get to the pit, special trains were run on market days and on Saturdays, and there were special excursions. For those who could afford to travel, large areas of the country were, as was noted in Chapter 2, within five miles of a railway station. However, it would be incorrect to conclude from this that travel across Wales was easy or regularly undertaken. The trains were not quick, nor were they frequent, and for many journeys there would be much changing of trains and waiting at stations.

The Chester & Holyhead Railway followed the coast for much of the way to Holyhead. Here a westbound train in LMS days crosses Cliff Road in Old Colwyn hauled by a 'Claughton' Class locomotive. *DD Coll.*

At the turn of the century, double-heading was a common practice on the LNWR. A heavy Bangor to Manchester train leaves Colwyn Bay, behind No. 1937, *Superb* and No. 1973, *Hood*. *GBJ Coll.*

LNWR 0-6-2T No. 7765 heads a local train from Bethesda to Caernarfon at Bangor, probably in the early 1920s.

S. Reid Coll.

An eastbound local train at Bangor hauled by a 2-4-2T No. 2218 (LNWR). The BR number, 46687, fixes the date at *ca.* 1949.

S. Reid Coll.

The unique 2-2-2 *Cornwall* leaves Colwyn Bay with a directors' special.
H. Gordon Tidey/S. Reid Coll.

The fastest trains ran across the south and the north connecting London to the two principal ports for Ireland. There were four other cross-country routes linking parts of England with Cardigan Bay or Swansea. From north to south, these were the GWR's Ruabon to Dolgellau line, the Cambrian's from Whitchurch to Aberystwyth and Pwllheli, the LNWR's Central Wales line from Shrewsbury to Swansea, and the Midland's line from Worcester also to Swansea. These were all slow and infrequently served, but there was at least a continuous service without having to find connections and change trains.

Each of these transverse routes was connected by lines moving generally in a north-south direction. The first group were from Menai Bridge to Afon Wen, from Llandudno Junction to Blaenau Ffestiniog and thence to Bala, and from Rhyl to Corwen. Then further south there were the Manchester & Milford, the Mid Wales, the Neath & Brecon and the Brecon & Merthyr. But, again, all these were characterised by slow and infrequent trains. The fastest north-south service was through Shrewsbury and Hereford. In Chapter 9 there is a description of a journey from north to south in 1899. Depending on the route chosen this could involve as many as 13 changes of train operated by six different railway companies, not to mention an overnight stop half way. The reason for this was not the absence of railway lines so much as a combination of the infrequency of trains and their slow speed.

In the early days of the twentieth century 'John Hick' Class 2-2-2-2 No. 1536 heads west with a light train on the four-track section from Colwyn Bay to Mochdre.
F. Moore/S. Reid Coll.

Another example of the use of 0-6-0 locomotives on passenger trains, this time a 'Special DX', leaving Colwyn Bay in a westward direction.
H. Gordon Tidey/S. Reid Coll.

No. 2056 *Argus*, a 'Dreadnought' Class 3-cylinder compound heads an 'up' express at Rhyl early in the twentieth century.
LGRP/S. Reid Coll.

There were no through trains between north and south Wales but in 1906 a new through train was introduced between Barry Docks and Newcastle-on-Tyne. The train, made up of Great Central coaches, was hauled in this case by 'Bulldog' Class No. 3708 *Sir Arthur Yorke*. The location is uncertain but Gloucester has been suggested.

J. Woodfin Coll.

A typical Edwardian south Wales express on the GW, hauled by what appears to be 'Bulldog' Class No. 3366 *Restormel*. *GBJ Coll.*

The New Milford to Paddington 'Cork Boat Express' leaving Box tunnel, headed by 4-2-2 No. 3028 *Wellington* on 29 September 1898. *WIMM/GW Coll.*

New Milford, &c., to London.]		62		[Great

NEW MILFORD, CARMARTHEN, SWANSEA, CARDIFF, NEWPORT, BRISTOL,

Up.   Week Days—*Continued on opposite page.*

Station	mrn	mrn	mrn	mrn	mrn	mrn	mrn	mrn	mrn	mrn	mrn	mrn	mrn	mrn	mrn	mrn	mrn	aft	mrn
New Milford ....dep.						4 3)										8 5			1020
Old Milford ... {arr. dep.														8 35	8 0				1015
Johnston														8 17					1032
Haverfordwest......					4 50									8 28					1045
Clarbeston Road ...														8 41					1057
Clynderwen 67														8 53					1110
Tenby 66 .....dep.														8 20					1030
Whitland 66														9 10					1132
St. Clears														8 30 9 23					1145
Sarnau														8 40 9 33					
Carmarthen Jn. 66..arr.														8 55 9 44					12 5
Carmarthen {arr.														9 0 10 5					1225
66, 343 {dep.					5 3)								8 20 9 15	9 30					1145
Carmarthen Junc. ..dep.					5 39			6 35					8 24	9 47					1210
Ferryside								6 48					8 39 9 30						
Kidwelly								6 57					8 49 9 39						
Pembrey and Burry Port.								7 7					9 69 50						
Llanelly 67					6 9	6 55		7 18					9 13 10 0	1016 1115					1242
Loughor						7 2		7 26					9 22	1124					1b2
Gowerton 342, 343..						7		7639					9b35						
Cockett						7 15							Stop	1138					
Landore 49					6 55									11 0					1 33
Swansea (High {arr.					7 10	Stop		8 10				10 5 mrn	1119	Stop				1 50
St.) 476, 343 {dep.					6 45			7 5	8 30			9 40	1050		1150			1 25
Landore					6 55			7 10	8 35		Stop	9 49	11 4		1154			1 40
Llansamlet												9 56						
Dynevor												10 2						
Neath 56, 476					7 13			7 24	8 51			1010	1119		12 8			1 58
Briton Ferry 72								7 32				1018			1215			
Port Talbot §.......								7 40	9 2			1025		1132	1223			d
Pyle 57...............								7 52				1038			1236			
Bridgend 67, 69								8 3	9 22 8 53			1049		1152	1248			d
Pencoed								8 14				11 0						
Llanharan								8 21				11 7						
Llantrisant 70, 71..								8 28		9 14		1114				1 6		
Peterston								8 35		9 22		1122						
St. Fagan's								8 41		9 28		1128						
Ely (for Llandaff) ..								8 45		9 32		1132						
Cardiff 70, 69, 348, {arr.				8 7	mrn	8 54	9 52 9 40	mrn	1141	aft	1225		1 25		2 50
344 {dep.	6 10 6 42	8 0	4 15 8 50	9 0	9 58 10 5	1015	1038 1146	1210 1233		1 30		2 55
Roath			8 3		9 5		1014 1150			1 36		
Marshfield		6 54		9 12					1 58		
Newport 56, 68, 345, 349	6 317	8 8 22	4 36 9 13	9 28	1018 1025	1036 11 5	1210 1232	1255	1 25 1 57		3 18
Llanwern		7 18		9 38					1 36		
Magor	6 467 28					1129			1 44		
Severn Tunnel Jn. ¶ 65.	6 517 31		9 309 51		1041		1240	1 49 2 13		
Stapleton Road ¶ 22	7 29	9 11	10 01041		1122 12 5		1 24	2 52	4 5
¶ Bristol † 10, 24, 18 arr.	7 35	9 20	10 7 1050		1152 1215		1 35	3 0	425
Bath 11 ″	8 9	9 52	1130		1142 1255		2 20	3 35 4 36 4 25
Portskewett	7 39		Stop		Stop		1 24 2 8	
Chepstow 59	7 48		10 0				2 9	
Woolaston	7 53		1010	1055			2 20	
Lydney 449	8 5		1020				1 40 2 27	
Awre (for Blakeney)	8 15		1028	11 7			2 37	
Newnham	8 22		1039				1 57 2 44	
Grange Court 59 ...	7 19	8 28		1047				2 51	
Oakle Street	7 26	8 36		1054				3 0	
Gloucester 458, 455, 56..	7 35	8 47		11 2					
Cheltenham 50 {arr.	8 19	9 45	4 36	11 11	1137		2 18 3 10	
(St. James's Sq.) {dep 6 50	7 20	8 30	11 0 mrn 1155	1230	mrn	2 53 3 43	
Hereford 59 ....dep.	6 25		9 20 1020 1110	1110	1140	2 10 2 50	
Gloucester ....dep.	7 45	8 57	45 9e25 1132		1145 e 1040		2 36 3 20	
Stonehouse 1	c	9 13			12 0		3 36	
Stroud * 476........	8 6	9 22		1155	12 8		2 59 3 45	
Brimscombe	c	9 30			1215		4 0	
Chalford	8 36				1221			
Cirencester 72 {dep	8 10	9 40		12 0			3 10 3 55	
(Sheep Street) {arr.	8 50	1018		1235			3 45 4 37	
Kemble 52	8 34	9 59		1222			3 28 4 20	
Minety	8 10	10 9		1241			4 30	
Purton	8 23	1018		1251			4 39	
Swindon 11, 2, 20 .. arr.	8 33 8 53 9 55 1027 1043	1040	1250			3 50 4 48 4 36 5 18	
Didcot 11 ......arr.	9 40 9 31 9 31	11 0	0 15		1 54	2 46	4 37 5 7	
Oxford 11 & 34.. ″	8 48 10 2 10 2	12 7	12 7 1233		2 33	1 10	5 31	
Reading 11 ″	9 43 9 56 9 56	1145	1145	24		2 15	2 45	3 50 4 45 5 45 45	
London (Pad) 11 ″	1025 1032 1032 1015	1235	235 0		2 15	2 45	3 50 4 45 5 45 45	

Taking first the frequency of operation, a glance at a timetable of the period reveals a marked contrast between the density of trains on the inter-city routes between London, the Welsh cities and the Irish ports and the scarcity on the cross-country lines. For example, from Cardiff to Paddington there were the following 14 trains each week day:

6.10 a.m. via Severn Tunnel and Bristol
8.00 a.m. via Severn Tunnel and Bristol
8.15 a.m. via Gloucester
9.00 a.m. via Gloucester, from Swansea
9.58 a.m. via Severn Tunnel, non-stop from Newport. Luncheon car express with corridor
10.05 a.m. via Gloucester
12.10 p.m. via Severn Tunnel and Bristol
12.32 p.m. via Gloucester from New Milford
1.30 p.m. via Severn Tunnel and Bristol
2.55 p.m. via Severn Tunnel and Bristol from New Milford. Corridor
4.02 p.m. via Gloucester from Swansea
5.25 p.m. via Severn Tunnel and Bristol
6.08 p.m. via Gloucester from New Milford. Corridor
10.37 p.m. via Gloucester from New Milford. Sleeper

Table 128

Saturdays

16 January to 20 February

West Wales, Swansea and Maesteg → Cardiff

Route Diagram - see first page of Table 128

	WW	GW	GW	GW	WW	WW	GW	WW	WW	GW	WW	WW	WW	WW	GW	WW	WW	GW	WW	WW	WW	WW	GW	WW
							A		A	B				C						D	B			E
Rosslare Harbour .... d		21b50																						
Fishguard Harbour ..... a		01 20																						
Fishguard Harbour .... d		01 45																						
Milford Haven . ... d	23p59									06 29					07 11									09 15
Johnston .... d	00x06									06x36					07x18									09x22
Haverfordwest .... d	00 13									06 44					07 26									09 30
Clarbeston Road .... d	00x21									04x52					07x33									09x37
Clunderwen .... d	00x28									06x59					07x39									09x43
Pembroke Dock ...... d										06 50														
Pembroke . ... d										06 58														
Lamphey .... d										07x01														
Manorbier . ... d										07 09														
Penally .... d										07x14														
Tenby .... a										07 17														
Saundersfoot .... d										07 19														
Kilgetty .... d										07x26														
Narberth .... d										07x28														
										07x37														
Whitland .... a	00 35	02 16								07 05	07 46				07 47									09 49
d	00 35	02 16								07 06					07 51									09 50
Carmarthen .... a	00 54									07 24					08 08									10 06
d					06 00			06 39		07 29					08 11		09 03							09 35 10 09
Ferryside .... d					06x08					07 38					08 20									09 45
Kidwelly .... d					06x13					07 44					08 26									09 50
Pembrey & Burry Port .... d					06 19		06 57			07 52					08 34		09 20							09 57 10 26
Llanelli . ... a	02 52				06 24		07 02			07 57					08 39		09 25							10 02 10 31
d	02 52				06 25		07 04			07 58					08 40		09 26 09 34							10 03 10 32
Gowerton .... d										08x05							09x41							
Swansea .... a	03 11				06 43		07 21			08 18					09 16	09 30 09 48		09 43 09 57						10 21 10 49
d	03 20	04 55	05 30		06 57	06 45	06 57		07 30 07 40	08 23		08 30			09 16 09 30 09 48				10 07	10 30 10 55				
Llansamlet .... d						→			07 47						09 23			09 57		10 14				
Skewen .... d									07 51											10 16				
Neath . ... d	03 32	05 07	05 42				06 57	07 08	07 42 07 55			08 34		08 42			09 42			10 22 10 42 11 06				
Briton Ferry .... d									07 58											10 25				
Baglan .... d									08 02											10 29				
Port Talbot Parkway .... d	03 45	05 14	05 49			07 04	07 15	07 49 08 06			08 42		08 49			09 49				10 33 10 49 11 13				
Pyle .... d							07 22			08 13							09 40			10 40				
Maesteg .... d						07 12			08 12						09 15				10 15					
Maesteg (Ewenny Road) .... d						07 14			08 14						09 17				10 17					
Garth (Mid Glamorgan) .... d						07 17			08 17						09 20				10 20					
Tondu .... d						07 26			08 26						09 29				10 29					
Sarn . ... d						07 29			08 29						09 32				10 32					
Wildmill .... d						07 31			08 31						09 34				10 34					
Bridgend .... d	03 57	05 25	06 00	06 50		07 15	07 30	07 35 08 00 08 21	08 35	08 56		09 00	09 38 09 48	10 00 10 17					10 38 10 47 11 00 11 26					
Pencoed .... d				06 56				07 41			08 41			09 44					10 44 10 53					
Pontyclun .... d				07 03				07 48			08 48			09 51					10 51 11 00					
Cardiff Central .... a	04 18	05 47	06 22	07 16		07 37	07 52	08 03 08 22 08 42	09 04	09 17		09 23	10 05	10 11 10 22 10 38					11 04 11 15 11 22 11 47					
Cardiff Queen Street .... a								08 11											11 11					
Newport (South Wales) .... a	04 32	06 01	06 37	07 32		07 52	08 07		08 37 08 57	09 18	09 42		09 37	10 20 10 27 10 37 10 57					11 37 12 12					
Bristol Temple Meads .... a	05 18	06 39	07 14				08 39		09 18	09 56 10 16			10 16 10 56		11 17 11 49				12 16 12 50					
Bath Spa .... a	05 40	06 56	07 35			08 39	08 56		09 27	10 16 10 33			10 26 11 18		11 29				12 26 13 14					
Southampton Central .... a										12 00									14 45					
Portsmouth Harbour .... a										12 47														
Gloucester .... a														11 20										
Birmingham New Street .... a														12 24										
Manchester Piccadilly .... a			10 38					11 59									13 59							
Reading .... a	06 51	08 08	08 55			09 53		10 52			11 37			12 40					13 36					
London Waterloo .... ⊖a						11 08																		
London Paddington .... ⊖a	07 24	08 45	09 30			10 25		11 24			12 08			13 15					14 08					

For general notes see front of timetable

A Advance seat reservations (available free) are compulsory for all journeys east of Bath Spa
B To Coryton (Table 130)
C To Westbury (Table 123)
D From Crewe (Table 131)
E To Brighton (Table 188)
b Previous night

From time to time it is necessary to undertake extensive engineering work at weekends. This frequently affects Saturday night/Sunday services and passengers are advised to look for specific announcements of possible diversions and delays making a final check at stations or telephone enquiry bureaux.

Changing styles of timetable presentation for the south Wales main line, Bradshaw in 1899 and Railtrack in 1999.

PRO: RAIL 903/113 and Railtrack

On the other hand, between Moat Lane and Brecon, a strategic north-south line through the centre of Wales, there were three. On the Midland's line from Hereford to Swansea, there were only two, one of which contained a through carriage from Birmingham. Two more trains operated only between Brecon and Hereford. Between Oswestry and Aberystwyth and between Ruabon and Dolgellau, both lines across the heart of the country, there were six and five, respectively. Between Carmarthen and Aberystwyth there were only three, and all required a change at Pencader. From Brecon to Newport there were also three.

BR Standard 2-6-4T No. 80080 with a short train in the picturesque Dee valley, August 1964. *J.B. Snell*

In the north the pattern was repeated. Thus along the strategic line from Bangor to Chester there were 10 trains:

3.03 a.m.	Irish Night Express
7.55 a.m.	for Chester
9.10 a.m.	from Holyhead to Euston
11.10 a.m.	from Holyhead, stopping train to Chester
1.14 p.m.	from Holyhead for Chester
2.30 p.m.	for Chester
3.20 p.m.	Irish Day Express
4.15 p.m.	from Holyhead, stopping train to Crewe
7.17 p.m.	from Holyhead, stopping train to Chester
9.03 p.m.	from Holyhead, boat train.

In addition, there were the two Irish Mail trains from Holyhead at 12.22 and 2.10 a.m., neither of which stopped at Bangor; one fast to Chester and the other fast to Crewe. By contrast, between Afon Wen and Bangor there were four trains, as also from Denbigh to Corwen.

There were exceptions. In the densely populated area served by the Taff Vale there was a fairly frequent service. Thus between Treherbert at the head of the Rhondda valley and Pontypridd there were 10. From Pontypridd to Cardiff there were 20 and from Cardiff to Penarth there were 23. From Barry, the Barry Railway ran 25 services to Cardiff, but only three to Pontypridd and Porth.

Even out in the country, there were cases where efforts were made to provide some frequency over shorter distances between country towns. Thus between Builth Road and Builth Wells there were eight trains, the through trains being augmented by a shuttle. Between Carmarthen and Cardigan there were six possibilities, four by changing at Whitland, on the south Wales main line, onto the Cardigan branch, and two by taking the train to Newcastle Emlyn and transferring there to a coach. This was, incidentally, one of the few remaining scheduled stage-coach services left in operation anywhere in Britain. In the Vale of Clwyd there were eight trains from Denbigh to Rhyl, and the same number to Chester.

It is these comparatively low frequencies which distinguish the services offered 100 years ago from what is available now, over a much reduced network. Seating capacity per train has seen little change. For instance, a high-speed train seats 480 people, while 400 has been assumed for the capacity of a main line 10-12 coach train of bogie carriages in 1899, and the capacity of a '156' class two coach multiple unit at 160, compares with the 200 assumed for ordinary trains in 1899. A 'Pacer' has comparable capacity to that of a small local train of four- and six-wheelers. As the tables in Appendix I & II demonstrate, it is the increase in frequency, rather than seating capacity, which has enabled passenger numbers and seat miles to be sustained in spite of the reduction in route mileage.

The appendices illustrate the seat miles offered each weekday on the Welsh railways in 1899 and 1999. Even allowing for errors in the assumptions about the seating capacity of trains, especially those in 1899, it seems that the seat/mile capacity offered today is considerably higher in spite of the reduction in route mileage. Something of the order of 4,000 day/seat/miles in 1899 has risen to some 5,000 in 1999. The fact that this latter figure happens to be similar to that between London and Southend is a coincidence which places the tables in perspective.

The increased frequency which has made this possible has been achieved partly by higher speeds and modern signalling, but a key influence has been the reduction in the range of train speeds. This has been made possible by closing minor stations on main lines and by the big reduction in the number of slow moving and frequently stopping freight trains, some of which were described in Chapter 4. Thus Pontypridd, in 1999, had 126 weekday passenger train departures. Even Treherbert, at the far end of the Rhondda valley, had 28. Before 6.00 a.m. every weekday morning, six trains head east from Cardiff for London, Exeter, Bristol (2) and Manchester (2). During the course of a day, 103 trains leave Cardiff for Newport, and there are 22 departures for London, two of which are for Waterloo. All

these now have a journey time of about two hours. Frequency has also been increased on the north Wales main line which now has the following pattern from Bangor eastward:

1.08 a.m.	NW	Holyhead to Chester
2.11 a.m.	NW	Holyhead to Birmingham
4.43 a.m.	NW	Holyhead to Birmingham
5.51 a.m.	WW	Holyhead to Cardiff
6.18 a.m.	Virgin	Holyhead to Euston
6.35 a.m.	NW	Bangor to Manchester
6.55 a.m.	NW	Holyhead to Crewe
7.08 a.m.	NW	Holyhead to Birmingham
8.09 a.m.	NW	Holyhead to Crewe
8.36 a.m.	NW	Holyhead to Manchester
9.05 a.m.	NW	Holyhead to Birmingham
9.20 a.m.	Virgin	Holyhead to Euston
10.16 a.m.	NW	Holyhead to Crewe
11.16 a.m.	NW	Holyhead to Birmingham
12.22 p.m.	NW	Bangor to Crewe
12.46 p.m.	NW	Holyhead to Llandudno Jc.
1.22 p.m.	NW	Holyhead to Crewe
1.51 p.m.	NW	Holyhead to Manchester
2.08 p.m.	Virgin	Holyhead to Euston
2.22 p.m.	NW	Holyhead to Birmingham
2.46 p.m.	NW	Holyhead to Llandudno Jc.
3.22 p.m.	NW	Holyhead to Crewe
3.30 p.m.	NW	Bangor to Llandudno Jc.
4.22 p.m.	NW	Bangor to Crewe
4.55 p.m.	NW	Holyhead to Llandudno Jc.
5.18 p.m.	NW	Holyhead to Birmingham
6.22 p.m.	NW	Bangor to Crewe
6.46 p.m.	NW	Holyhead to Crewe
7.22 p.m.	NW	Holyhead to Llandudno Jc.
8.22 p.m.	NW	Bangor to Chester

That makes a total of 30 departures from Bangor, three times the frequency in 1899, and, in addition, eight departures from Llandudno for Manchester. Noteworthy is the single train for the south of Wales.

Turning now to the speed of travel, in 1899 a mere 20 m.p.h. was normal. This was the average speed for branch line trains, stopping at all stations, as for example between Whitland and Pembroke Dock, and between Pencader and Aberystwyth. These trains and those over the Midland's line between Swansea and Hereford averaged about 20 m.p.h. On the Amlwch branch the average for 17 miles was 22.6 m.p.h., while the similar distance between Denbigh and Corwen was covered at 21.4 m.p.h.

The 'up' Irish Mail hauled by No. 1968, *Cumberland*, a 'Renown' and George V No. 2197 *Planet* heads east through Bangor. The date is early 1920s as *Cumberland* was converted from an 'Alfred the Great' Class 4-cylinder compound.
S. Reid Coll.

'Greater Britain' Class 2-2-2-2 No. 2053 on the Irish Mail at the turn of the century.
W.G. Rear Coll.

But there were large variations. One of the Irish Mail trains achieved an average of 48 m.p.h. between Holyhead and Crewe. The other averaged 46 m.p.h. non-stop between Holyhead and Chester, while a train stopping at all stations only achieved 26 m.p.h. over the same distance. This was the same average speed as the Cambrian achieved between Welshpool and Pwllheli. Over the 27 mile line from Bangor to Afon Wen the LNWR achieved an average 34 m.p.h. with a semi-fast, but only 15 m.p.h. stopping at all stations. Three and a quarter hours was the time for the fastest train of the day between Cardiff and Paddington, the 9.58 a.m., stopping only at Newport, and taking

advantage of the Severn tunnel, but as yet without the benefit of the Wootton Bassett cut-off. By contrast, the 9.00 a.m. stopping train via Gloucester took five hours, twenty minutes.

In spite of the fact that some trains in 1999 were theoretically capable of 125 m.p.h., in reality there is less difference in the speed of travel than might be expected and no track in Wales has been cleared for 125 m.p.h. running. The fastest train between Holyhead and Crewe now achieves an average speed of 50 m.p.h., not much of an improvement on the fastest of 1899, though with six intermediate stops. Between Cardiff and Swansea the high-speed train averages 48 m.p.h., whereas on the branch line between Whitland and Pembroke Dock the average speed is now about 25 m.p.h. Between Shrewsbury and Pwllheli the speed has been raised to 34 m.p.h. and on the Llandudno Junction to Blaenau branch 27 m.p.h. is achieved, but a local train from Treherbert to Cardiff takes an hour to cover the 22 miles. The biggest improvement, that between Cardiff and London, has been achieved not only by increasing train speed but also by shortening the route.

Another area of improvement is in the journey time between Cardiff and Manchester. Whereas this now takes just over three hours with no change of train, the fastest train in 1899 took over five hours and, by travelling over the Rhymney Railway and LNWR by way of Brynmawr, it was possible to extend the journey time to more than eight hours. In this instance the reduction is partly due to the elimination of time lost changing trains. The railway historian will note, with a wry smile, the reincarnation in 1999 of the Manchester & Milford Railway in the form of through trains betweeen the two places. Sadly, they are routed by way of Cardiff rather than mid-Wales.

On a wet day in August 1959 a southbound train leaves Pontypool Road behind an unidentified 'Hall' Class locomotive. In 1900 most passenger services on this line between Shrewsbury and Newport were joint GW/LNW, though operated by the GWR. *Steam & Sail/courtesy E.S. Owen Jones*

The limited frequency of scheduled trains in 1899 was augmented by a large number and variety of special and excursion trains offering day trips for fairs, races and *eisteddfodau* or just a visit to the seaside. These were offered at discounted prices and their large number contributed significantly to the erosion of average passenger traffic receipts. To convey this unscheduled trade, the railway companies had to hold a large number of carriages in reserve. These were normally ancient and lacking the latest facilities, and a characteristic of the time, no longer seen on the modern railway, was the large number and variety of these carriages held in waiting on sidings at the more important stations.

0-6-0 'Cauliflower' No. 439 with what was probably a returning excursion train of at least 14 carriages leaving Colwyn Bay.   *S. Reid Coll.*

Railway day excursions survived until the end of locomotive haulage. Here a Tredegar to Barry Island day excursion wends its way through the junction at Penrhos behind ex-LNWR 0-8-0 No. 49121 on 13 July 1958.

C.H.A. Townley/J.A. Peden

Monday, Sept. 23rd Continued.

27 Excursion to Belle Vue Gardens, Manchester.

As announced by Handbills from Pwllheli, Dolgelly, Aberdovey, and intermediate stations, by **Specials** as under :—

UP.		Pass a.m.	DOWN.		Pass a.m.
Pwllheli ....dep		2 40	Wrexham ....dep		12 10
Afon Wen.............. ,,		2 50	Ellesmere ....arr		12 40
Criccieth .... ,,		3 0	,, ...dep		12 50
Portmadoc .... ,,		8 10	Oswestry ....arr		1 5
Minfford .... ,,		3 15	,, ...dep		1 10
Penrhyndeudraeth ...... ,,		3 20	Welshpool .... ,,		1 40
Talsarnau .... ,,		3 25	Moat Lane ....arr		2 17
Harlech................ ,,		3 32	,, ...dep		2 20
Llanbedr and Pensarn.... ,,		3 42	Talerddig Top .... ,,	z	
Dyffryn .... ,,		3 50	Machynlleth ......arr		3 5
Barmouth ....arr		4 0	,, ... dep		3 10
,, ...dep		4 2	Aberdovey .... ,,		3 30
Barmouth Junction ..... arr		4 7	Towyn ... . ,,		3 38
,, ...dep		4 10	Tonfanau .... ,,		3 43
Llwyngwril .... ,,		4 22	Llwyngwril ...... ,,		3 51
Tonfanau .... ,,		4 30	Barmouth Junction..arr		4 2
Towyn .... ,,		4 35	,, ... dep		4 5
Aberdovey .... ,,		4 45	Barmouth .... ,,		4 10
Machynlleth ....arr		5X10	Dyffryn .... ,,		4 20
,, ...dep		5 15	Llanbedr & Pensarn ,,		4 26
Cemmes Road .... arr		5X26	Harlech ... . ,,		4 36
,, ...dep		5 29	Talsarnau ... ... ,,		4 45
Moat Lane.............arr		6 10	Penrhyndeudraeth.. ,,		4 50
,, ...dep		6 13	Minfford .... ,,		4 55
Newtown .... ,,		6X21	Portmadoc ....arr		5 0
Montgomery........ .... ,,		6X38	,, ...dep		5 5
Forden .... ,,		6X42	Criccieth........... ,,		5 15
Welshpool .... ,,		6w50	Afon Wen .... ,,		5 25
Pool Quay .... ,,		6X59	Pwllheli ....arr		5 35
Oswestry. ....arr		7 18			
,, ...dep		7 23			
Ellesmere ....arr		7 37			
,, ...dep		7 46			
Wrexham .... arr		8X15			

(*Tuesday Morning, September 24th.*)

DOWN column note: Collect Tickets same as of Ordinary Trains, except that Barmouth and Portmadoc will collect their own Tickets, Messrs. Wellings and Roberts arranging.

Run in front of 5 10 a.m. ex Machynlleth.

Pass 2 25 a.m. ex Whitchurch at Cemmes Road.

Pass 4 0 a.m. ex Oswestry at Newtown.

Pass 6 0 a.m. ex Welshpool at Montgomery.

Pass 5 30 a.m. Special ex Oswestry at Forden.

Pass 6 15 a.m. ex Oswestry at Pool Quay.

Loco. Dept. to provide Engine.

Inspector Parry to provide the required Carriages, Brake-power and Guards.

If the train exceeds 10 Vehicles, a Van must be marshalled in middle, so that the train can be divided and run in duplicate from Wrexham.

An example of a Cambrian Railways Excursion Service offering a long day out in Manchester in 1899.

Ifor Higgon Coll.

Another feature of travel at the time was the early rising often called for. A 2.00 a.m. departure from Pwllheli was necessary in order to enjoy a visit to the Belle Vue Gardens in Manchester, returning 24 hours later and with no possibility of finding a sleeping car, or even a couchette, and almost certainly in obsolete stock with few comforts. However, early morning departures were by no means confined to specials. The only LNWR train of the day between Shrewsbury and Abergavenny Junction left Crewe at 1.40 a.m. Ten minutes earlier, at 1.30 a.m., the North & Cardiff Express had left, due at Cardiff GW station at 5.38 a.m. The North & West Express left ten minutes before that, reaching Bristol at 5.15 a.m.

LNWR poster promoting rail travel in north Wales to the French.   *NLW*

Interior of LNWR restaurant car of the period.
F. Moore/S. Reid Coll.

The LNWR publicity department published postcards bearing the statement, 'The LNWR is noted for punctuality, speed, smooth riding, dustless tracks, safety and comfort, and is the oldest established firm in the railway passenger business'. The comfortable First Class compartment illustrated bore out at least one of these claims.   *DD Coll.*

A characteristic of most rail travel in Wales in 1899 was the primitive character of the carriages in use. Many of the features of a modern carriage had been introduced by 1899 but these were by no means universally employed. They were confined to a few long-distance prestige trains. The bogie, the corridor, lavatories, the connection between carriages,

sleeping cars, dining cars, and electric light had been introduced during the previous 25 years. Steam heating had not yet been introduced, so the foot-warmer was still the sole source of heat. Even on the main south Wales line to Paddington, the presence of a corridor connection between carriages called for special mention in the timetable. The ability to move

Cambrian Railways composite coach built in 1895, recently restored and here seen on its way into storage at Nantgarw near Cardiff on 28 August 1998.   *E.S. Owen Jones*

At Barmouth a close-up of part of Cambrian Railways 4-wheeled Third Class carriage No. 55, built at Oswestry in 1884. The locomotive is one of the Sharp Stewart 'Small Goods' Class.   *Ifor Higgon Coll.*

from one carriage to another had first been introduced by the Great Eastern for its Harwich boat-trains in 1891. The Great Western was close behind and introduced such a continuous train on the Birkenhead line, also in 1891. For south Wales trains, in 1895, the GWR introduced the first central gangway carriages linked by a corridor connection. These were also remarkable for having electric lighting. In the First Class carriages there were only single seats on either side of the gangway, each discretely secluded behind elaborate wooden screens. On faster trains with few stops, luncheon or dining cars were provided at appropriate times, and on both routes to Ireland sleeping saloons were provided. Passengers on the night train from south Wales to London were invited to break the journey at Gloucester and take an early morning train next day.

In the absence of a corridor connection, and in order to provide flexible arrangements within a carriage which could be shunted between trains on cross-country services, elaborate configurations of compartments and lavatories were tried. On the Cambrian a complex and compact arrangement was introduced in 1890; this accommodated one First, one Second and two Third Class compartments, all in the six-wheel carriage, together with a luggage compartment and four lavatories. The First and Second Class compartments at either end of the carriage had only one row of seats facing, if unlucky, a fine view of the adjacent carriage. These carriages were employed especially on through trains from Cardigan Bay over the LNWR and GWR and had the advantage of being self-contained. On the GWR a slightly different arrangement was introduced in 1893 in a rather longer carriage carried on bogies. Here three Third Class compartments were connected to a lavatory by a side corridor. Another adjacent lavatory led into a Second Class compartment, and the whole was completed by two First Class compartments, each with its own lavatory. The end one of these also offered the possibility of observing the view, provided, that is, the carriage was marshalled at the end of the train. The Cambrian then brought out a bogie carriage of similar dimensions but with four Third Class compartments and only one First, no doubt reflecting the relative affluence of its clientele. This, too, offered the occupants of the First Class compartment an unrestricted view of the end of the next carriage. Similar arrangements were provided by the Midland on its through carriages to Swansea.

A suburban train of the period on the Taff Vale Railway at Tonypandy & Trealaw station in May 1909. This station had just been renamed having opened a year previously as Trealaw. In 1973 BR named it Tonypandy, and thus it remains. The locomotive is one of the 4-4-2T engines, No. 172.   *DD Coll.*

On all the local lines, the carriages would have been a mixture of four- and six-wheelers without a corridor. The frequent stops offered some compensation for the absence of buffet cars and lavatories.

The price of this service was not cheap. The cost of the 132 miles across Wales on the Cambrian main line from Whitchurch to Pwllheli was 20s. 3d. for a First Class single. This works out at 1.87d. per mile. It is necessary to multiply 1900 prices by 60 to obtain an approximation of value in today's terms. It was still normal practice on the GWR and LNWR to quote a Second Class fare at about two-thirds of First

Class, and Third Class fares were quoted at the so-called 'Government rate'. This was originally known as the 'Parliamentary rate' as, under Gladstone's famous Act of 1844, each railway was required to operate at least one train a day at 1d. per mile, stopping at every station and providing covered accommodation. By 1899 most railways were accommodating parliamentary rate passengers on all stopping trains, but on the Manchester & Milford, between Pencader and Aberystwyth, one train a day was described as the 'Government train'. Although not the fastest of the day, it was not the slowest. The rate quoted was exactly 1d. per mile.

At Cardiff Riverside TVR 0-6-2T No. 40 with a uniform rake of carriages forming a local train from Penarth; 11 August 1913.
LCGB/Ken Nunn Coll.

45 years later, a local train at Penarth Town with locomotive No. 6411; 19 April 1958.   *Ian L. Wright*

Edwardian travel on the Kerry branch of the Cambrian Railways. The little saddle tank was probably No. 36 *Plasffynnon*. *Ifor Higgon Coll.*

This photograph taken in 1959 shows a train little changed in nearly 100 years. Ffestiniog Railway locomotive *Prince* hauls original carriages of the 1860s. *R. Wood*

The archetypal Talyllyn train with No. 2 *Dolgoch* at Abergynolwyn in 1952.

R. Wood

The LNWR also described Third Class fares as 'Government fares' and quoted fares at exactly 1d. per mile, irrespective of distance and for both single and return journeys. On the other hand, the First Class fare for the 264 miles from Holyhead to Euston was 42s. 6d. which is 1.93d. per mile. The return First Class fare at 75s. was discounted to 1.7d. per mile. A distance scale was operated such that the 24 miles from Holyhead to Bangor were at a First Class single rate of 2.16d. per mile and the 3.5 miles from Holyhead to Valley were at 2.28d. per mile. The rate of 2d. per mile was hit at a 40 mile journey like that from Holyhead to Llandudno Junction.

A colourful selection of tickets of the period.
Chris Green and DD

Early in the twentieth century the railways responded to road competition by developing rail-cars, tram-like single carriage trains. This early steam powered version was employed by the LNWR on the Dyserth branch.
S. Reid Coll.

A Cardiff Railway steam rail-car at Rhydyfelin.
Ian L. Wright Coll.

Steam rail motors, as they were called by the GWR, were later replaced by auto trains, which had the advantage of leaving the passenger accommodation available for use while the power source was being serviced. They lasted until steam was replaced, their successors being the diesel multiple unit. In this example locomotive No. 1471 and auto coach wait at Tonyrefail with a train for Llantrisant; 31 May 1958
Ian L. Wright Coll.

No premium was charged for the use of a faster train, but there were many discounts for groups, excursions and special services. The Cambrian operated a voucher system whereby a number of miles of First Class travel could be bought in advance at a rate of approximately 1d. per mile. These low fares were widely advertised on posters and in leaflets and were available only on special trains. It was therefore normal that in any class of carriage, whether on a regular scheduled train, a workmen's train or an excursion, all were paying at the same rate. This can be compared with the position in 2000 where, broadly, those who are paying for themselves travel in the lower class and those whose fare is paid by another organisation travel First. However, within the group who pay for themselves there is a bewildering range of discounts available. These are conditional on travelling at certain times on certain days, booking and paying early, and being a student, a child or a pensioner, but the result is that any one passenger can be paying a quarter of the fare paid by his neighbour for an identical service.

In 1899 there were low fares for workmen on specified trains. For instance, between Cardiff and Pontypridd, lower fares were available on the 5.15 a.m. from Cardiff and the 6.20 p.m. arrival in the evening. A workman's ticket cost 3s. 6d. for a week's travel compared with an ordinary Third Class single of one shilling and a halfpenny or 2s. 1d. return. An excursion ticket was available on special offers at 1s. 3d. return.

As a result of the promotions and the lack of serious competition from alternative means of transport, relatively large numbers of tickets were sold. In 1903, Cardiff GW alone sold 1.25 million against 1.7 million sold at Paddington. The three stations at Pontypool sold nearly 400,000. This was not much less than the GW's share at Swansea (plus Landore), which was dwarfed by Newport's 850,000, rising to over 1 million by 1913. In the Swansea valley the Midland sold over 600,000, compared with 900,000 at St Pancras. Even at Blaenau Ffestiniog the GW alone managed to sell 50,000.

The main eastbound departure platform at Rhyl with generous provision of space and shelter for the large number of passengers handled in the season; viewed looking to the west in the early days of the twentieth century.   *LNWR Soc.*

A quiet time on the main 'down' platform at Newport in 1911. This station, at its peak, sold over 1 million tickets a year and was substantially rebuilt in the 1920s. *NRM/GW Coll.*

A GWR country station of the period, Pontyrhyll, looking up the line towards Blaengarw. Between 1898 and 1932 this little place was served by two railway companies, the GWR and the Port Talbot, the latter employing a steam rail motor from 1907. The lines joined at a junction a short distance behind the photographer, whence the PTR had running powers up to Blaengarw. The GWR's service ceased in 1953. *GBJ Coll.*

But as was noted above, it was probably only a small proportion of the population who travelled at all, and the trains, though infrequent, were not generally crowded. The early morning mail train on the Mid Wales, which featured in the accident at Tylwch described in Chapter 8, had a seating capacity of about 150 with only 12 passengers on board. We saw earlier that an average of about three passengers per train mile was typical on the GWR and on several of the Welsh railways. Only the Taff Vale reached a figure over 10. No doubt the evening trains from Cardiff and Newport up the valleys on a Saturday were well patronised, and commuting put pressure on services in the Cardiff rush hour, but it looks as though it was normally possible to find a seat.

Less satisfactory was the time-keeping and general reliability. Although a conscious effort was made to run the more prestigious long-distance trains to time, attitudes with regard to cross-country and local trains were more relaxed. The worst excesses of the Cambrian had been cured by a new management. No longer did they operate mixed passenger and goods trains requiring the passengers to wait during shunting at intermediate stations. But newspapers of the period contain many references to anger and frustration at the general level of railway time-keeping and efficiency. Both trains involved in

the collision at Tylwch were running over a quarter of an hour late early in the morning on a single track line. Both had run only a short distance from the start of the journey and, in the case of the excursion train, as predictable a factor as the time taken to load passengers had been the main cause of the delay. Quite apart from this relaxed attitude to the timetable and the likelihood of mechanical breakdown, the complexity and lack of tight scheduling of slow-moving freight trains, as illustrated in Chapter 4, must have made it difficult to run passenger trains to time. Although the method of operating has changed, this is one aspect of railway travel which would be only too familiar in 1899 to a traveller of today.

An LNWR poster of 1907 by Norman Wilkinson showing the transfer of passengers at Holyhead.

Victoria & Albert Museum

However, there are other aspects of travel in 1899 which would cause quite a shock. In case the reader is in danger of forming a romanticised and rosy view of life at the turn of the twentieth century, it may be as well to recall a number of features of the time which tend to be forgotten. The poor lighting at night would

probably be the first thing to be noticed. Stations and trains still largely relied on gas lighting which would cast a dim pool of light around the source and leave many sinister shadows. Smells would be strong, of primitive drains and sewage systems, of horses in the street, and of smoke from factories, domestic

A wet day at Ebbw Vale Low level, the former GWR station; 12 July 1958. *H.C. Casserley*

fires and locomotives. Pipe smoke would surround many of the men, though they could only smoke in designated compartments on the trains.

Most people would have travelled to the train on foot, on horseback or in an open carriage. As a result, there was a strong probability that their clothes would be wet. The clothing of Third

The bookstall at Llandovery during the summer of 1901. *NLW/DCH Coll.*

Class travellers would, in any case, tend to be old, worn and smelly. Second Class was pervaded by mothballs, clean-living and sensible clothing, while in the First Class carriage there were fine clothes, eau-de-Cologne, and perhaps a little eau-de-vie for the journey. But, mixed with the damp, dirt was everywhere, from smoke, from coal dust and from mud or dust on the roads, and there was only rough soap to fight it. Shoes and boots would be scuffed and muddy. Without modern detergents and cleaning fluids, floors, stairs, platforms and carriages would be swept but generally dirty. Windows would be grimy. The trains themselves would be dusty and steeped in the sweet smell of engine smoke, fish crates, stale clothing and, from time to time, boiled cabbage and gravy.

It is not all bad in 2000.

This approach to Llanishen station was virtually unchanged for 100 years; only the parked scooter betrays the date; 27 February 1960.
Ian L. Wright

Pontshôn Norton, Pontypridd. A Taff Vale Railway train bound for Cilfynydd and Nelson c. 1905.

National Museums & Galleries of Wales, Department of Industry

Cwm Prysor; Bala to Blaenau Ffestiniog line mixed train, c. 1935.

CHAPTER 6

MOTIVE POWER

Steam engines undoubtedly contributed large volumes of smoke, dirt and noise to the world of 1900. But they were also colourful, ornately finished and brightly polished. Photographs of the period rarely show a dirty locomotive, whether passenger or freight. Many would say the locomotive of the period 1890 to 1910 was at the epitome of its aesthetic and mechanical appeal. Bright colours, brass fittings, large wheels and the whole generally well-tended made them the schoolboy cynosure of the age. Every boy had a toy engine, or wanted one. The sight of one of these hissing monsters at the front of a train of finely crafted carriages entering a gloomy station on a cold and dark night was a cheering and thrilling experience. On a sunny day, spinning through the mountains or beside the sea, it was a delight.

The turn of the twentieth century marked a time when both passenger and goods train loads were increasing, the former due to the larger and more comfortable carriages, the latter because locomotive design was making it possible. On the Great Western, the period saw the beginnings of a major change in locomotive design policy leading to the building, early in the new century, of the first modern locomotives in Britain. Outside cylinders, large taper boilers and a high running-plate caused many an eyebrow to be raised. On the LNWR, the end of the nineteenth century witnessed the final decline of an unsuccessful experiment in compounding leading to a reversion to traditional simple-expansion.

On the Great Western, for the previous 30 years, the locomotives for the goods trains and

No. 3543 of the GWR's much rebuilt '3521' Class of 4-4-0 tender engines; these started life as broad gauge 0-4-4T engines. At the turn of the century nearly half the class were allocated to south Wales.

GBJ Coll.

No. 2601, the 'Kruger' 4-6-0 goods engine, was built in 1899. Designed to cope with larger trains, especially of south Wales coal, it was not a success and the solution lay with the development of the 'Aberdare' 2-6-0, first produced in 1900, and the subsequent '2800' Class 2-8-0s.

GBJ Coll.

local passenger trains in Wales, over lines often with severe gradients, had been almost exclusively of the same wheel arrangement, 0-6-0 saddle tanks, and later 0-6-0 tender engines. In spite of a superficial similarity, variations in design were such that there was a serious need for a policy of standardisation. There was also a need to increase power.

At the end of the first decade of the twentieth century the GWR adapted the highly successful '2800' Class 2-8-0s for working coal trains in the more confined space available in the south Wales valleys. The '4200' Class was the result, of which Nos 4286 and 5224 stand in Duffryn Yard, Port Talbot on the 23 July 1961.
S.A. Leleux

After the grouping GWR 'Barnum' Class 2-4-0s were introduced into mid-Wales to replace former Cambrian locomotives; No. 3216 was at Barmouth Junction on 7 November 1935.
Ifor Higgon

Churchward's 2-cylinder 4-6-0 express engines first appeared in 1902 and established a pattern followed on the GWR for nearly 50 years. The contrast with previous designs was marked.
GBJ Coll.

South Wales had an allocation of 'Stella' Class 2-4-0s at the turn of the century. No. 3519 is seen here at Machynlleth, *ca.* 1925.

J.P. Richards

There was an allocation of Class '3232' 2-4-0 locomotives in south Wales at the turn of the century. No. 3245 is seen here.

GBJ Coll.

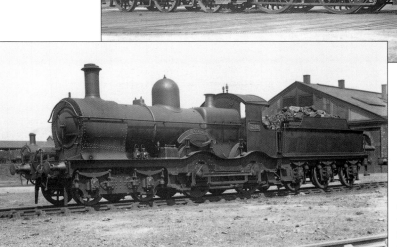

'Duke' Class 4-4-0 *Chough*. This class was also represented in south Wales in the early 1900s.

GBJ Coll.

With a view to increasing the load capacity of freight trains, the GWR in 1899 introduced the 'Kruger', a 4-6-0 double-framed goods engine developed from a similar design of 1896. This was followed later in the same year by a 2-6-0 version of which another six were made, very much with the Welsh coal trains in mind. None of these locomotives was a sufficient success to be developed further. Instead, in 1900, the first 'Aberdare' 2-6-0 was introduced and this was such a success that it was followed

by another 40 before the end of 1902. The first outside cylinder 2-8-0 followed in 1904. This was a truly modern engine, the product of Churchward's fresh thinking and search for designs which would become standard, and it was these locomotives which hauled the long-distance coal trains for the next 50 years. This development dramatically increased the haulage capacity and the distance run, without having to replenish water.

As to GWR passenger engines, Churchward, the father of the modern British locomotive, was at the turn of the century still acting as assistant to the elderly William Dean, and the first modern outside-cylindered 4-6-0 express engine did not appear until 1902. The increasing weight of GWR express trains was being handled by a mixture of older types and some new. Neath had two Class '3232' 2-4-0s for the main line and there were 10 'Stella' Class 2-4-0s at sheds along the coast. Cardiff had one of the famous 4-2-2 'Dean Singles'. By 1901 two of these were also based at Newport for the non-stop run to London.

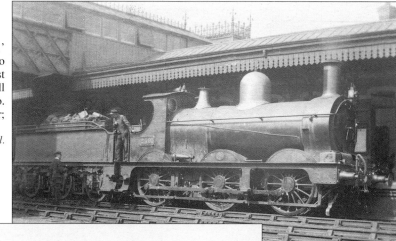

Dean's ubiquitous '2301' Class of 0-6-0 proved to be among the most successful of all locomotive types. No. 2491 was at Gloucester; *ca*. 1900.

GBJ Coll.

'Atbara' Class No. 3387 *Roberts* was built in 1900. At this time a few representatives of the class were allocated to south Wales.

GBJ Coll.

At the turn of the century half the GWR locomotives based in Wales were of the 0-6-0ST type. Here No. 2075 is seen at Abermule on the Kerry branch train, 7 June 1930.

Ifor Higgon

The GWR's 'Metro' tank, a 2-4-0T, was to be seen on local trains all over the system around 1900.   *GBJ Coll.*

Double-framed inside-cylinder locomotives of the 4-4-0 arrangement, with which Dean and Churchward together were constantly experimenting, had started to appear. 59 'Dukes' were built between 1895 and 1899 and one was allocated to Cardiff. Their construction was followed by 19 'Badmintons' between 1897 and 1899, 40 'Bulldogs' in 1898, two of which were at Pontypool Road by 1901, and a 'Waterford' Class in 1899. Of 26 '3521' Class 4-4-0's converted from broad gauge 0-4-4Ts between 1899 and 1900, 11 were scattered along the south Wales coast as far as Pembroke Dock and New Milford. In 1900, 40 additional 'Bulldogs' were started and 29 'Atbaras'. By 1901 Cardiff had four 'Atbaras', mainly used on

trains to Birmingham, and one was at New Milford. So Swindon was busy.

On the secondary lines, Aberdare had two recently built 'Metro tanks', while Bala and Corwen had 0-4-2Ts of the '3571' Class.

At this time there were about 600 GWR locomotives based at engine sheds in Wales and nearly half were 0-6-0 saddle tanks. The busiest shed was Newport with over 100 locomotives, closely followed by Pontypool Road with over 90. Then came Cardiff with over 70 and, as an indicator of the coal traffic emerging from mid-Glamorgan, there were over 40 at Tondu.

The LNWR presented a total contrast to the GWR position. Here, ever since Ramsbottom's regime as locomotive engineer in the 1850s and

A nicely staggered line-up of former LNWR engines at Abergavenny Brecon Road Shed during the late 1920s. Both the 0-6-2T and the 0-8-0 were widely used in Wales.   *J.P. Richards*

At Rhyl at the turn of the century, an LNWR 0-6-0 No. 1061 of the 'Special DX' Class, a class found all over the LNWR system on all types of train. They were rebuilt by Webb from an original Ramsbottom design, of which a staggering 943 were made.

LNWR Soc.

A Webb 4-cylinder compound 0-8-0, considered to be the most successful of LNWR compound engines; *ca*. 1910.   *S. Reid Coll.*

'60s, standardisation had been the core policy. 260 0-6-0ST 'Special Tanks' were built between 1870 and 1898, all to the same design. Some of these were used on the Merthyr, Tredegar and Abergavenny line when that reached Rhymney. But most amazing of all, no less than 943 0-6-0s of the 'DX' Class were built between 1858 and 1874. This was the largest single class in Britain until the GW pannier tank exceeded this number in the middle of the twentieth century. Webb continued the policy and built 500 0-6-0 'coal engines' between 1873 and 1892 and 310 0-6-0 'Cauliflowers' between 1880 and 1902. He then rebuilt 500 of the 0-6-0 'DX' Class between 1881 and 1890. He also built 300 0-6-2T 'coal tanks' over a similar period. When he applied compounding to freight engines, he built 111 three-cylinder 0-8-0 locomotives between 1893 and 1900 and 170 of a four-cylinder version

between 1901 and 1904. Both the three- and four-cylinder versions were used on coal trains originating on the MTA, and some were based at Abergavenny Brecon Road Shed. At the turn of the century this was probably the largest LNWR shed in Wales, with nearly 100 locomotives based there. Other sizeable sheds were Swansea Paxton Street and Bangor.

For passenger locomotives the story was similar, and Ramsbottom was responsible for a class of 60 small 2-2-2 engines known as the 'Problem' Class. He also built 96 of a 2-4-0 class known as the 'Newtons'. These were the basis of his successor Webb's two very successful classes, the 70 'Precedents' and 40 'Precursors', also 2-4-0s built from 1874 onward. These simple but reliable locomotives, often double-heading with other classes, provided an alternative to the subsequent compounds even on express trains long after they should have been eclipsed by their successors. Webb clearly appreciated the qualities of these simple 2-4-0s as he rebuilt 166 of them between 1886 and 1901. For normal passenger service, 50 2-4-0T and 160 2-4-2T tank engines were built new or rebuilt.

LNWR 2-4-2T No. 6666 at Llandudno Junction; 3 June 1932. In north Wales these locomotives were mainly in use on local trains, but both there and on the Central Wales line they did a certain amount of main line work too.   *H.C. Casserley*

Another 2-4-2T No. 2148 at Llanberis, probably in the 1920s.   *S. Reid Coll.*

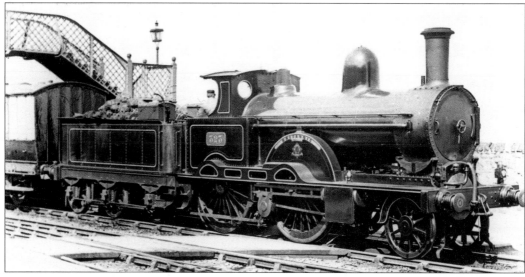

No. 323 *Britannic*, one of 30 members of the 'Experiment' Class, Webb's first class of 3-cylinder 2-2-2-0 compounds, built for the LNWR in 1884 and seen at Llanfairfechan in June 1895. All had been withdrawn by about 1905.   *LNWR Soc.*

Less successful were Webb's experiments with compounding. In 1882 he produced the first of 30 'Experiments'. Similar in size to a 'Precedent' but compound, with three cylinders and a 2-2-2-0 wheel arrangement, they were poor performers and were succeeded by 40 'Dreadnoughts', similar but larger and a little better. Then in 1889 came 10 of the even larger 2-2-2-0 'Teutonic' Class. These were followed by the 2-2-2-2 'Greater Britain' Class of which 10 were built between 1891 and 1894, all of which had been scrapped by about 1907. Then came the worst of all the three-cylinder compounds, the 10 'John Hicks'; these too were 2-2-2-2s and also had a short life spent mainly on light trains around Shrewsbury. The last came out in 1898 and all had been scrapped by 1912.

In 1897 Webb started producing his first four-cylinder compound, the sluggish 4-4-0 'Jubilee' Class of which 40 were made up to 1900. There then followed, between 1901 and 1903, 40 of the larger 'Alfred the Great' Class. These were unreliable and double-heading even of these large engines was often required. At the turn of the century it is probably fair to say that the LNWR was having a struggle to maintain a competitive timetable for its express trains.

However, salvation was at hand. Just after Churchward had begun his trend-setting reign at Swindon, in 1903, Webb was succeeded by Whale. Faced with a poor performing collection of express engines, he proceeded to reverse the compounding policy. In doing so he retained standardisation as an objective and reverted to the traditional British (and LNWR) inside-cylinder simple locomotive. Within a year the first of 130 of a new 'Precursor' Class of 4-4-0s were emerging from Crewe Works. In the meantime, the compound system on the 'Alfred the Great' Class was altered and the modified engines became known as 'Benbows'. The compound 'Experiments', 'Dreadnoughts' and 'Teutonics' were scrapped and from 1908 the 'Jubilees' were converted into two-cylinder simple engines, known as 'Renowns'.

The locomotives which found their way into Wales were examples of many of these different types. The Irish services demanded speed and sustained running with heavy trains over relatively level track. Many, at the turn of the century, would have been double-headed, a testimony to Webb's failure to keep pace with the demands of greater speed and heavier trains. A typical locomotive type for the period on these services would have been a 'Precedent'

'George the Fifth' Class No. 1481 *Typhon* at Rhyl. This class, a superheated version of the LNWR's traditional four coupled 2-cylinder simple, came out in 1910, and was as popular with modellers as with railwaymen.

S. Reid Coll.

Built for hauling both passenger and coal trains in south Wales, Beames' 0-8-4T came out in the first year of the LMS. No. 380, the first of the class is in ex-works condition, early 1923. *S. Reid Coll.*

2-4-0 with a 'Problem' Class as pilot engine but there is photographic evidence of 'Dreadnought' 2-2-2-0s, the unfortunate 2-2-2-2 compounds and the four-cylinder 'Jubilees'. The minor passenger services and goods trains would have attracted anything from a 'DX' to a 'Cauliflower' and 2-4-0T, 0-6-2T and 2-4-2T tank engines.

The position on the Midland was different again. Johnson was the locomotive superintendent from 1873 until 1903. He had successfully built 343 simple 4-4-0s and 95 4-2-2s, the last in 1900, and in 1901 introduced the Midland's first compound express locomotive. This became the most powerful type of express locomotive on the Midland until

The Midland relied almost exclusively on 0-6-0 tank engines for its Welsh operations. Here No. 7258, built in 1899, is seen at Upper Bank, Swansea on the 27 August 1928.   *H.C. Casserley*

the grouping, as, contrary to experience on the LNWR, compounding was considered a success. Even so, only 10% of the Midland's 4-4-0s were built as compounds. The Midland had a small engine policy consistent with a commercial policy of running frequent light passenger trains. Double-heading was employed if necessary, and indeed frequently in the case of the heavy London coal trains. This may explain why in 1922 the Midland had more locomotives than any other company and twice as many per mile as the GWR. In 1899 a general shortage of sufficiently powerful locomotives across Britain, exacerbated by an engineering strike, caused the Midland to make a controversial purchase of 40 American 2-6-0s. Standardisation was never achieved to the same extent as on the LNWR, so although there were altogether 1,127 0-6-0s, they had many minor variations.

However, in Wales most of the work was done by tank engines. Johnson built 205 0-4-4T tank engines between 1875 and 1898 and four of this type handled most of the passenger trains between Hereford and Swansea. They were

based at Brecon. He also built 340 0-6-0T tank engines between 1874 and 1902. The largest class of these, consisting of 280 locomotives, was built between 1874 and 1899, and the first of the class were sent to Swansea when the Midland took over the Swansea Vale in 1874. Some 20 of these and later derivatives eventually covered all requirements in Wales until the closure of the Midland lines in BR days. They were mainly based at Upper Bank in Swansea, though a few were at Gurnos, near Ystalyfera.

Turning to the locomotives of the Welsh railways at the turn of the twentieth century, in the valleys of the south there was a large variety within the broad trend which was to use the tank engine and, increasingly, the 0-6-2T wheel arrangement. The reason for this lay in the geography of the narrow and crowded valleys. This limited the space available for the provision of turntables, so bunker-first running was common. As it became customary to run bunker-first down the valleys, a trailing axle was particularly advantageous. Furthermore, distances between coaling and watering points were not great and passenger trains tended to stop frequently at the many stations, so they needed adhesion and acceleration rather than sustained high-speed capacity.

The Rhymney, which had 123 locomotives at the time of the grouping, had already by the turn of the century discovered the virtues of the 0-6-2T, though it had a number of representatives of the ubiquitous 0-6-0ST and its last 0-6-0 tender engine was not withdrawn until 1915. Five unusual 2-4-2ST engines had been introduced to haul passenger trains in 1890.

Rhymney Railway 0-6-0ST No. 18, built in 1861 and withdrawn in 1911.
G.H. Platt Coll.

The Rhymney had five of these unusual 2-4-2ST locomotives. This one, No. 64, was built in 1891 and was converted to 0-6-2T in 1906; it is seen at Merthyr around 1900.
G.H. Platt Coll.

The final development of the 0-6-2T on the Rhymney Railway, No. 38 was introduced in 1921. It is seen here at Caerphilly in BR days.

R.K. Blencowe

At the turn of the century the Brecon & Merthyr had 23 0-6-0STs, more than any other type. This one, No. 8 built in 1884, is seen shunting at Rhydycar near Merthyr. *GBJ Coll.*

Between 1894 and 1905 the Brecon & Merthyr bought four of these rather unusual 0-6-2ST locomotives. No. 20 was photographed at Oswestry as GW No. 1677 in the summer of 1924. *GBJ Coll.*

The Brecon & Merthyr only had 30 engines of which the majority at the turn of the century were of the 0-6-0ST arrangement. It had six 2-4-0Ts similar to the GWR 'Metro' tanks for passenger trains and four unusual 'stretched' 0-6-2STs for mineral trains. After the turn of the century it became the fourth owner of a strange 4-4-0PT and later a former LSWR 4-4-2T. The trend towards the 0-6-2T was followed and 14 were built new by Robert Stephenson.

As one would expect, the Barry was different from the others. A smart red-brown livery with polished brass dome and copper chimney cap distinguished its locomotives and, at the turn of the century, passenger trains were being hauled by four 0-4-4T engines and 13 2-4-2Ts. For freight trains, the Barry followed the trend and by the time of the grouping had as many as 72 of the inside-cylinder 0-6-2T type. Even here it took an independent line and, when in 1899 it was unable to procure sufficient in Britain, bought five outside-cylinder engines of the same wheel arrangement in America. But it also broke new ground in other ways. It was the first British company to employ eight-coupled tender engines when four 0-8-0s of a class originally destined for Sweden were bought. It also introduced the first British 0-8-2Ts. Later, in 1914, the Barry bought 10 powerful engines of the 0-6-4T arrangement.

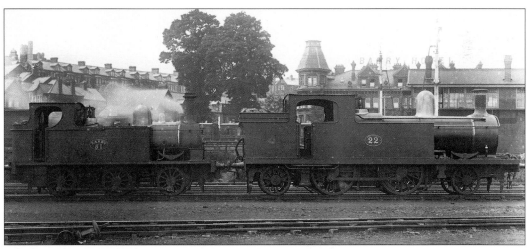

At Barry a pair of locomotives constructed for the opening of the Barry Railway in 1889, 'E' Class 0-6-0T No. 51 and 'C' Class 2-4-2T No. 22. Probably about the turn of the century.   *GBJ Coll.*

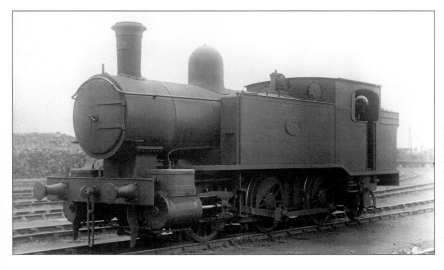

No. 119 was one of a class of five locomotives which were imported by the Barry from America in 1899; at that time British suppliers could not meet the order.
GBJ Coll.

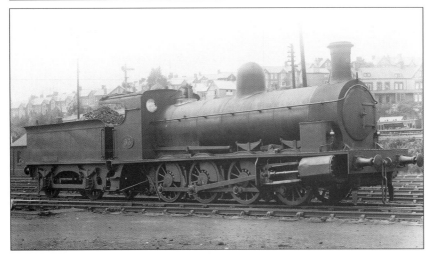

Barry Railway No. 93 was originally delivered to a financially unsound railway in Sweden; it was bought by the Barry in 1897 when a Swedish court ordered its return to Sharp Stewart, the builder. The Barry had four of these 0-8-0s.

GBJ Coll.

The Barry had seven of these handsome 0-8-2T engines built in 1896 by Sharp Stewart.

GBJ Coll.

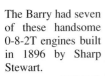
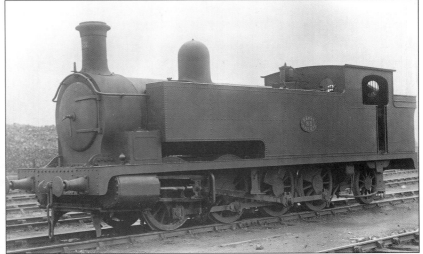

The final class of locomotives purchased by the Barry consisted of 10 0-6-4T engines delivered in 1914. They had a tendency to derail and the GWR kept them for only two years. By October 1926 they had all been withdrawn.

GBJ Coll.

Taff Vale 0-6-0 goods engine No. 339. The Taff Vale persisted with tender engines more than the other valley railways of south Wales as it valued the greater braking effect.   *Real Photographs-Ian Allan Ltd.*

The Taff Vale had six 4-4-2T engines for passenger trains; with good acceleration they were useful locomotives and some were adapted for auto trains. No. 170 was built in 1888. All were withdrawn by 1927.
Real Photographs-Ian Allan Ltd.

The Taff Vale was the only company in south Wales to build its own locomotives and these had, by the turn of the century, set the tone in that the majority were tank engines of the 0-6-2T arrangement. This type was used for hauling both passenger and freight trains. The Taff used tender engines more than the other railways, partly because of the benefit of the greater braking power; indeed, it was not unknown for coal trains to be operated without brake-vans if hauled by a tender engine. There were also some 0-6-0STs, but generally the Taff had a less varied selection of types than its junior brethren. Three 4-4-0T engines were employed on branch passenger trains and there were six inside-cylinder 4-4-2Ts; these were very efficient at hauling main line passenger trains as they had good acceleration. By the time of the grouping, the Taff had over 250 locomotives.

Taff Vale No. 16 of the first group of 0-6-2Ts, introduced in 1886. This locomotive was photographed about the turn of the century, before being rebuilt with a larger boiler.   *GBJ Coll.*

No. 402 was the ultimate design of 0-6-2T on the Taff Vale, here seen at Merthyr in the early 1920s.
LCGB/Ken Nunn Coll.

The Cambrian differed from the lines in the south Wales valleys in having a greater preponderance of passenger traffic, greater distances travelled and less constraint on space. Therefore, tender engines were more widely used. Of the 99 locomotives handed over to the GWR in 1921 over half were tender engines, mainly Sharp Stewart 4-4-0s but also 0-6-0s and a few 2-4-0s. All locomotives except two, which were built at the company's works at Oswestry, were purchased new from outside contractors or second-hand from other railways.

The Cambrian had more tender engines than the other Welsh railways. In GW days No. 23, an 0-4-4T, is seen at Barmouth with a train for Ruabon.
Ifor Higgon Coll.

A typical Cambrian passenger locomotive of the turn of the century was the 'Large Bogie' 4-4-0 built in 1894. No. 69 is seen at Oswestry.
Ifor Higgon Coll.

Cambrian 2-4-0 locomotive No. 29 *Pegasus*, built in 1863 for the Oswestry & Newtown Railway, on the turntable at Barmouth, from a postcard dated 1908. The photograph was taken sometime after a rebuilding necessitated by the locomotive being swept into the sea at Friog on 1 January 1883. It had been subsequently salvaged and survived until 1913.
R. Warner Coll.

The other standard gauge companies had a mixed bag of locomotives, often bought second-hand. From 1903 there were three ex-Mersey Railway 0-6-4Ts and seven 2-6-2Ts on the Alexandra Docks Railway. The Port Talbot followed the lead of the Barry in buying five 0-8-2Ts and there were two 0-6-6-0 Fairlie engines on the Burry Port & Gwendraeth Valley, but the 0-6-0ST was the mainstay.

One of the more unusual locomotives on Welsh railways in 1900 was this double Fairlie on the Burry Port & Gwendraeth Valley. It had originally been delivered to a railway in Queensland, Australia in 1866, but when it proved unsatisfactory was returned to Britain. It turned up in south Wales in 1873 and survived as No. 8 *Victoria* on the BP & GV until 1903.   *GBJ Coll.*

The Port Talbot was the third railway in Britain to have recourse to American locomotives in 1899. This 0-8-2T No. 21, like five 0-6-2Ts on the Barry, was built by the Cooke Locomotive Co. of Paterson, New Jersey. The GWR fitted a standard boiler in 1908. Three more were bought from Sharp Stewart in 1901. Port Talbot, 25 April 1910.   *LCGB/Ken Nunn Coll.*

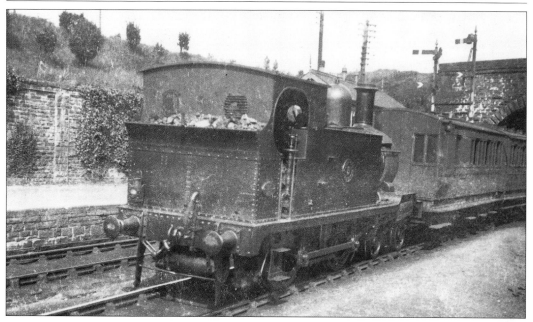

At the turn of the century the principal passenger locomotive on the Neath & Brecon was No. 5, a 4-4-2T seen here at Neath Riverside sometime between 1921 and 1923. This locomotive was built in 1871 as No. 4 and worked on the N & B for about 50 years. It hauled trains between Neath and Colbren Junction and only rarely on to Brecon, as from 1877 this was a Midland preserve. *W. Clifford*

Manchester & Milford 0-6-0 *Aberystwyth*, seen here at the turn of the century at Aberystwyth, was built by Manning Wardle in 1868. In the words of the makers it was 'renewed' in 1897/8, only to be cut up by the GWR at Neath in 1906. *Ifor Higgon Coll.*

On the narrow gauge lines in the north there was a wide variety of locomotives. The majority were simple industrial tank engines, but the need to maximise load-hauling capacity without increasing the gauge or doubling the track called into use the Fairlie type. The earliest steam engines on the narrow gauge were two 0-4-0 tender engines on the 4 ft gauge Padarn, built as early as 1848 with a 10 ft wheel-base.

Linda sister engine to *Blanche* on the Penrhyn Railway, was built in 1893 and is seen here at Port Penrhyn as an 0-4-0T. It survives in 2000 on the Ffestiniog Railway where it has been modified by the provision of a trailing pony truck and a small tender; August 1961.   *GBJ*

Some of the derelict steam engines of the Penrhyn system at Coed-y-parc, Bethesda in August 1961. Most survive in 2000.   *GBJ*

Linda pausing at Port Penrhyn before setting off for Bethesda with sleepers and empty slate waggons; August 1961.
GBJ

On the 4 ft gauge Padarn Railway *Velinheli* built in 1895, at Gilfach Ddu. This locomotive was scrapped in 1963.

GBJ Coll.

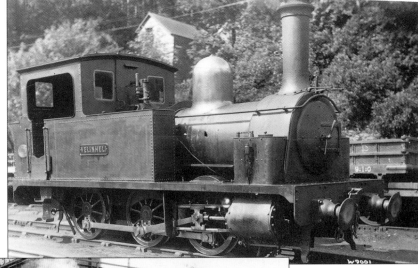

Apart from the oil tank (and the colour photography) this view might have been taken at any time in the last 100 years, though the locomotive *David Lloyd George* is virtually new; Porthmadog, October 1999.

DD

The Welsh Highland 2-6-2T *Russell* built in 1906 for the North Wales Narrow Gauge Railway (NWNGR), awaits restoration, at Tywyn in 1959. Few locomotives have been named after a company receiver and second mortgagee, but James Cholmeley Russell was also for a time chairman of the NWNGR, manager of the Manchester & Milford and a promoter of the Vale of Rheidol.

R. Wood

One survived until after 1900. In 1863 the Ffestiniog introduced six 0-4-0 tender engines with saddle tanks. Subsequently, the Talyllyn followed with one 0-4-0T and another with a trailing axle for greater stability. This policy was followed by the Ffestiniog & Blaenau who built two 0-4-2Ts which did not survive beyond 1883. The Corris bought three 0-4-0Ts, which were quickly converted to 0-4-2Ts, and the Penrhyn bought ten 0-4-0Ts with vertical boilers. The Padarn bought three. Then the Penrhyn bought ten more normal 0-4-0Ts and the Padarn 12. The Padarn finally went in for three 4 ft gauge 0-6-0Ts, now all scrapped.

The Ffestiniog broke new ground in a search for more power and in 1869 introduced the first double Fairlie, followed by three more and one single Fairlie. The North Wales Narrow Gauge bought two single Fairlies and a more conventional 0-6-4T. Unique were the four rack engines on the Snowdon Mountain Railway. There were, in addition, three 0-4-2T steam

tram-engines on the Glyn Valley and two 0-4-0 saddle tanks on the Swansea & Mumbles. In all, that amounted to about 66 engines.

Perhaps surprisingly, 100 years later there are surviving more Welsh narrow gauge steam engines than were operating in 1900. Eight are in the Penrhyn Castle Industrial Railway Museum, but there are now seven on the Snowdon Mountain Railway, 12 on the Talyllyn and in its museum, eight on the Welsh Highland (Porthmadog), successor to the North Wales Narrow Gauge, 13 on the Ffestiniog, and four on the Llanberis Lake, successor to the Padarn. This total has been further helped by the arrival after 1900 and subsequent survival of the Vale of Rheidol with three, the Welshpool & Llanfair with seven, and the Fairbourne with four. Among newcomers, all of which operate over former standard gauge track-bed, the Brecon Mountain has five, the Welsh Highland (Caernarfon) four, and the Bala Lake three from the Padarn. That makes nearly 80 altogether, to

The much photographed Talyllyn locomotive No. 2 *Dolgoch* at Tywyn Wharf in 1951. At this early date in the history of railway preservation only the addition of the name-plate betrays the activities of preservation enthusiasts.   *R. Wood*

A characteristic scene on a preserved railway with former GW 2-8-0 No. 2859 awaiting attention; Llangollen, *ca*. 1990.   *GBJ*

which may be added those survivors from the Penrhyn and Padarn which have found their way to other parts of the world.

On the standard gauge, the number of surviving steam engines varies as they are moved about from one owner to another. With about nine in various states of repair on the Gwili, five on the Swansea Vale, up to 14 on the Llangollen, possibly six on the Pontypool & Blaenavon and about 11 on the Vale of Glamorgan, there are altogether in Wales about 45. In any case, there are fewer standard gauge locomotives than narrow gauge.

On the surviving main line railways, most of the motive power is slung beneath the carriages. Only for freight trains and some of the passenger trains between Crewe and Holyhead and between Cardiff and Rhymney are there any locomotives; those based in Wales amount to 10 diesel locomotives for hauling passenger trains and about 100 for freight. The latter, although based in Wales, operate all over Britain. The passenger train diesels are unlikely to survive beyond the year 2000.

CHAPTER 7

EVENTS AT THE TURN OF THE CENTURY

This chapter highlights some of the events which occurred around the turn of the twentieth century. Some of them were minor but all were part of an important trend or process. They illustrate wider tendencies and demonstrate how railway managements were tackling them. The problems associated with small struggling branch lines, the development of sea links, the increasing power of organised labour, the last outburst of competitive frenzy in the scramble to transport coal to the ports, and the upgrading required to cope with the heavier trains of the Edwardian era, were all features in evidence at the turn of the century and most continued to be serious management concerns for the first half of the twentieth century.

FISHGUARD

On the 1 July 1899, the small town of Fishguard was at last connected to the railway network, over 50 years after Brunel and the South Wales Railway had envisaged its harbour as a new and competitive port for Ireland. The way this came about casts interesting light on the haphazard way the railway network was developed and on the role of individuals in Victorian Britain. One of the key players, the Hon. Margaret Owen, died a month too soon to witness the opening. She had been left a widow three times, on the last two occasions by the two men who successively had most to do with bringing the railway to Fishguard.

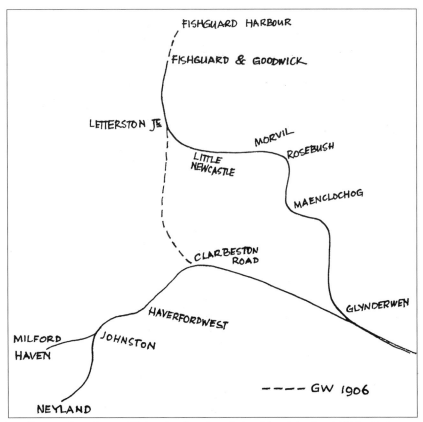

A map of the railways of south-west Wales showing the relationship of the South Wales Railway main line to the 'Maenclochog', the Rosebush & Fishguard, and the eventual extension to Fishguard Harbour.   *GBJ*

Construction of the line to Fishguard, planned to be a competitor to what became the LNWR's route to Holyhead, had been halted seven miles short of the objective in 1851 by the effect on financial markets of the Irish famine. The South Wales Railway's progress westward was diverted instead towards Milford Haven. The original authorisation had included a branch from Whitland to Pembroke on the south side of the Haven, but it was much cheaper to gain access to the Haven by building a short line from Haverfordwest, reached in 1854, to the north shore.

Milford Haven was already in use as a port for mail ships to Waterford. The first Milford mail coach had set out from London in 1785 and was taking 33 hours to cover the 256 mile journey. Milford Haven had been founded in the latter part of the eighteenth century on land owned by the husband of Nelson's Lady Hamilton. Nelson himself visited the town in 1802 and was impressed by the harbour and its emerging role as a naval base. Unfortunately, a

land dispute caused the Admiralty to move in 1814 to the south side of the Haven at Pembroke. Milford remained a base for a group of American immigrants who operated whaling ships and for a time exploited the market for sperm whale oil as a fuel for street lamps.

When Brunel surveyed the north shore, looking for a site for a terminal for the short branch from Haverfordwest, he decided not to use Milford Haven but to create an entirely new terminal to the east, at Neyland. The railway reached Neyland in 1856 and connections with ships for the Irish ports were made from a pontoon jetty established in 1857. It was called New Milford from 1859 to 1906, when it reverted to Neyland. Milford Haven obtained a branch railway in 1863, yet, until its closure in 1964, the Neyland branch remained the main line and Neyland the terminus for London trains. For a time there were hopes of Milford Haven becoming a base for transatlantic shipping but it failed to compete with Liverpool. Its economic base changed again

The jetties at Neyland, at that time known as New Milford, near the turn of the century.   *NLW*

Neyland had a single, curved platform with a columned arcade seen here on what, from the absence of activity, may be deduced to be a wet Sunday afternoon, probably in the late 1930s. *GBJ Coll.*

when, at the beginning of the twentieth century, it became an important trawler port. Just as this declined, the oil industry became attracted to the deep water haven and saved the town again by establishing refineries in the area. This has ensured the continuation of the railway connection up to 2000.

Meanwhile, Fishguard was bypassed by the railway, and so it might have remained had it not been for the enterprise of a few idiosyncratic investors. The first of these was Edward Cropper. Already in his seventies and a former MP and gentleman of Kent, he decided late in life, and while still suffering the after-

The engine shed and sidings at Neyland, 24 July 1938. *C.A. Appleton/J.A. Peden*

Clynderwen was the junction for the 'Maenclochog' and was formerly called 'Narberth Road'. Early 1900s.
NLW

effects of a stroke, to invest in slate production in west Wales. He privately financed and built an eight mile line from the main South Wales Railway at Narberth Road station, Clynderwen, west of Whitland, to the slate quarries at Rosebush. This place lies on the southern slopes of the Presely Hills and Cropper felt tourists could also be attracted to use the railway. Accordingly, this steeply-graded and winding

industrial line was opened to passengers in 1876 as the Narberth Road & Maenclochog Railway (NR & MR), commonly known as the 'Maenclochog'.

In 1848 Cropper had married for the third time a widow, Margaret, whose husband had been the younger brother of the famous poet, historian and politician, Lord Macaulay. Margaret's son by her former marriage, Joseph

A distant view of Rosebush station with a short train in the late nineteenth century. The flank of Foel Cwmcerwyn, the highest point of the Presely Hills, can be seen in the background.   *NLW*

Babington Macaulay, was engaged as general manager of the railway by Cropper, but he and Margaret also had sons of their own, Edward Denman Cropper who became a soldier, and James who stayed at home. Edward Denman inherited the railway when his father died in 1876, shortly after the opening. Margaret then married for the third time the son of a local landowner, John Owen.

Her son Joseph was enthusiastic about the prospect of continuing the railway further west and was instrumental in promoting the Rosebush & Fishguard Railway (R & F) to construct a 14 mile extension. This company was authorised in 1878 and was backed by Sir Hugh Owen Owen of Rosebush, father of Margaret's third husband John. He became the first chairman. John was also a director. Margaret was thus in an interesting position as wife of John, a director of the R & F, daughter-in-law of Sir Hugh, the chairman, and mother of the deputy chairman, Joseph Babington Macaulay. She was also mother of the new owner of the Maenclochog. Initially, Edward Denman Cropper was also a director of the R & F but he resigned a year later, allegedly to facilitate the development of the relationship between the two neighbouring companies. However, he was not the man his father was and appears to have had not just a lack of vision as to the future of the railway, but a determination to forestall its progress. While he was away in the army, his younger brother James allowed the railway to deteriorate and it had to close at the end of 1882, ruined partly by the excessive charges made by the GWR for access to Clynderwen.

The staff of Rosebush station in the early 1900s. *GBJ Coll.*

There followed a desultory game of poker between the two family companies with offer and counter-offer, one part of the family being dog in the manger, the other pushing for expansion. One can imagine difficult family parties in the early 1880s dominated by the differences of opinion between Edward Denman Cropper and James Cropper on one side of the table, step-brother Joseph Macaulay and step-father John Owen on the other, and their mother at the head of the table trying to keep the peace. In 1884 the railway was reopened but had to close again in 1888. In 1889 it was put up for auction but there were no bidders. There was no agreement until 1894, when the Croppers were fortunate enough to sell their shares for £50,000, but only because of the improved fortunes of the extension over which James had been so obstructive. To understand how this change in fortune came about we need to revert to 1878, two years after the opening of the Maenclochog.

Back in 1878 a public meeting called by the R & F in Fishguard had been 'largely attended' and had given 'hearty support' to Owen and Macaulay's projected railway from Rosebush to the town. However, the company had difficulty in raising money and in paying the contractor for the work on the short first section from Rosebush to New Inn near Morfil. In 1881, the R & F was authorised to acquire the Maenclochog and was granted an extension of time. An approach was made to the GWR for financial help, but Grierson, the general manager, was initially interested only if he could work both the railways and then only once they had both been completed. At this point, Cropper was prepared to accept £20,000 for the NR & MR but the money could not be found. Then, at a second meeting, Grierson offered to assist with a new line from the GWR at Clarbeston Road to Morfil, which was at that time the limit of the R & F. This would have taken a fairly circuitous route towards Fishguard, though it foreshadowed the line eventually built by the GWR. It had some appeal to the R & F as it would have cut out the Maenclochog altogether; it thus provided some much needed negotiating leverage with the Croppers. On the strength of this, they were asked for a £10,000 guarantee.

One can imagine Margaret struggling to keep her difficult relatives under control, but this solution also failed and in 1883 a contractor called Jackson & Co offered to build the rest of the R & F for £10,000 cash, £20,000 in bonds and £20,000 in shares, to purchase the NR & MR and to hand it over to the R & F on completion. Unfortunately, the cash was still not available, so another contractor was found. In July 1883 Maddison & Co offered to construct the line as far as Letterston for all the capital, namely £78,000 in ordinary shares and £30,000 in debentures. They would take over existing liabilities up to £7,000, buy all the land needed and then pay for the line onward to Fishguard.

This was readily accepted and in 1884 application was made to Parliament for a further extension of time, powers to increase the share capital and authority to change the company's name to the North Pembrokeshire & Fishguard Railway (NP & FR).

Early in 1885 no progress had been made with Maddison and the company reopened talks with the first contractors, Appleby & Lawton, who were still owed £4,987. It was decided to try to interest the GWR again and a lawyer called Cave was engaged as negotiator with the GWR. He emerges from the record as a smooth-talker and made optimistic noises about the prospects. On the strength of this he was made joint solicitor to the company. He worked with another solicitor called Harris, who seems to have been more of a realist. Harris put forward three solutions to the practical problem which stood in the way of progress: how to gain access to the site for construction in the face of the difficult neighbour, James Cropper:

1. Start the line at Fishguard and move back towards the existing line
2. Run plant and equipment to Clarbeston Road on the GWR and then use carts for conveyance by road to site
3. Try to force the running powers over the Maenclochog and gain access that way.

Cave could only wring his hands and say it was all very difficult, that without the GWR no contractors were interested and, without a contractor, the GWR were not interested either.

On 27 May 1885 a significant development was reported by Harris who had been to see the Rosslare Harbour Board. They were seeking to discuss with the GWR a line from Clarbeston Road to Fishguard, with a view to establishing a sea link between Fishguard and Rosslare. He had then been to see Gooch who was also interested. In August, Cave reported that the GWR would work the line for 5% and Appleby & Lawton would build the line if the GWR were thus involved. Since this was no more than had been established some months previously by Harris, Cave was summarily dismissed. A new negotiator was appointed, one Le Hunte, who based himself at the Oxford & Cambridge Club in London.

A period study of the station and its surroundings at Clarbeston Road about 1900. The well-groomed appearance of the railway infrastructure compares favourably with the roughness of the street. The width of the railway bridge and the space between the tracks bear witness to the original broad gauge of the South Wales Railway.   *NLW*

It was now decided to put another Bill to Parliament with the intention of constructing a line from the GWR at Clarbeston Road to the present limit of the line at Little Newcastle. The GWR were willing to operate the line for 60% on the basis of a sea link to Wexford being established. However, it proved difficult to interest a contractor and the idea collapsed.

Nothing appears to have been done until the end of 1891 when a Colonel Joseph O'Kell contracted to extend the line to Fishguard and to buy the Maenclochog; he was to be paid partly in shares. At this point, two entrepreneurs, Rowlands and Cartland (grandfather of the late Dame Barbara), saw the potential for a new harbour at Fishguard and of reviving the concept of a short sea link with Ireland. They acquired shares and when O'Kell became bankrupt in 1894 took over his contract. In March 1894 they were instrumental in, at last, purchasing the Maenclochog, but now had to pay £50,000 for it, though only in NP & F preference shares.

The NP & F was now in much better shape. Indeed, the new management had become so confident that, in October 1894, it submitted plans to Parliament for an eastward extension from Clynderwen (as Narberth Road was now called), through Narberth and then southward in a great loop towards Pendine. A new station was

proposed in the centre of Carmarthen, just behind the cattle market; the line then went right through the town, destroying in the process a fine row of houses in Picton Terrace, to a connection with the LNWR line near Abergwili. This spectacular plan was approved but, in the absence of support from the LNWR, was replaced by an even more adventurous plan in 1897, to extend to Swansea and Aberdare. This fantasy did not even reach Parliament, but now the boot was really on the other foot; the GWR was enquiring whether it could interest the company in a direct line from Clarbeston Road to Letterston.

The reason for this more positive attitude on the part of the GWR was its involvement with the moves initiated on the Irish side of the water. In 1898 these led to a company, which had been formed in 1894 and 1895, to develop the harbours and sea connections of Rosslare and Fishguard, making an agreement with the GWR and the Great Southern & Western of Ireland to complete the two harbours and provide steamers.

In the light of these developments the GWR realised that the NP & F had to be taken seriously and agreed to take it over for £150,000. The NP & F became part of the GWR by an Act of 20 June 1899 and the first through train from Fishguard to Clynderwen ran on 1 August.

A general view of Fishguard & Goodwick station, in the late 1930s, looking east, with a handsome Austin Saloon parked in the forecourt.   *WIMM/GW Coll.*

Two auto trains in Fishguard & Goodwick station, probably 1950s.   *GBJ Coll.*

By the winter of 1899 Bradshaw had squeezed into a page of assorted Welsh train services a timetable of trains over the NP & F as far as Goodwick. From 1904 this station was known as 'Fishguard & Goodwick'. Closed in 1964, it reopened in 1965, only to be closed again in 1972.

PRO: RAIL 903/113

The short connection to Fishguard Harbour and the new sea terminal were completed in 1906. In order to speed the boat trains, the GWR built a direct line from the original south Wales main line at Clarbeston Road to Letterston. Gooch had discussed such a link in 1885 and it was indeed similar to the idea discussed with Grierson as far back as 1881. It had the effect of bypassing most of the NP & F line and the Maenclochog altogether. They had served their purpose; they had created the opportunity, and were now redundant. Nevertheless, passenger traffic survived with interruptions until 1937, and goods traffic, despite closures during the Second World War, lasted until 1949. During closure the line was used for a number of non-railway functions by the RAF. One of these involved the use of a tunnel on the old Maenclochog as a practice target for Barnes Wallis' 'dam-buster' bouncing bombs.

Fishguard Harbour station opened in 1906 was photographed shortly afterwards.
GBJ Coll.

R.M.S. *Mauretania* at Fishguard with tender and boaters, *ca.* 1910.   *PRO: RAIL 1014/53/11*

Poster advertising the Transatlantic possibilities at Fishguard, *ca*. 1910. *WIMM*

Thus it was almost by accident that the GWR acquired what, for some years, it subsequently made great efforts to promote as a prestigious international connection; it even persuaded Cunard to make Fishguard a transatlantic port of call for the few years leading up to the First World War.

It is as a cross-channel ferry terminal that it survives as a railhead in 2000. Happily, The Hon. Margaret Owen's memory is preserved by the tank engine named *Margaret* which stands in a museum in Pembrokeshire.

The former NP & F 0-6-0ST *Margaret*, named after Margaret Owen, was built in 1878 and sold by the GWR in 1923. It resides at Scolton Manor Museum in Pembrokeshire; 1997.   *DD*

THE TAFF VALE RAILWAY STRIKE

The last decade of the nineteenth century witnessed an increase in labour unrest, leading to employee militancy, the emergence of trades unions and the birth pangs of the Labour Party. The hard but effective rule of business, which had brought about the industrial revolution, was no longer uncriticised. Attitudes which had been seen as unexceptional and essential to the achievement of a successful business were now more widely unacceptable. Conditions of work and living and the rights of employees were being openly discussed. Dependence upon the uncertain and sometimes quixotic charity of the

employer was ceasing to be enough. Even the then generous provision of a free pension after 25 years' service did not assuage the TVR employees' dissatisfaction, though it was one of the factors which mollified their attitude later.

In south Wales the Taff Vale Railway became an early victim of labour unrest. The Boer War put pressure on living costs and during 1899 pay rises were negotiated on the Barry, Cardiff and Rhymney Railways. The Taff Vale, under an extremely tough management, resisted the pressure. For some time, it had been criticised by the public and investors.

Its financial performance, once scintillating, had declined, and its management was perceived as being arrogant and difficult to deal with. Perhaps, therefore, it was not entirely accidental that the Taff was the early focus of industrial confrontation. In February 1900, the chairman, R.G.L. Vassall, when reporting to shareholders, 'ventured to think it passed the wit of man to conceive any ground for requiring the company to pay a higher price for labour'.

In September 1899 a local committee of TVR employees gave notice of a meeting to be held on 1 October in Cardiff, with the purpose of formulating demands to be placed before the company. This was stimulated by articles in the trade union press notifying workers that, since the reservists were being called-up for the war in South Africa, there was likely to be a labour shortage, so the time was ripe for securing an increase in pay; as much as a 70% increase was wildly spoken of. The Taff refused to negotiate with a union and, accordingly, the workers' committee organised a ballot on calling a strike. It was decided that, since less than 90% of the workers were in favour of negotiating through the union, the strike could not go ahead.

However, on 6 August 1900, 400 men gave notice of strike action independent of the union, and on the 19th nearly all the TVR locomotive men, signalmen and train men gave notice of a strike to start in 14 days time.

As the Amalgamated Society of Railway Servants (ASRS) was not involved until the strike had begun, it reprimanded the Taff men for acting without its agreement but, mainly because one of the complaints was against the dismissal by the TVR of a signalman who was on sick leave, the union agreed to back the strike. This unfortunate man, John Ewington by name, had been a TVR employee for 20 years and was at the time signalman at Abercynon. He was also a representative of the ASRS. The company wished to move him to Treherbert, but he asked to be excused from uprooting and moving to another valley. The company insisted, whereupon he fell sick with rheumatic fever and while he was away from work, both of the jobs, at Abercynon and Treherbert, were given to other men. According to Herepath, he was later offered another job as deputy signalman without requiring a move, but by then the damage had been done.

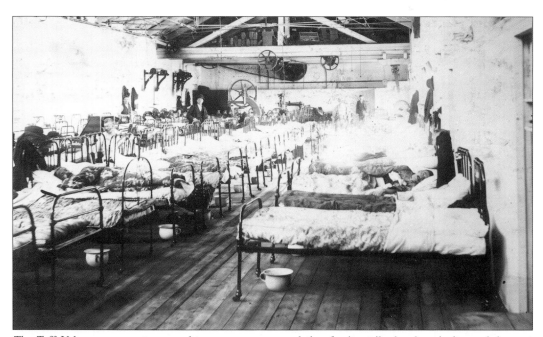

The Taff Vale management arranged temporary accommodation for its strike breakers in its workshops at Cardiff.
PRO: RAIL 1057/1791

Pickets near the Cathays Works in Cardiff, with a conveniently located convenience of the period.

WIMM 77. 1076

The Woodville Hotel near a gate into Cathays Works. The publican provided liquid sustenance to the pickets and no doubt a location for 'entertaining' the strike breakers as they arrived from other parts of the country. The pub still stands in 2000.

WIMM 77. 1078

Pickets on Cardiff General station platform ready to meet strike breakers arriving by train from as far away as Scotland.

WIMM 77. 1088

The strike was not without unpleasantness and there was some violence, particularly over blacklegs. Twelve men were brought by the Taff management from as far away as Scotland. One train-load who were brought into Cardiff were met by 30 strikers and escorted to the hotel, where the strikers had their headquarters; there they were 'entertained' and most returned whence they had come. On 20 August a driver and fireman were forcibly removed by strikers from the cab of the locomotive they were taking out of the yard at Pontypridd. They were then taken, with their arms tied, to strike headquarters in Cardiff. Many who wanted to work dared not leave their houses. But the behaviour of the TVR management was fairly inflammatory and some strikers were evicted from company housing. Richard Bell, the general secretary of the ASRS, gave the strike strong personal backing and added his own weight to the campaign. The flavour of his contribution towards coping with blacklegs is reflected in a message he sent to the strikers at Aberdare: 'You must have much trouble up there with this scum of hell. Keep your men well to the line.'

On 23 August, the TVR applied to the High Court for an injunction to stop picketing. This was granted on 30 August. Meanwhile, public pressure, including a letter to *The Times* from the former TVR chairman, James Inskip, had forced the management to agree to negotiate. The strike ceased on 1 September, and the ASRS paid the strikers the expenses incurred, which amounted to £2,548 12s. 2d. Many of the items were in connection with the escorting of blacklegs away from the area. James Taylor, a local organiser, included two items in his expense claim for tips to the police, one of a shilling and sixpence, the other of just sixpence, as there had been much extra need for policing. All the strikers were offered reinstatement but the company managed to avoid having to dismiss instantly the blackleg labour.

The importance of the case in industrial history is that, on the strength of words attached to the court's injunction restraining picketing, the TVR sued the ASRS for £24,626, in respect of loss of profits and additional costs incurred as a direct consequence of the strike. The

Mr R. Bell, MP for Derby and secretary of the Amalgamated Society of Railway Servants; from *The Railwaymen* by Phillip Bagwell.
George Allen & Unwin

finding in favour of the company, ultimately on appeal to the House of Lords, led to the enactment in 1906 of the Trades Disputes Act which provided trades unions with certain legal immunities. The over-rigorous reaction by the company in the end produced a more disadvantageous result than a balanced and reasonable attitude might have achieved. But that is with the benefit of hindsight and in the light of the eventual modification of the Act in the 1980s.

RHYMNEY RAILWAY V. BRECON & MERTHYR TYDVIL JUNCTION RAILWAY

One of the processes in train at the turn of the century was a prolonged legal battle between two of the companies who had been deadly rivals 35 years previously but had then managed to find an accommodation. Their rivalry was revived by the maverick Barry. In the language

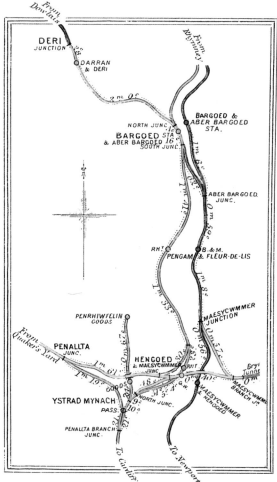

of today's tabloid press, two neighbouring villains, who had carved up the trade in the Rhymney valley, fell apart when one of them was seduced by a gangster from the other side of Cardiff.

In 1864, the Rhymney main line ran down the west side of the Rhymney valley to near Caerphilly, whence it made connection with the Taff Vale at Walnut Tree Junction, for access to Cardiff docks. It was keen to develop its own line to Cardiff direct from Caerphilly, and also wanted to establish a connection with the LNWR line from Abergavenny at the head of the Rhymney valley. The B & M also had eyes on Abergavenny from its line from Brecon to Dowlais, but had just acquired the so-called Old Rumney Tramway which ran down the east side of the Rhymney valley and then over the hills to Newport. It was also keen to gain access to Cardiff. After a struggle which occupied hours of parliamentary committee time they reached a compromise. The B & M

The Rhymney Railway (pink) and the Brecon & Merthyr (blue) running in parallel down the Rhymney valley. The map illustrates how, between Deri and Bargoed, the B & M was dependent on access over the Rhymney to complete the link between Brecon and Newport.   *RCH*

The point at which the original Rhymney Railway main line joined the Taff Vale at Walnut Tree Junction, Taffs Well, June 1978.   *GBJ*

Cefn On Halt and the tunnel under Caerphilly Mountain which carried the Rhymney's direct line to Cardiff.
Locomotive No. 4121, 22 May 1961. *Ian L. Wright*

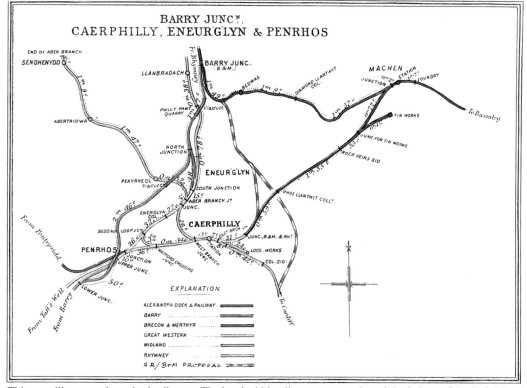

This map illustrates the point in dispute. The hatched blue lines represent the original plans of the B & M and
the Rhymney to link the B & M to the Rhymney's direct line to Cardiff. The orange line of the Barry is what
caused the Rhymney to go to court. *RCH/GBJ*

A view up the upper Rhymney valley above Bargoed with the track-bed of the B & M branch to New Tredegar visible on the right and the Rhymney Railway still in operation on the left; 1964.

G.H. Platt

withdrew its projected line from Caerphilly to Cardiff in return for running powers from Caerphilly to both Cardiff and Walnut Tree Junction over the Rhymney. In addition, in clause 11, they agreed to share receipts, less 30% for working expenses, on coal movements from New Tredegar as far as Caerphilly. New Tredegar lay on the east side of the Rhymney valley, and was linked to the Rhymney on the west side of the valley over a link line already in place. From Caerphilly to Cardiff the business was to be for the Rhymney account alone. In clause 17 they made an agreement, which today would almost certainly be judged to be in restraint of trade, which bound them not to build any more links across the Rhymney valley with the intention of taking traffic one from the other. A strategic weakness in the

B & M position was that its only link between Dowlais and Newport was by way of running powers over the Rhymney from Deri in the Bargoed Taff valley to just south of Bargoed.

Moving on to 1898, the Barry was seeking to increase throughput at Barry Docks by tapping more of the coal-bearing valleys; the Rhymney valley was rich and tempting. The Barry already had a link to the Rhymney at Penrhos Junction, on the west side of Caerphilly, and now had a proposal before Parliament to extend that connection across the valley to the Brecon & Merthyr. Simultaneously, the B & M were negotiating with the Rhymney for the creation of two additional connections between their systems in the neighbourhood of Caerphilly which would have moved additional coal to Cardiff over the Rhymney. However, the Barry

The B & M line passing the Pengam collieries south of Bargoed; 1950s.

GBJ Coll.

managed to persuade the B & M to switch the new connections to the Barry Railway, so that the coal trade in question would find its outlet at Barry Docks rather than at Cardiff. The deal was made attractive by promises of cash and a contribution towards the cost of doubling the B & M main line.

The RR then wrote to the B & M and declared that in view of this proposed breach of clause 17 in the 1864 agreement, they considered the whole agreement null and void. This is no place to enter into the legal arguments which carried the case through Chancery to the Court of Appeal. As so often, the clarity of the argument was muddied by inconsistent behaviour by both parties; the RR had themselves ignored clause 17 when submitting earlier proposals for a line across the valley, which were in fact thrown out by Parliament, and they had never submitted any accounts to the B & M for the New Tredegar to Cardiff coal movements. Furthermore, the B & M had made scant use of the running powers to Cardiff, nor had they built the lines

The Rhymney Railway station at Hengoed seen from the higher level Vale of Neath line station; 1959. The multiple junctions at this important crossing enabled the switching of coal trains between valleys.　*G.H. Platt*

The Barry Railway's Walnut Tree viaduct over the Taff with No. 5671 on a Barry-bound excursion; August 1959.　*Steam & Sail/E.S. Owen Jones*

The Barry Railway's Llanbradach viaduct striding across the valley, over railway and river.   *WIMM/GW Coll.*

A close-up of the Llanbradach viaduct showing the quality and massive proportions of the structure. The Rhymney Railway may be glimpsed in the lower left corner of the picture.   *GBJ Coll.*

for which they negotiated so hard at the head of the valley. Nevertheless, the Chancery judge held that clause 17 had been breached and that the RR was entitled to consider the agreement at an end. The Court of Appeal, on the other hand, held that the breach of clause 17 did not give cause to consider the whole contract terminated. In particular, the lords justices pointed out that it would have been excessive if, as a result of such a conclusion, the running powers from Deri to Bargoed were also terminated. It was held that the RR's correct recourse lay in damages, once the line was open, and that the B & M was entitled to the costs of the appeal. The case was prepared for appeal to the House of Lords but it appears that, before it was heard, it was concluded that the Master of the Rolls had said all there was to be said in the Court of Appeal, and there is no record of the case being heard in the House of Lords.

The new link was eventually opened in 1905 and involved the construction of the impressive Llanbradach viaduct. So soundly was this built with such excellent bricks and such effective mortar that, when it was pulled down 50 years later, the demolition contractor seriously underestimated the cost. The abutments alone bear silent and massive witness to this dramatic piece of civil engineering, the construction of which cost the company £250,000.

THE TANAT VALLEY LIGHT RAILWAY AND OTHER LIGHT RAILWAY ORDERS

Since the introduction of the street tramway in the 1860s, the railways had been losing much of the inner urban passenger traffic which they, in turn, had taken from the horse bus 20 years earlier. One of the reasons for this was their inability to compete with the cost of operating trams. In France and Belgium, many railway projects, particularly those in rural areas, were recipients of direct state subsidies. In Britain the first response to this idea was the Local Government Act of 1888, which for the first time allowed local authorities to raise income direct from ratepayers and to consider how to spend it. This led to the Light Railways Act of 1896 by which, under certain circumstances, what was termed a 'light railway' could be created, with obligations and operating standards rather lower than those applicable to normal railways. This prompted a large number of projects all over Britain, with several in Wales. They ranged from what today looks more like a tramway partly on segregated track with electric trains, to what was almost entirely indistinguishable from a railway, on a segregated standard gauge track with steam locomotive propulsion. In Wales, at about the turn of the century, there were a number of such projects, ranging from the Merthyr Tydfil Light Railway, at 3' 6" gauge with electric traction and partly on segregated track, to the Llandudno & Colwyn Bay Light Railway, mainly running in the street, the Rhyl & Prestatyn, the Pwllheli & Nevin, and the Llanelly & District, all electric. The Welshpool & Llanfair was to be a steam-hauled narrow gauge line, as was the Vale of Rheidol, both mainly on segregated track, and one, the Tanat Valley Light Railway, 14 miles long, steam-hauled and standard gauge, was almost indistinguishable from a railway. This was to link Llangynog to the Cambrian Railways at Porthywaen. The first sod was turned on 12 September 1899.

The Tanat Valley Light Railway was a good example of a line made possible by the Light Railways Act, as an earlier project to reach Llangynog, the Oswestry & Llangynog, which had been authorised in 1882, had not proved viable. However, even the more relaxed requirements of the new act were insufficient to make the Tanat Valley an economic success. Its sources of finance suggest that conventional investors had given it a thumbs down, for 36% of its expected capital investment came in the form of loans from seven local authorities and 35% was direct from HM Treasury. The company struggled until it was taken over by the Cambrian in 1921, its status as a light railway being insufficient to enable it to operate economically and repay its loan capital. Like other latecomers, it was one of the first to lose its passenger trains, in 1951; goods traffic continued over part of the line until 1964.

It is interesting to compare the fate of the Tanat Valley Light Railway with that of the two others started at about the same time and both under construction at the turn of the century. These were the Welshpool & Llanfair (2' 6" gauge) and the Vale of Rheidol (2' gauge), mentioned above. In spite of being latecomers, both survive in 1999.

On 8 September 1899 the Welshpool received its Light Railway Order. It was constructed under contract by the Cambrian, who also operated it from opening in 1903. It therefore became part of the GWR at the

Llangynog station at the head of the Tanat Valley line seen in 1947 with locomotive No.1196. The closure of passenger services four years later was prompted by a national coal shortage.
IRS/ K.J. Cooper Coll.

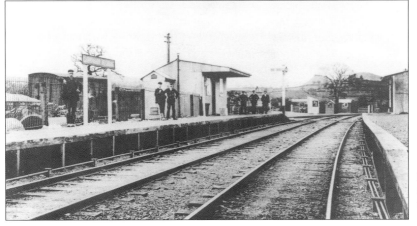

Llanrhaiadr Mochnant station in the Tanat valley.
Lens of Sutton

Track flooding at Blodwell Junction at the lower end of the Tanat Valley line; August 1957. The locomotive is No. 46513. Further flooding here in 1960 precipitated the final closure of the line.

Steam & Sail/
E.S. Owen Jones

Mellowed reminders of the Tanat Valley line; January 1986. *GBJ*

grouping. However, this was no great advantage as passenger services were replaced by a GWR bus service in 1931, though goods services continued until 1956. As a line carrying local and agricultural produce only, with no mineral or other industrial works anywhere in the vicinity, it can only have survived so long due to the uncritical financial analysis of branch lines, first by the GWR and then by British Rail. But survive it did, and just long enough to be caught up in the emerging wave of enthusiasm for preservation started on the Talyllyn in 1950. By 1959 a preservation society had been formed and in 1963 the Welshpool & Llanfair was rolling again. It is now an important tourist attraction.

Welshpool & Llanfair locomotive *The Earl* with a train at Llanfair shortly after the opening of the railway in 1903.   *LCGB/Ken Nunn Coll.*

A quiet evening on the Welshpool & Llanfair nearly 100 years later as the level crossing gates are closed behind the last 'down' train of the day; October 1999.   *GBJ*

The Vale of Rheidol Railway has avoided closure, except on a temporary basis during the Second World War. Locomotive No. 7 *Owain Glyndwr*. August 1961. *GBJ*

August 1897 saw the Vale of Rheidol Railway's Light Railway Order, and it opened in 1902. From the start there was some bread-and-butter mineral trade but the tourist potential at Devil's Bridge was foreseen early on. Accordingly, the railway was sufficiently successful to be able to sell out to the Cambrian in 1913. It therefore passed to the GWR and its steam engines eventually became the last on British Rail. Goods traffic ceased in 1937 but, although the whole line was closed down during the Second World War, passenger traffic started again in 1945, and continues in 2000. BR sold the line to private operators in 1989. Its survival is probably due to careful management taking advantage of its scenic route, the use of steam engines and the continuity of operation, but no doubt it has benefitted from the survival of other narrow gauge steam lines in north-west Wales. They all share the advantage of lower capital and operating costs compared with those on a standard gauge railway.

The Vale of Rheidol Railway in BR days; the engineman demonstrates his versatility as he tries his hand with the points; 1969.   *Ian L. Wright*

THE GOLDEN VALLEY LINE AND WORSE

On 1 July 1899 the GWR acquired for £9,000 18 miles of standard gauge railway that had already been closed for a year. It ran north-westward from Pontrilas on the main line of the Newport, Abergavenny & Hereford Railway, by then part of the GWR, and terminated at Hay. Only a small part of the line was therefore strictly Welsh. The first stage of 10 miles, as far as Dorstone, was authorised in 1876 and the extension onward to Hay, on the Midland's line from Hereford to Brecon, a year later. The first part opened in 1881 and the complete line in 1889. Nine years later it was all closed.

Sir Richard Green Price, MP for Radnor and a local landowner was chairman of the company and a backer; he had visions of a link across country to Monmouth and even Bristol, but the line only cut the distance from Brecon to Abergavenny by 15 miles and when, after 1893, the change of trains necessary at Hereford could be made using only one station, the incentive to use the line was very small. When trade declined in 1894, the line was offered to the GWR for £30,000. This was rejected, as was a reduced offer of £20,000 made in the following year. When it eventually agreed to buy the line in 1899, the GW was able to make some improvements in earnings, mainly by promoting through connections, and went on to run passenger trains until 1941. Thereafter there was some goods activity from time to time until Pontrilas station was closed in 1958.

This was a railway whose viability was suspect from the start, and whose survival depended on cross-subsidy. As Jack Simmons has pointed out in *The Railway in Town and Country*, the railway companies were slow to analyse the profitability of the different parts of their systems and were dominated by respect for the network and a desire to reach the maximum number of potential clients. A similar attitude was manifest by the oil companies in the 1960s. Their desire to ensure representation everywhere led to a proliferation of petrol pumps in remote corners, convenient but eventually unprofitable.

In even worse shape than the Golden Valley line and also starting in England, was a line closed as early as 1880, the Shropshire & Montgomeryshire Light Railway, which ran from its own station near the abbey in Shrewsbury to Llanymynech, with branches to 'granite' quarries. By the turn of the century it had been idle for 20 years and was due to

remain so for another 10, but then, almost miraculously, with the help of a Light Railway Order, it was revived by, among others, Colonel Stephens. Almost as miraculous was its subsequent survival, on and off, until 1960.

From the above examples it might be concluded that, at the turn of the century, almost any project was worth floating. However, there was one that was bad enough to be abandoned, even in 1899. It had been thrown out by the House of Commons in 1898. It was to link the Manchester & Milford Railway, east of Aberystwyth, with the Mid-Wales Railway near Rhayader; it was then to find its way to a crossing of the LNWR's Central Wales line north of Llandrindod Wells, and was finally to make an end-on junction with the Kington & Eardisley at New Radnor. Scenic it would certainly have been, but uneconomic.

The year 1900 also witnessed another attempt to develop Porthdinllaen as a port for Ireland. This place, on the north coast of the Lleyn peninsula, has a particularly sheltered north-east facing harbour. It had been seriously considered as an alternative to Holyhead, avoiding the crossing of the Menai Strait, as early as 1837 and again in 1845 by Brunel. In May 1900 a six mile line from Pwllheli, called the Pwllheli & Nevin Light Railway, was projected but withdrawn. By November it had become an 11 mile line entitled the Pwllheli, Nevin & Porth Dinlleyn Light Railway. This was approved in 1901 but later withdrawn.

The motor car succeeded where the railway failed, in this case at Porthdinllaen in August 1938. This quiet spot might have been the ferry terminal for Ireland in place of Holyhead if various schemes put forward over more than half a century had come to anything. The last was thrown out in 1901.
WIMM/GW Coll.

AN EARLY LINE CLOSURE

The upper reaches of the Plynlimon & Hafan Railway as it approached the dramatic incline up the rocky mountainside. The locomotive *Talybont* with a waggon is visible in the middle distance; *ca*.1898.　　　*NLW*

It would be incorrect to infer from the preceding examples that any line operating at the turn of the century was likely to continue indefinitely. In 1899 the Plynlimon & Hafan Tramway was closed, having been open for barely two years. This narrow gauge 2' 3" line ran for just over 7 miles from Llanfihangel, north of Aberystwyth, through Talybont and into the hills, to haul lead-ore and stone from the quarries. It qualifies for mention because for some five months in 1898 it operated a passenger service once a week, hauled by steam engines. It was remarkable if only for

The Plynlimon & Hafan's vertical boiler locomotive *Victoria* at Talybont, *ca.* 1898.　　　*NLW*

A close-up of the steeply-inclined plane and the rather opulent bogie carriage provided for a sparse train service; *ca.* 1898.   *NLW*

The two locomotives *Talybont* and *Victoria, ca.* 1898.   *Ifor Higgon Coll.*

the fact that neither the line itself nor its passenger train operations had any official authorisation. In some records it is oddly referred to as the Plynlimon & Hafan Toy Railway. Locally it was referred to as 'y lein fach'.

In 1914 efforts were made to interest the Cambrian and even the LNWR in reopening the line as far as Talybont, as either a standard gauge line (still at that time referred to as the 'broad gauge') or on the original narrow gauge. The Cambrian's engineer, who inspected the site, considered the curves too sharp for a standard gauge line and since restoring the narrow gauge would require transshipment the prospects dwindled. The start of the First World War seems to have finally put paid to the idea.

Halt at Sugar Loaf Summit

In 1899 the LNWR placed two short wooden platforms at the summit of the Central Wales line situated between Llanwrtyd and Cynghordy, and just north of the 1,000 yard tunnel. At 820 ft with a climb of 3 miles at 1:80 from the north and 4 miles at 1:60 to 1:70 from the south, the increasing traffic made it necessary to provide a loop and two sidings. That required signalmen, and a box was erected on the north side of the track. In view of the distance from civilisation, houses were provided for the signalmen and a ganger. The main platform, for the use of the men and their families only, was on the north side but there was also a smaller version on the south side.

In 2000 the larger platform survives but its purpose is now as a halt for tourists. The smaller platform is also believed to exist, beneath the cover of some undergrowth. The LMS subsequently extended the loop to cope with longer trains. During the Second World War nearly 1 million tons a year was moved up the Central Wales line, so this would have been a busy place. By the time they reached the summit, northbound footplatemen would have been gasping for air, especially if they had been on the banker, pushing through the long single bore on a climb of 1:60.

Barry Pier

The creation of the docks at Barry and subsequently of the Barry Railway, built to ensure the flow of coal, was essentially the work of one man, David Davies of Llandinam. A statue stands outside the Dock Office at Barry which now accommodates the Vale of Glamorgan Council. In a shareholders' meeting of the Rhondda & Swansea Bay Railway at Swansea in August 1899, the retiring chairman Sir John Jones Jenkins MP reported that David Davies had said, before work on the Barry Docks had started, that if the Blaenrhondda tunnel had been built at a lower level out of the Rhondda valley, there would have been no reason to build the docks at Barry at all. The

growth in coal trade would have been taken up by Swansea and, to a lesser extent, Port Talbot. However, by 1889 the Barry Docks were a reality and the Barry Dock and Railway Company, controlling both dock and railway under one management, was able to exploit the competitive advantage it gained from its modern facilities and its simplified command structure. In spite of having to invest heavily in its infrastructure, it became highly profitable.

On 27 June 1899, the Barry Railway completed an extension from Barry Island to Barry Pier, with a view to enhancing Barry's appeal to the better class of holiday-maker. This involved the digging of a tunnel 280 yards long

The Barry Railway's pier-head station on Barry Island, with the harbour used by the passenger ferries; *ca.* 1895.

GBJ Coll.

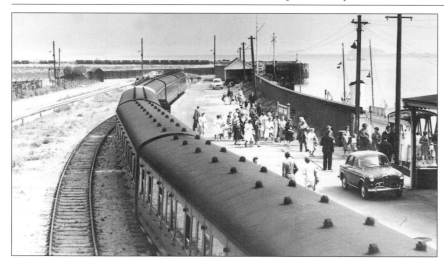

Barry Pier station close up in BR days; 18 August 1963.

S. Rickard

and the construction of a two-platformed station. A landing pontoon was placed in a position such that passengers could make a convenient transfer to ferries for trips across and along the Bristol Channel. This service was initially provided by an already existing shipping company, Campbells, but their ferries also called at Cardiff and were overcrowded. In 1905, therefore, the Barry Railway obtained authorization to operate its own fleet which by 1907 consisted of four paddle-steamers, named *Gwalia*, *Devonia*, *Westonia* and *Barry*. Unfortunately, the conditions of the parliamentary approval were very restrictive; the vessels were confined to the passenger trade, to certain named ports in England and only to Barry in Wales. After attempts to get round the restrictions, the Barry gave up and sold them in 1910. Thereafter Campbells continued alone.

The end of the nineteenth century marked a turning point in the fortunes of Barry as a town. Hitherto it had been a squalid place dominated by the contractors engaged in building the docks. In the new century it began to be a pleasant residential and holiday town.

Passenger carriage sidings at Barry Island station on the site occupied in 2000 by the Vale of Glamorgan Railway; *ca.* 1910.

GBJ Coll.

Sadly, during the twentieth century its fortunes have declined. Coal shipments ceased in the 1960s, and the holiday trade became dominated by day-trips. The use of the old dock sidings as a store for condemned steam engines seemed to bear witness to the slow death of Barry itself.

However, by the close of the century there are signs of revival. The injection of European and national funds into the redevelopment of the docks for leisure pursuits, the creation of a transport museum around the remains of the old railway to Barry Island, and the construction of housing and commercial premises on the old port area promise new hope. Even the old tunnel to the pier, now in use as a shooting range, may one day echo again to the sound of steam trains.

Dai Woodham's scrapyard in the Barry Docks which turned out to be a resting place rather than a mortuary; July 1971.   *GBJ*

Locomotives in the scrapyard at Barry. Of 288 locomotives delivered for scrap in the ten years from 1959, over 200 have survived, the first being removed in 1968. Photographed in 1976, a year in which eight locomotives were removed for restoration.   *GBJ*

SELECT COMMITTEE ON WORKMEN'S TRAINS

In 1900 a parliamentary select committee published a report on Workmen's Services. They were of particular importance in the south Wales valleys because, by 1900, many coalminers were being taken to work by special workmen's trains. In the early days, workers' housing had grown up close to the iron-ore deposits. These happened to be high up at the head of the valleys. As steam coal came to be found lower down the valleys, the coal owners preferred to bring in their labour from existing residential areas, rather than run the risk of investing immediately in the building of new houses. There was also a reluctance on the part of the men to move to initially uncomfortable temporary accommodation near the new pits. So the railway offered a solution which suited both parties.

There were two types of arrangement. The first was statutory under the Cheap Trains Act of 1883. A local petition would in the first instance cause a three month's trial to test the market and the profitability; special trains with spartan accommodation would operate to suit colliery shifts and were not in the public timetables, though the Barry and the Rhondda & Swansea Bay attached workers' carriages to scheduled trains. In 1899, 23 such workers' trains a day were running on average more than 8 miles on the Taff Vale. By 1900 they were also being operated by the Neath & Brecon and the Port Talbot. One of the longest journeys was from Llandovery to Ammanford.

Cambrian Colliery workmen's train, perhaps in the 1920s. In the days before bath-houses were provided at the collieries these trains were notoriously spartan.
GBJ Coll.

The Rhymney Railway branch to Senghennydd served a close-knit and settled mining community, most of whom walked to work. The locomotive is No. 53, *ca.* 1910. *GBJ Coll.*

The second type of arrangement applied in the early days mainly in the start-up phase of a mine and was contractual. The owners contracted with the railway companies to provide the trains and could thus choose how much to subsidise the charges to the men. Later, as large companies began to dominate mining, particularly in Monmouthshire, most of the colliery trains were contractual. For instance, miners were taken down the Sirhowy valley from Tredegar until well after the First World War and, as a result, the lower part of the valley remained relatively free of housing. Similar situations developed in the Rhymney and Ebbw valleys. The opening of the Brynmawr & Western Valleys line in 1905 enabled residents of Brynmawr to catch a colliers' train down the Ebbw Fach.

In an article on this subject in the 1970 volume of the *Journal of Transport History*, Philip Jones emphasised the social importance of this facility as well as its economic benefit. It enabled greater stability of residence in addition to the enormously increased flexibility of labour.

Commuting is one of the few activities in the valleys that has persisted until the end of the twentieth century. As the extractive industries have been replaced by light and service industries, the pool of labour has had to find work wherever it is located. Initially, this was in new collieries but, during the Second World War, armaments factories were built and later factories for new industries, and offices for both the private and public sectors. This has often meant commuting from the narrow valleys, which do not lend themselves to ease of access for either goods or workers, and this has given a new lease of life to some of the railways which might otherwise have had to close. Indeed, some lines, such as those to Aberdare and Maesteg, have been reopened after a lengthy period of closure. The advantage of the railway for transport in difficult terrain has been evident. It has also been able to keep alive valley communities whose local sources of income had dried up.

RED WHARF BAY

On 1 August 1899 Parliament authorised a 7 mile railway from a point called Holland Arms, on the Amlwch branch in Anglesey, to Red Wharf Bay on the east coast. This was thought to be an area with increasing tourist potential although, at the time, it was still pleasantly unspoilt. The projected line finished some distance from Red Wharf Bay and stopped short of the village of Benllech. A year later a new act

modified the terminal point by shifting it to a compromise location halfway between the two places at a lonely crossroads. The LNWR were in no hurry to build the line; after all, it had first been projected as early as 1812 as the 'Anglesea [*sic*] Railway' which, as noted by *The Railway Magazine*, was only the fifteenth railway ever authorised by Parliament. However, the first 5 mile section to Pentraeth

The junction for Red Wharf Bay called Holland Arms; 21 July 1934.
R.M. Casserley

was opened in 1908. *The Railway Magazine* could think of no other railway project so long delayed between its first authorization and eventual opening, nearly 100 years later. The rest followed in 1909. The expected development of the area did not occur, though the line survived with an auto-train passenger service until 1930. Thereafter there was a

reprieve on summer Saturdays when the bus service was unable to cope with passenger numbers due to a weight restriction on the Menai Bridge; this was corrected by 1940. Freight traffic ceased in 1950.

In 2000 only the Irish boat trains keep any railway operating on Anglesey although there is talk of reopening the Gaerwen-Amlwch branch.

SWANSEA'S LAST STATION

On 7 May 1899 the Rhondda & Swansea Bay Railway extended its line from Danygraig for a mile to the site of a new passenger terminal, called Swansea Riverside, on the east bank of the Tawe river. This was the last of six terminal

stations in Swansea, more than in any other city in the British Isles outside London.

The reason for this proliferation lay in the arrangements surrounding the construction of the first station. This was built as a terminus

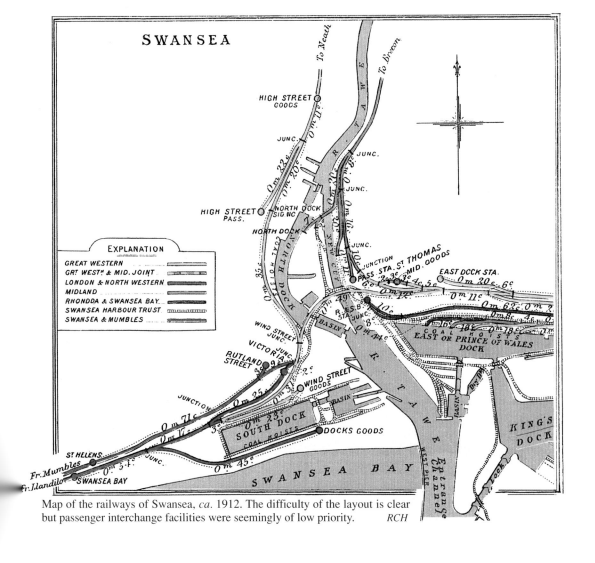

Map of the railways of Swansea, *ca.* 1912. The difficulty of the layout is clear but passenger interchange facilities were seemingly of low priority.   *RCH*

because the main objective of the South Wales Railway was the short sea connection with Ireland from a terminal to be built at Fishguard. With that in mind, and the need to minimise the cost of crossing the river Neath, the line was constructed across the north of Swansea. The line to High Street, completed in 1850, became a mere branch in 1852 when the main line was pushed on from Landore to Carmarthen. Landore station became the station for through trains; here it was necessary for Swansea-bound passengers to change onto a branch line train to High Street. In 1899, Swansea Corporation put pressure on the GWR to build a new through line and, as it was ambiguously expressed at the time, 'to place Swansea on the main line', but the company argued that it would be uneconomic as it would cost £500,000 and involve a long tunnel under the town. They therefore enquired whether the corporation would make a contribution to the cost. The idea came to nothing. Instead, in 1906, a west loop was put in, creating a triangle at Landore which enabled trains to proceed westward from High Street, but it was still necessary for through trains to reverse.

Since 1807 there had been in existence a railway conveying passengers between Swansea and Mumbles using a terminus at Rutland Street. Apart from a period of closure between 1827 and 1860, this was in operation until 1960. Although the Swansea & Mumbles Railway carried freight as well as passengers for many years, its main role was as a local passenger tramway. It therefore had little influence on the layout of the railways of Swansea.

The second terminal (or third, if Rutland Street is considered a railway station) opened in 1860 at St Thomas, on the east side of the river. This was when the Swansea Vale started conveying passengers up the Tawe valley to Pontardawe. This was a standard gauge line laid on the track-bed of old tramways and had no connection with the broad gauge South Wales at High Street. Indeed, when built, the two lines crossed on the level, and although provision was made by Parliament for mixed gauge track to be laid, this was never done. This station became part of the Midland Railway in 1876

and for a period received through carriages from as far away as Birmingham and even St Pancras.

In 1863 the Vale of Neath Railway completed its Swansea & Neath line with mixed gauge track. This crossed the river Tawe from east to west and a temporary terminus was built at Wind Street on through lines belonging to the harbour trustees. This station was perched on the top of a viaduct carrying mixed gauge track from near High Street to the new South Dock. The Vale of Neath became part of the GWR in 1865 and Wind Street continued in use until 1873, serving as a terminus for trains from as far away as Hereford. At that date a combination of congestion and pressure from the harbour trustees seeking more space caused the GWR to close it and divert the Vale of Neath trains over the South Wales main line to High Street.

In the meantime, the Llanelly Railway arrived at its new terminus at Victoria in 1867. This station was close to Wind Street on the west side of the river but, like Rutland Street, was at a low level. The approach to Swansea had been from Llandovery over the Llanelly company's main line to Pontardulais and then along the coast from the west. The possibility of switching onto the South Wales line at Gowerton had been considered and indeed earthworks on a spur were begun, but the different gauge necessitated mixed gauge track and this, together with a shortage of space at High Street, prevented that possible concentration from being developed. In 1867 the LNWR started operating to Victoria over the Central Wales line with trains from as far away as Shrewsbury and even Euston.

Efforts were made in 1865 to get agreement between the companies on building and using a general station. A Bill was prepared for Parliament which combined Wind Street and Victoria in one enlarged site with lines at two levels and a hotel. The participation of the GWR was felt to be essential and negotiations were carried on, but the project died. No doubt the shortage of space was a major problem; this would have made it difficult for the GW to use it as a terminus and would therefore have

The interior of Swansea Victoria, late 1950s. Under-utilised even at the peak, it was a monument to railway company rivalry.

NMRW

necessitated their running through trains over the Llanelly Railway to Gowerton, requiring the laying of a broad gauge rail. In any case, the GWR may already have been expecting the Llanelly's line to be absorbed by the LNWR and would therefore have been wary of giving away any competitive benefit.

The failure of this project to unite at least three of the stations in a centrally located site was the end of the matter. In 1881 a new station for the Vale of Neath line trains was opened at East Dock, on the east side of the river, not far from St Thomas. This was a small two-sided platform with a modest wooden shed at one end which survived until 1936. This finally put paid to the idea of a single station serving trains from east and west. The arrival of the R & SB at Riverside in 1899 further emphasised the divide. This was a two-platform terminus unobtrusively tucked away in the dock area near East Dock and served trains from Neath and the Afan and Rhondda valleys.

The Rhondda & Swansea Bay Railway's Swansea Riverside station, the last to open and the first to close; 8 September 1951. *H.C. Casserley*

By 2000 concentration has been achieved but at the expense of losing most of the lines. Riverside was the last in and was first out, in 1933. From that date, trains from Treherbert were diverted to East Dock until 1936, when that too closed. After the Second World War the GWR and LMS discussed station rationalisation but there was no coordinated plan. St Thomas was closed in 1950 and its remaining services were transferred to Victoria by way of Pontardulais. Rutland Street closed in 1960, soon followed by Victoria in 1964. High Street, which was modernised and extended in the 1920s, survives as the only station and is still a terminus.

SECOND CLASS TRAVEL

In 1899 the Cambrian Railways restored Second Class travel, having abolished it as a rationalisation measure following an initiative of the Midland Railway. In 1872 the Midland had announced that they would henceforth offer Third Class accommodation on all trains at the so-called 'parliamentary rate' of 1d. per mile. In 1875 this was followed by the abolition of Second Class travel altogether. In practice, it was First Class fares which were abolished together with Second Class accommodation. Henceforth, Second Class fares covered First Class accommodation. These changes call for some explanation.

Different classes of travel on the railways stemmed from practice on ships and, later on, stage coaches. The distinction here was between travelling outside or inside. It was impractical on the railway to travel on the roof of a carriage, partly because of the greater speed but also because of the sparks and cinders from the engine's chimney. Nevertheless, Third Class accommodation was provided initially in open trucks. However, in 1844 Parliament decreed that there should be at least one train a day on every line providing covered accommodation and stopping at all stations at a fare of no more than 1d. per mile. As a result, this level of service was normally provided in a separate train and faster more comfortable services were operated for First and Second Class passengers only.

By the 1870s most railway companies carried First, Second and Third Class accommodation in the same train, though James Allport, the Midland's general manager, had abolished Second Class travel in 1850 when he was general manager of the Manchester, Sheffield & Lincolnshire Railway. Following the Midland's initiative, only on the Cambrian, South Western, Great Eastern, Great Northern, North Eastern and in Scotland was Second Class abolished. The Great Western and North Western and the railways in the south-east of England retained Second Class, but in upgrading their Third Class to compete with the Midland they were in danger of reducing the differential between their Second and Third. Perhaps the distinction lay more in the class of clientele than in the facilities offered. But the trend was inevitable. By the turn of the twentieth century 95% of all passengers travelled Third Class compared with 41% in 1845. On many of the other Welsh railways there was only one class of travel.

So it would appear to be somewhat reactionary for the Cambrian to be reintroducing Second Class. It was almost certainly due to the extensive cooperation exercised with the LNWR and GWR in providing through services between England and the Cambrian coast. As has been noted elsewhere, at the turn of the century the Cambrian was pursuing a strategy of developing the coastal resorts, in competition with Cornwall and Devon, and it no doubt proved a delicate matter to handle the interface between Second Class and a choice of First or Third. In any case, Second Class was finally abolished on the GWR in 1910 and on the LNWR in 1912.

THE SPELLING OF 'LLANFIHANGEL'

One of the unique problems faced by the English railway companies operating in Wales was the spelling of Welsh place-names. On 1 January 1900 the GWR changed the more usual Welsh spelling of the common place-name 'Llanfihangel' (Church of St Michael) to the Anglicised version 'Llanvihangel'. This was the name of the station at Llanfihangel Crucorney, a village a few miles north of Abergavenny on the old Newport, Abergavenny & Hereford main line. The only other railway station called 'Llanfihangel' was on the Cambrian Railways, but that changed its name completely to Llandre in 1916. However, while it was still called 'Llanfihangel' it was always spelled with an 'f'. Quite why the GWR decided to celebrate the turn of the century by a reversion to Anglicised spelling at Llanfihangel Crucorney is unclear, though the existence of a private waiting-room for the use of the local landowners, the Baker-Gabb family, may have had something to do with it. It also seems to fit with practise in Monmouthshire not confined to the railway where, until it became generally acknowledged

The South Wales Pullman approaches Llanvihangel (*sic*) station with a Cardiff to Liverpool Football Special on a grey day in February 1964. This station was closed to passengers on 9 June 1958, too soon to have the spelling corrected.
John Beardsmore

Llanvihangel Signal Box with 0-6-2T No. 5659 which has just dropped off a train it was banking from Abergavenny; 29 February 1964.
John Beardsmore

as part of Wales, the more Anglicised 'v' was preferred to the 'f' in every appropriate case. The only other station with the use of a 'v' instead of 'f' after the 'Llan' was called 'Llanvair', but it only existed from January to October 1854. Perhaps it was significant that it, too, was on the old Newport, Abergavenny & Hereford, in Monmouthshire. Elsewhere in Wales the use of the 'f' after 'Llan' was universal. The GWR locomotive department, however, found this whole subject confusing and, not realising that 'Llanvair Grange' was in fact the same place as 'Llanfair Grange', followed a safe course and named two locomotives, numbers 6825 and 6877, after the same house!

Elsewhere the trend has generally been in the direction towards a greater Welshness. Thus, in the 1920s, after the grouping, when a number of Welsh stations had to be renamed to avoid duplication or confusion, the opportunity was taken to restore more normal Welsh usage. For example, 'Hirwain' near Aberdare became 'Hirwaun'. Later, the British Railways Board was even more rigorous. No doubt as a nationalised body they were desirous of being found to be politically correct; after 'Blaenau Festiniog' had been spelled by all its railways with only one 'f' for 117 years, in 1982 the BRB introduced for the first time the correct Welsh spelling 'Ffestiniog'. Accordingly, the eponymous railway did the same for the name of the station and for the company, though to change its statutory title from 'Festiniog' would require an Act of Parliament.

Spelling has clearly been a problem for the railway companies, whether Welsh or English. Sometimes it appears to have been simple carelessness in dealing with unfamiliar names. An example can be found on a GWR luggage label which bears the destination of 'Aberdovery', presumably somewhere between Aberdovey and Llandovery. When the Taff Vale Extension of the Newport, Abergavenny & Hereford Railway, a London-based company, was opened to Quakers Yard in 1858, 'Llancaich (*sic*) & Nelson' station was thus spelt in spite of the fact that it was partly named after the ancient and historic Llancaiach House.

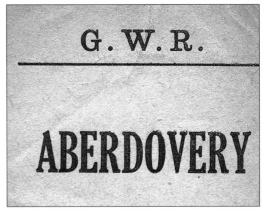

The schizophrenic luggage label.   *GBJ Coll.*

The misspelling had been corrected by the turn of the century when 'Nelson' was dropped and the station became simply 'Llancaiach'. This was odd because only a few years later, in 1912, it was renamed 'Nelson & Llancaiach' in deference to the increased importance of Nelson.

The problems were not confined to the English railways. The Barry Railway spelt 'Dinas Powis' thus when the station was opened in 1888. In 1904, someone must have complained that it was not sufficiently Welsh because it then became 'Dynas Powis'! By 1922 it had been decided that the original spelling was not so bad after all. In 1980 the BRB decided that change was needed, and that the Barry had been right to put in a 'y' but had put it in the wrong place. It became Dinas Powys, and so it remains. In retrospect, it is hard to understand why anyone ever thought 'Dynas' was right.

English people are frequently puzzled to find that what looks to them a pure Welsh name, like 'Abergavenny', is in fact an Anglicised version of the Welsh, in this case 'Y Fenni'. For many years the companies tended to Anglicise Welsh names, 'Dolgelley' for 'Dolgellau' and 'Cemmes Road' for 'Cemaes', and made no attempt to use genuinely Welsh place-names, even in parallel. With examples like Pontnewydd and Pontnewynydd on the same line near Pontypool, English board members may have felt that one Welsh name per station was sufficient. Even the most ardent Welsh

Dinas Powys station in Barry Railway days.   *GBJ Coll.*

Dinas Powys on 12 May 1999, the ultimate in minimalism, but full marks for spelling.   *A. Jarvis*

patriot may feel that for the Fairbourne Railway to change 'Golf House' to 'Gorsafawddach-a'idraigddanheddogleddolonpenrhynareurdraeth ceredigion' was overdoing it, even on a miniature railway.

But the BRB have been conscientious and have offered Welsh place-names alongside the more widely known Anglicised versions. In so doing, a clear distinction has been made in the colour and typeface. This is, incidentally, a distinct improvement on the practice of the highways authorities whose road signs in Wales are confusingly full of names, all in the same typeface.

However, sometimes it is hard to resist the conclusion that railway naming was intended to confuse. 'Bargoed' on the Rhymney was renamed 'Bargoed & Aberbargoed' in 1905. It reverted to plain 'Bargoed' in 1924. Meanwhile, nearby 'Aberbargoed' on the Brecon & Merthyr was renamed 'Aberbargoed & Bargoed' in 1905 and 'Bargoed & Aberbargoed' in 1909. It reverted to 'Aberbargoed' in 1924. 'Bargoed' alone survives.

The GWR's difficulties were not confined to Welsh place-names and the area of Milford Haven clearly presented a problem. The station at the end of the first line to be built opened as 'Milford Haven' on 15 April 1856, but was renamed 'Neyland' in February 1859. In November 1859 it was named 'New Milford', until 1 September 1906 when it became 'Neyland' again, until eventual closure.

Meanwhile, the station on the nearby branch at Milford Haven opened on 7 September 1863 as just 'Milford'. By 1902 it had become 'Old Milford' but by 1910 'Milford Haven'. Thus it remains in 2000. If that were not confusion enough, the junction station where the two branches met was opened as 'Johnston' on 15 April 1856, but changed to 'Milford Road' in November 1859, though only until 7 September 1863, when it reverted to 'Johnston'.

The railway companies were slow to use Welsh on public notices, and as the fortunes of the Welsh language have changed, the railway companies have slowly followed. In 1891 over 54% of the population of Wales could speak Welsh, though this proportion was in decline. Even so, there were more Welsh speakers at the end of the century than at the beginning. In 1901, 15% of the population could understand only Welsh. In the north-west, only half the population could understand English. It is therefore odd that it was as late as 1883 that the LNWR first set up trespass notices in both Welsh and English. This coincided with a national revival of interest in the Welsh language, but it was the only action taken by the English companies. The Welsh companies were hardly better, and it was not until the politically correct BRB introduced bilingual notices in the 1970s that it can be said that the railways were acknowledging seriously that the Welsh language is used by at least 20% of the population.

The final solution: Bargoed station with a Newport to Brecon train headed by No. 3706; *ca.* 1960.

GBJ Coll.

CHAPTER 8

MISHAPS AT THE TURN OF THE CENTURY

In the last 100 years there has been a major change in the state of medicine and health and hence life expectancy in the Western world. This has influenced our attitude to safety, whether at work or at leisure, at home or when travelling. Accordingly, we are inclined to be shocked when we first see Victorian accident statistics. At the turn of the century, there had been some improvement over earlier years but in 1899, in England and Wales, 953 people were killed by trains and 6,168 received injuries. In addition, there were 40 deaths on railway property not involving trains and a massive 10,494 injuries. Out of the English and Welsh total, passenger deaths were 131, which represented one death for every 79 million passenger journeys. There were 405 deaths of railway company employees, and the balance was composed of contractors, suicides (119), trespassers (208) and others.

Of the deaths, 40 were in Wales, including only 6 passenger deaths but 13 of railway employees. The worst offender was the Taff Vale with its intense operations. Shunting operations were particularly dangerous and contemporary newspapers bear frequent reports of death through trespass.

One indication of the improvement in safety is the fact that in the last 50 years, there have been 13 years with no passenger deaths at all on the railways of Britain. By contrast, the Chief Inspector of Railways has pointed out that road deaths in Britain in one year are about the same as the cumulative number of railway deaths since 1820. In 1996 there were 196 deaths on the roads of Wales. Even though that figure appears high, it actually represents one of the lowest levels in Europe per head of population, and is bettered only by England, Norway and Sweden.

A general view of Tylwch station at roughly the time of the accident. The mail train was standing at the platform where the five men are sitting; the excursion train approached from beyond the bridge.   *GBJ Coll.*

During 1899 in England there were 96 collisions between trains and two in Wales. One of these on 16 September 1899 was on the Cambrian and caused the death of a passenger. It was a case of a SPAD (a Signal Passed At Danger, an acronym which earned a gloomy familiarity in 1999) and led to a particularly interesting report by the railway inspectorate.

The accident occurred at Tylwch, a pretty little place on the Mid Wales line. The whole line, like most of the Cambrian, was single track and at Tylwch there was a passing loop. A north-bound passenger train ran into the southbound mail train as it stood in the station. This occurred because the train ran past a red signal; the driver claimed he could not make the

This is believed to be No. 49, the locomotive which hauled the excursion train, and whose driver passed a signal at danger.   *Ifor Higgon Coll.*

An official Sharp Stewart & Co. photograph of 'Large Bogie' 4-4-0 No. 65 which was stationary at the platform at the head of the mail train when the crash occurred.   *Ifor Higgon Coll.*

The first two vehicles of the excursion train after the accident.
Railway Magazine

vacuum brake work. To compound the problem, the points at the southern end of the loop had been set to permit the exit of the mail train from the loop onto the single track. As so often, the accident was the result of a coincidence of errors. The report is reproduced in full, not only as a model of carefully presented argument and clarity of prose, but also for the light it casts on life and practices on a country railway running through the heart of Wales in 1899:

THE REPORT INTO THE ACCIDENT AT TYLWCH BY THE BOARD OF TRADE.

CAMBRIAN RAILWAY.

Board of Trade (Railway Department),
8, Richmond Terrace, Whitehall, London, S.W.,
October 6th, 1899.

SIR,

I HAVE the honour to report, for the information of the Board of Trade, in accordance with the Order of the 18th September, the result of my enquiry into the collision that occurred at 6.17 a.m. on the 16th idem, at Tylwch Station, on the Cambrian Railway.

In this case, the 5.10 a.m. up excursion train from Builth Wells, when approaching Tylwch Station, over-ran the up home signal, which was at danger, and owing to the loop points being set for the down line, came into collision with the 5.30 a.m. down mail train *ex* Moat Lane, which was standing at the down platform.

One passenger in the excursion train was killed, and seven others, of whom five were excursionists, received injuries, which however were not serious. The driver and fireman of the excursion train were cut and bruised, and the driver of the down mail received a slight shock.

The excursion train consisted of a six-wheels-coupled goods engine, four-wheeled tender, and 11 coaches, viz. :—

								Wheels.
Brake,	No.	6 having	...	...	...	..	6
Bogie composite,	,,	266	,,	...	...	...	...	8
Third class,	,,	204	,,	...	...	...	...	6
,, ,,	,,	206	,,	...	...	...	...	6
Composite,	,,	40	,,	...	...	...	...	4
Third class,	,,	168	,,	...	...	...	...	6
,, ,,	,,	186	,,	...	...	...	...	6
,, ,,	,,	174	,,	...	...	...	...	6
,, ,,	,,	38	,,	...	...	...	...	4
,, ,,	,,	39	,,	...	...	...	...	4
Brake van,	,,	105	,,	...	...	...	...	6

The train was fitted with the automatic vacuum brake, which worked blocks on all the wheels of the engine and tender, and on all the wheels of the train except the middle wheels of the six-wheeled coaches. There was also the usual hand-brake on the tender. The brake pipes are said to have been properly connected up through the train.

The down mail consisted of a four-wheels-coupled bogie passenger engine, six-wheeled tender, and four six-wheeled vehicles, viz., two third class, one composite, and a brake van. It also was fitted with the vacuum brake.

The two engines were badly damaged, but the injury to the rolling stock was not as extensive as might have been expected. The two leading vehicles of the excursion train, viz., the van and composite, were telescoped, the trailing end of the former and the first three compartments of the latter, in one of which was seated the unfortunate woman who was killed, being completely smashed. Two other vehicles of this train received slight injuries, the remainder being undamaged.

The three front carriages of the mail train had their headstock and buffer castings broken.

Full particulars of the damage to the engines and rolling stock are given in the Appendix.

Little harm was done to the permanent way, only one chair being broken and 11 sleepers split.

The force of the collision was sufficient to drive the mail train backwards about 19 yards.

Description.

The Cambrian Railways are for the most part single, and are worked on the electric tablet system, Tylwch being a passing station of the usual description, with up and down loop lines and up and down platforms. The length of the loop lines from facing point to facing point is 260 yards.

The place is correctly signalled and interlocked in accordance with modern practice, there being distant, home, and starting signals in each direction. The points at each end of the loop lie for the proper or left-hand road, and each home signal only requires the facing points nearest to it to be locked in the proper position, before it is lowered, and is altogether "free" of the points at the other end of the loop. The signal-box is situated at the north end of the up platform, and at the middle of the same platform are the station-master's office, booking hall and waiting rooms.

At the time of the collision the engine of the mail train was standing at the down starting signal, which is situated at the south end of the down platform, 70 yards from the signal-box. From here to the up loop points the distance is 78 yards, and the up home signal is 19½ yards outside (*i.e.*, south of) these points, while the up distant signal is 801 yards south of the up home. From personal observation I have ascertained that a driver approaching Tylwch from the south obtains a good view of the up distant signal 335 yards before he reaches it, and of the home signal 559 yards from it.

The next station towards the south is Pantydwr, which is 3 miles 74 chains away, and from this place to Tylwch the line is on a falling gradient which for nearly a mile has an inclination of 1 in 110. At the down distant signal the inclination is 1 in 123; at the spot where the home signal first comes into view it is 1 in 143, and so it remains to within about 120 yards of the home signal, where it changes to 1 in 324.

The following are extracts from the rules adopted by those railway companies who employ the vacuum brake :—

"The guard . . . . must see that a proper amount of vacuum* is registered in his van before giving the engine driver a signal to start."

"The engine driver must accept the signal to start given by the guard . . . . as an assurance that the brake is in proper order, and that the gauge in the rear van indicates the required vacuum. He must also satisfy himself before starting that the gauge on the engine indicates the required vacuum."

"Should the engine driver not be able to create the required vacuum, he must, after satisfying himself that his engine is all right, at once inform the guard and station staff, so that an examination may be made of the train, and the brake on any vehicle shut off, or such vehicle detached, or any other steps taken that may be necessary."

"If during the journey the guard finds that the gauge in his van shows less than the required vacuum, he must be prepared to apply the hand-brake as may be required."

"If the engine driver is unable to work the vacuum brake it must be cut off, and the train worked by the hand-brakes only, the speed being so regulated as to enable the driver to have full control of the train by the hand-brakes. In such cases the guards must be on the alert, and assist in stopping the train with their hand-brakes."

* The amount of vacuum required by the rules of the Cambrian Company is 18 inches.

" Engine drivers must satisfy themselves that the vacuum brake is in proper working order before starting . . . . It must be tested before descending steep inclines, and before passing the distant signal of any . . . . crossing station on a single line at which the train has to stop, and the speed of the train must be reduced by it. . . . . and guards must watch the speed of the trains, and assist the engine drivers by the use of the hand-brake when necessary."

" Unless the vacuum brake is working properly when tried, the driver must whistle for the guard's hand-brake, stop the train, and inform the guard that the vacuum brake is out of order, and that the hand-brake must be relied on for working the train. Special care must be taken in approaching stations at which the train has to stop."

Evidence.

James Davies, station-master, Tylwch, says : I am 33 years of age, and have been in the Company's service 20 years. I have been station-master at Tylwch since January 13th last ; previous to that I was goods clerk at Welshpool for four years, and prior to that in the general offices at Oswestry, and chief parcels clerk at Newtown for about eight years ; during the latter time I took duty every alternate week in taking charge of the tablet working for the morning trains. I came on duty at 5 a.m. on Saturday, September 16th. At 6.2 a.m., Llanidloes had tablet for the down mail, and the train was put on section at 6.9. Pantydwr had tablet for No. 2 (5.10 a.m.) special *ex* Builth Wells at 5.50. I received entering section for the excursion at about 6.9½. The down mail arrived at Tylwch at 6.14 a.m. This train whistled for the signals to be taken off, and I admitted it into down loop ; at this time both the up distant and the up home signals were at danger. I drew over levers Nos. 9, 6, and 2 in the order named ; No. 2 is the down home, No. 6 is the lock-bar, and No. 9 is the up facing points, the normal position of the latter being for the up road. I was under the impression that unless the up facing points were pulled over, the down home signal could not be lowered ; I have always been under this impression and acted accordingly. I was on the down plat-form when the down mail arrived. I took the tablet from the driver, and dealt with two or three passengers who arrived by the train. There were no passengers booked forward from my station by this train. I then went across to up platform to put tablet in instrument, and obtain another for the up excursion. Immediately I got there, I heard the engine of the up excursion whistle sharply, as I thought for the brakes to be applied, but before I could look around it had come into collision with the down mail, standing at the down platform. I at once phonophored to Llanidloes for the doctors and assistance, and a train with doctors and assist-ance arrived from Llanidloes at Tylwch at 7.0 a.m. The engines of both trains were seriously damaged, and could not be moved. On examining the train, I found several pas-sengers injured ; Margaret Rowlands, who appeared to have been travelling in the front compartment of the bogie coach next to the van in front of the excursion train, was just alive and nothing more. She was completely buried by wreckage. Another man and woman were in the same compartment, the woman was not injured in any way, but the man had his face and leg injured. The excursion train to which the mishap occurred left here at 7.32 a.m., being worked by the engine which had arrived from Llanidloes. No. 4 excursion passed through at 8.2 a.m., and the down mail left at 9.0 o'clock. I did not see the up excursion come round the curve. The first that I saw of it was when it was in close proximity to the down mail. It was impossible for me to know whether the brakes were applied on the up excursion as the time was so short from the moment I saw it

until the collision occurred. After the mishap I had a conversation with the driver to the follow-ing effect : " Well, Sam, how did this happen ; how did you run against the signals ? " And he replied, " I could not get the brake to work, no vacuum." Before hearing the engine of the up excursion whistle sharply, as I thought, for the brakes to be applied, I heard nothing whatever of his whistle, nor did I know he was approaching the station. At the time of the collision the driver and fireman of both engines were on their respective engines.

Samuel Hopkins, driver, says : I am 40 years of age, and have been in the Company's service 15 years. I am stationed at Llanidloes, and have been a temporary driver three years, and a regular driver since June last. I was the driver of the No. 2 excursion train leaving Builth Wells at 5.10 a.m. on September 16th. I was off duty the day before and travelled to Builth Wells on the Friday night in order to work the train. I came on duty at 4.20 a.m., on the date in question, and took charge of the engine at the shed. I examined my engine, tested the brake and found 15 inches of vacuum in it ; I then took the engine out of the shed, proceeded to the station, took water, and then hooked on to the train. I arrived at the platform at about 5.5 a.m. The train consisted of 10 vehicles from Builth with one guard. My fireman coupled the engine to the train, and I then applied the large ejector, but failed to get more than 14 inches of vacuum. I was booked to stop at all stations except Builth Road, and the brake was applied at each stopping place in the ordinary manner. I knew that I had to cross the mail train at Tylwch, and on approaching the distant signal I saw it was against me, and applied the vacuum brake. I found, however, that the gauge showed no vacuum. I then applied the large ejector and blew the brake up to 14 inches of vacuum, and applied the brake again suddenly. The vacuum then again immediately disappeared. I applied the vacuum brake a second time opposite the old factory, and on finding it would not act I began to pop with my whistle, at the same time telling my mate to apply the hand brake, which he did with all his force, and immediately after-wards I opened the sand valves. I cannot see the home signals just before getting to the old factory, but can see it on passing that place. Shortly afterwards I sighted the home signal which was at danger, and soon afterwards I saw the points which were set for the down loop. I then reversed my engine and put steam on, but was unable to avoid a collision with the down mail, which was standing in the loop. Both I and my mate remained on the engine. I clutched the reversing lever, but was dislodged from this position by the impact, and sustained a badly bruised hip, right arm, and strained my back. I was not, however, so badly hurt that I could not rescue my mate, who was thrown on the foot-board and covered with coal. I had no conversation with anybody afterwards, to the best of my recollection. I then proceeded as a passenger by train on to Llanidloes, by instructions from my foreman, Mr. Watson, and was not examined by any doctor. I had a copy of the Rule Book, and am acquainted with the rules therein. I am aware of the rule that when a driver has no confidence in the vacuum brake he must keep his train under such control as to be able to stop it with the hand brake. I depended upon my vacuum brake, and when I wanted it, it failed to act. After reversing, I considerably reduced the speed of my train, and am under the impression that, if the points had lain for the up road, I could have stopped before I had reached the signal box. At the time of the collision I was not running more than five miles per hour. There was a drizzling rain and the rails were in a slippery condition. I have done all my firing and driving over this portion of the line, and am thoroughly acquainted with the road. I expected on sighting the home signal to find it off. I have never been stopped at this home signal before. After whistling for the brakes to be applied, I did not perceive whether the guard had put his brakes on or not. We were running without steam after leaving Pantydwr. I have always applied my brake when the distant signal has been against me. The home signal is visible immediately after passing the old factory. I do not remember speaking to the station-master after the mishap. We should have 18 inches of vacuum before starting, according to the rules. I made no examination of my train before starting from Builth Wells to ascertain why the necessary amount of vacuum was not being maintained. When at Rhayader I told the guard that my brake was a poor one, and he replied that he saw it was. The reason why I did not reverse my engine on seeing the home signal at danger was that I was sure that the points would lie for the up platform line, and that I should be able to stop at the platform. I did not think when at Rhayader, or at any other place, to wire foreman Watson for another engine. My engine was No. 49, six-wheels-coupled goods engine, with a four-wheeled tender. It was fitted with the vacuum brake, working blocks on all the wheels of the engine and tender. There was also a hand brake on the tender. The brake pipe was properly connected throughout the train. I had plenty of steam. I have occasionally driven this engine before on goods trains, but I have never worked it before on a passenger train, so far as I can recollect. If my brake had worked as well at Tylwch as it had done at other stopping places, I should have had no difficulty in stopping at the home signal. I did not reverse my engine as soon as I saw the home signal at danger, because I think this course would have been a risky one. When I saw the points were lying for the down road, I reversed my engine as being the last thing that I could do. I stopped my train without difficulty at Newbridge and Rhayader by means of the vacuum brake.

Richard Evans, fireman, says : I am 26 years of age, have been in the Company's service six years, and fireman about 15 months. On Saturday, the 16th inst., I was firing for Samuel Hopkins on the 5.10 a.m. excursion train from Builth Wells. I was off duty the day previous and travelled with Hopkins to Builth the night before, where I lodged and came on duty at 4.20 a.m. on the Saturday morning. I saw the driver test his brake before leaving the shed, and he made the remark to me that he had not got much of a brake. After coupling the engine on to the train

at the station, I noticed that there was only 15 inches of vacuum on the gauge, and I continued to notice about 15 inches during the journey from Builth to Pantydwr. The vacuum brake was used in the ordinary manner to stop the train at each stopping station ; it then seemed to work all right. My driver applied steam to start from Pantydwr, and after getting the train into motion, shut the steam off near the overbridge, and ran down the incline without steam. The driver pointed out to me that the vacuum brake only registered 15 inches just about the time that he shut steam off after leaving Pantydwr, to indicate to me that the brake was not very powerful. On nearing the distant signal for Tylwch, I saw that it was at danger, and the driver then tried his vacuum brake, and I noticed that both the index fingers of the vacuum gauge dropped to zero. I then applied my hand brake as hard as I could, upon instructions from the driver, and the latter opened the steam sand-valve. I never released my hand brake until the collision took place. I believe that my driver made several other attempts to put the brake on, but my attention was principally directed to minding the hand brake. I then sighted the home signal, which was at danger. I believe that my driver reversed his engine when about opposite the home signal. I saw the points were in position for the loop almost at the time we reached them. I retained my position on the engine and the next thing I knew was the driver releasing me from the coals under which I was buried on the footplate. The nature of my injuries was a wound over the right temple and another one on the back of my head, and a few bruises. I have been working over this portion of the line ever since I commenced firing. I think the speed, when the driver applied his vacuum brake at the distant signal, was about 15 to 20 miles an hour. I heard the driver whistle for the guard's brake. I have seen the distant signal at danger sometimes when approaching this station, when the home signal has been off to allow the train to run into the station. I had no occasion to use the hand brake at previous stopping places. The vacuum brake was sufficient.

William Hamer, relief guard, Builth, says : I am 26 years of age, have been six years in the Company's service and relief man for three years. On Saturday, the 16th September, it was part of my duty to work the 5.10 a.m. excursion from Manchester to Whitchurch. I booked on duty at 4.40 a.m., and my train was composed of seven third-class coaches, one compo., and a van at each end. On arrival at Rhayader there was a large number of passengers, and we picked up bogie No. 266. This made up my train equal to 11½ vehicles. We lost seven minutes at Rhayader loading passengers and picking up the extra coach, two minutes were lost from Rhayader to Pantydwr, and three minutes at Pantydwr getting in passengers. We left the latter station at 6.9 a.m. or 17 minutes after our booked time. Just as the train was passing the old factory I heard the driver give a loud whistle. I cannot now say what sort of a whistle it was, but my attention was specially called to it. I noticed that the index of the vacuum gauge in my van was completely down. When I took charge of my van at Builth the gauge showed 13 inches of vacuum, and when we left Builth it registered 14 inches, and it kept at about that figure throughout. The driver called my attention to the vacuum being wrong at Rhayader by saying that there was a very bad brake on, and I told him what the gauge in the van was, and I did nothing more. I knew that the gauge in the van should show 18 inches of vacuum, and I was also aware that I should report it if otherwise. I called out to the driver before leaving Builth that the vacuum was wrong, but I do not know whether he heard me. I did this in accordance with instructions contained in the Appendix to the Time Book. When I heard the sharp whistle, when approaching the up home signal at Tylwch, I at once put on my hand brake as tightly as possible, and after putting the brake on I went to the window and saw the home signal was up, and immediately afterwards I found that my train was in collision with another one. I was knocked against the side of the van, and on getting up and going outside, I found some passengers were hurt. I assisted in getting them out of the wreckage and helped to clear the road. I was making out my journal when passing the Tylwch up distant signal, and it had then turned 6.16 a.m. After the road was cleared and the injured passengers attended to, my train was sent forward with another engine at 7.40 a.m., and I went with it in charge. I had only received a very slight knock on the side of the head, and felt none the worse for the mishap. After leaving Tylwch the vacuum gauge in my van registered 20 inches, and continued to do so up to Whitchurch, up to which place the brake worked satisfactorily. The van in front of my train (No. 6) and bogie compo. (No. 266) were badly damaged, and these were left at Tylwch. I put third-class coach (No. 204) off at Llanidloes and third-class coach (No. 39) off at Moat Lane on account of minor damages. After the mishap I saw a workman who had travelled as a passenger from Rhayader in the front van, but do not know his name. He told me that there were five or six passengers in the van. I was not aware that they had travelled in that van, neither did I know anything about them. Mr. Jones, stationmaster at Rhayader, asked me if we were stopping at Llanidloes, and I replied that we were booked to stop there. He said something to me about some workmen, but I did not know that he was going to put them into the van. When testing the vacuum brake in the front van at Builth, I drew the driver's attention to the vacuum being very low. At the time the engine whistled near Tylwch up distant I should say we were travelling at about 10 to 12 miles per hour. It did not occur to me to apply my brake to steady the train down the incline from Pantydwr station, knowing the brake to be defective. I know the road between Llanidloes and Rhayader well. I had no need to apply my hand brake to stop the train at any previous station. The vacuum brake was sufficient. The injured passengers were in the third and fourth compartments of the bogie carriage. The passenger who was killed was in the third compartment.

Richard Jones, driver, Llanidloes, says: I am 50 years of age, have been in the Company's service 36 years, and a driver 28 years. On Saturday, the 16th inst., I came on duty at 4.30 a.m. to work the 5.30 a.m. down mail ex Moat Lane. We left Moat Lane 20 minutes late. I arrived at Tylwch at 6.18—being 18 minutes late—and my train was stopped on the down platform in order to cross the excursion train. The front end of my engine was close to the starting signal. My mate and myself were on the footplate, and whilst standing there we heard the excursion engine whistling. I think this was about a minute after we had arrived. My fireman shouted to me, "Look out, Dick, she is coming into us," and jumped on to the platform. I immediately took off the brake, and, whilst doing so, was run into by the excursion train before I had time to open my regulator

in order to set the train back out of the way. I received no injuries, but felt the effects of the shock slightly. I then left my engine and went to assist the driver and fireman of the excursion train, and also the passengers who were injured. I noticed that the home signal for the excursion train was at danger at the time driver Hopkins passed it. The latter complained to me that his vacuum brake was not in good working order. I saw the head of the excursion engine just at the same moment as I heard the whistle, and I had not heard any whistle previously. I did not notice in what position the up facing-points lay. The vacuum pipe in front of my engine was broken off by the collision.

Stephen Humphreys, fireman, Caersws, says: I am 22 years of age, have been in the Company's service six years, and have been firing 15 months. I was fireman on the 5.30 a.m. down mail ex Moat Lane on Saturday the 16th instant. My train was brought to a stand at Tylwch, and shortly afterwards I heard the driver of the excursion train whistle repeatedly for the brakes. I shouted to my mate "Look out, Dick, she is coming into us," and I jumped on to the platform. After the collision I went to render what assistance I could to the driver and fireman of the other engine. I did not hear the driver of the excursion whistle for either the distant or home signals. My engine was not blowing off, and the indicator showed 125 lbs. pressure.

John Jones, guard, says: I am 49 years of age, have been in the Company's service 29 years, and guard for 25 years. On Saturday the 16th instant, I came on duty at 5.0 a.m. to work the 5.30 a.m. down mail ex Moat Lane. Everything went well until we got to Tylwch at 6.18 a.m. by my watch. After the passengers had left the train I went down the latter and closed the carriage doors returning to my van to sort letters. Immediately upon getting into my van I heard the driver of the excursion train whistle for the brakes. I at once jumped out of my van and stopped the passengers from crossing the line, as I thought, in front of the excursion train. I had heard no previous whistle from the driver of the excursion train. Immediately after the collision I went along my train to see if there were any injured, but found but only a few had sustained slight bruises. I then went across to the booking office and communicated with Llanidloes to ascertain if medical and other assistance was being sent, and the reply I got was " Yes, and get the tablet put in so that we can get the train out." I then went out and met the station-master with the tablet, which he had taken from the driver of my train. After this I went to the rear to protect my train and to signal forward the engine which was on the road from Llanidloes. I should think there were about 12 passengers in my train, which was made up by engine, third, compo, third, and van. I think we had been at Tylwch about a minute or less before the collision occurred. I had not put on my hand brake while standing at Tylwch.

Edward Nichols, driver, says: I have been in the Company's service about 11 years, and I have been driver about two years. On the 15th September I was working No. 49 engine on goods trains. I found nothing whatever wrong with it. The vacuum brake was then working satisfactorily. I was able to maintain 21 inches of vacuum. The brake blocks were all right. I put the engine away at 4.15 p.m. that evening at Builth Wells. I knew when I put away the engine that evening that it had to work an excursion train the following morning. I have worked a passenger train with that engine ; this was about August 26th.

Arthur Owen, driver, Llanidloes, says : I am 50 years of age and have been in the Company's service 25 years, and driver about 12 years. I came on duty on Saturday the 16th inst. at 6.45 a.m. in order to work the Talyllyn goods. At 7.45 a.m. I received a message from Mr. Watson instructing me to be prepared to work the Man-

chester excursion, which was brought from Tylwch to Llanidloes, which place I left at 8.5 a.m., and I worked the train to Whitchurch with goods engine No. 10 fitted with vacuum brake. There were 10 vehicles on the train from Llanidloes and one was taken off at Moat Lane. I tested my engine before coupling on to the train, and got 22 inches of vacuum on the gauge, and after coupling and applying the injector I succeeded in getting 22 inches again, and this was maintained all the way to Whitchurch.

Conclusion.

The main facts in this case are clear enough, but some of the statements given in evidence require to be carefully weighed before an opinion is expressed as to the cause of the disaster.

The down mail left Llanidloes at 6.9 a.m. and arrived at Tylwch at about 6.16* being 16 minutes late. The distant and home signals were against the train until it had nearly reached the station, when stationmaster Davies, who alone was on duty at that hour, lowered the home signal to admit the train to the platform. The points at each end of the loop are constructed so as to be normally in position for the left hand road, i.e., the points at the north end lie for the down road, and those at the south end for the up road, and it was only necessary for Davies to lock the north points in position by pulling over No. 6 lever, before he could lower the down home signal. But for some reason or other Davies had got it into his head that it was also necessary to pull over No. 9 lever, so as to set the points at the south end of the loop for the down road before lowering the signal, and he accordingly did so. When therefore the down mail arrived at the platform the points at both ends of the loop were set for the down line ; the down home signal was "off" ; the down starting signal was at danger ; and the up home and distant signals were also at danger, the interlocking rendering it impossible for them to be lowered, so long as the down home signal was off, and the points at the south end of the loop set for the down loop line.

At 6.9 a.m. the up excursion train, which was booked to pass the down mail at Tylwch, left Pantydwr, it being then 17 minutes late. It arrived at Tylwch at 6.17, having occupied 8 minutes in traversing the distance (3 miles, 74 chains) between the two places, the average speed being about 30 miles an hour, which was correct according to the time tables. Driver Hopkins on approaching the distant signal found it at danger, and says that he at once applied the brake, and that it would not act properly. He made a second application with the same result, whereupon he told his fireman to put on the hand-brake and open the sand valves, he himself at the same time whistled for the guard's brake. By this time he was getting near to the home signal which, as already explained, was also at danger, and perceiving that the loop points were open for the down line, and that his train was not going to stop at the home signal, he made a final effort to check it by reversing the engine. But in spite of this his train over-ran the signal, and passing through the loop points on to the down line, was still moving at speed, said by Hopkins to have been 5 miles an hour, but which was probably a great deal higher, when it collided with the down mail train, which was standing 97 yards inside the signal.

The cause of the catastrophe was evidently the failure of driver Hopkins to stop his train at the home signal, and the question at once arises, whether this was due to any defect, as he alleges, in the vacuum brake, or to any error on his part.

Hopkins asserts that on taking charge of his engine that morning at Builth, he found that he could only produce 15 inches of vacuum in the brake apparatus, instead of 18 inches, as required by the Company's rule. After being coupled to his train and during the journey to Tylwch the brake-gauge only registered 14 or 15 inches of vacuum. He made no report of this to anyone at Builth, nor did he cause any examination to be made of his engine, as he should have done before starting, so as to ascertain what was wrong with it ; nor during the journey did he do more than exchange a casual remark at Rhayader with the guard, that he had a "poor" brake. Although he says that he had not the full

---

* The stationmaster gives the time of the arrival of this train as 6.14, whereas the driver thinks it was 6.17, but neither of these statements seems to be quite accurate. If, as appears from the evidence, the accident occurred at 6.17, the down mail must have reached the place about 6.16, as it is given in evidence that it had only been standing at the platform for a minute or less when it was run into.

amount of vacuum available, he admits that the brake worked satisfactorily at the previous stopping places, and that he was " depending " upon it when approaching Tylwch. He did not use any extra care when running down the long incline between Pantydwr and Tylwch, and made no attempt to get the train under control until after seeing that the distant signal for the latter place was at danger.

Guard William Hamer supports the driver in his statement that the vacuum before leaving Builth and during the journey was below the prescribed amount. But in spite of this Hamer took none of the necessary precautions for the safe working of the train. It might at any rate have been expected that having as he knew a " poor " brake, he would have been more than usually careful to watch for the signals and to stand by his hand-brake, so as to steady the train by its means down the incline into Tylwch. Instead of this he was sitting down making out his journal and never saw the distant signal for Tylwch at all, and he made no attempt to apply his hand-brake until the driver whistled for it, when he was close to the home signal.

In fact, both Hopkins and Hamer acted in all respects up to this time as though the brake was in perfect order, and it is clear that if any deficiency existed in the amount of vacuum registered by the gauges on the engine and in the van, they deliberately broke the rules* laid down for their guidance under such circumstances.

It is difficult to reconcile the actions of these men, as described by themselves, with their statements that the brake was wrong before they left Builth. If, as they say, they knew the brake was out of order, they convict themselves of a total disregard of all necessary care in working the train. If, on the other hand, we are to be guided by what they did, the conclusion is forced upon us that the brake was in good order, and their evidence to the contrary becomes quite unreliable.

But even 14 inches of vacuum, though not so powerful as 18 inches, would be capable of applying the brake blocks to the wheels with considerable effect, if it was made use of in sufficient time, and with due discretion. According to Hopkins' account he applied the brake as soon as he saw that the distant signal was at danger, but it altogether failed to act. He says that as soon as he turned the handle to the " Brake on " position " the vacuum immediately disappeared," which he and his fireman explained to me to mean, that both the pointers of the vacuum gauge on his engine fell to zero, indicating that the vacuum was destroyed not only in the train pipe, as it should be, but also in the vacuum chamber on the tender, as it should not be ; in which case the brake, so far as the engine and tender were concerned, would be inoperative. If this was so, it would disclose a serious defect in the apparatus, and one which could not previously have existed, seeing that Hopkins and the guard say that the brake had worked all right, though with less vacuum than usual, up to that time.

Unfortunately the engine was so much damaged that no test of the brake appliances could be made after the collision, and the question whether the apparatus suddenly and at a critical moment developed the defect, cannot be satisfactorily cleared up. But it will be seen from the evidence of driver Nichols, who was in charge of the same engine during the previous day, that the brake apparatus on it was then working satisfactorily.

Even if it be the case that the brake failed on the engine and tender in the way stated, it by no means follows that it was also inoperative on the wheels of the coaches composing the train. On the contrary, the fact that as soon as the handle was turned to the " Brake on " position, the pointer on the gauge connected with the train pipe fell from 14 inches to zero (as stated by Hopkins) shows that so far as the carriages were concerned the brake was working, though with less than the normal vacuum. And if Hopkins had reversed his engine directly he found that the engine brake was out of order, he could in all probability have got his train under sufficient control to stop it at the home signal. The reason he gave when first questioned on the subject for not having reversed was, that although the signal was at danger he felt sure " that the points would lie for the up platform line," and that he would be able to stop at the platform. He subsequently gave another and totally different reason, namely, that he thought it was a very " risky " proceeding to reverse while the engine was in forward motion, and he therefore postponed doing so until he became aware that the points were lying for the down line.

I have gone thus fully into this question of the condition of the brake, because the mere statement of a driver in a case of collision to the effect that his brake failed must always be received with caution.

In the present instance I am unable to attach much importance to the allegations as to the condition of the brake, and I believe that the true explanation of the occurrence is

---

* These rules are quoted earlier in this report.

to be found in the admissions made by Hopkins, that he expected to find the home signal "off," and that even if the signal was at danger, the points at any rate would lie for the up line.

It doubtless sometimes happens at passing places on single lines, especially at times when there is only one man on duty to work the signals and attend to platform duties, that the signals are kept at danger longer than is necessary or desirable, and are only lowered at the last moment to admit a train into a station. Hopkins was expecting every moment to see the home signal lowered, and I have little doubt that he did not make any serious effort to get his train under control until it was too late. Thinking that it would not be necessary for him to stop until he reached the platform, he regulated his speed accordingly, and he was clearly taken by surprise at finding the loop points open for the down road. He then probably realised for the first time the mistake he had made, and did all he could to stop, but was unable to do so in time to avert a collision.

If the points had been in their proper position, i.e., for the up line, as Hopkins expected, no collision would have occurred; and although the train might have passed the signal at danger it is probable that nothing would have been heard of the matter. If, on the other hand, the signal had been lowered at the last moment, the question would never have been raised whether the train could have been stopped at it or not. But a driver has no right to expect or assume anything. When he finds a distant signal at danger his duty is to take immediate steps so to reduce speed as to be able to stop at the home signal, and under no circumstances should he pass the home signal at danger. It is not necessary for him to know why the signal is at danger; all he has to do is to stop.

On this occasion the train had 1,136 yards to run on a falling gradient from the spot where the distant signal first became visible up to the home signal, and as the speed at that place was probably not much above 30 miles an hour Hopkins should, if he had managed properly and received the assistance to which he was entitled from the guard, have been able so to control his train as to stop at the home signal. His failure to do so, due, as I believe, to his having postponed the application of the brake until too late, in the expectation that the signal would be lowered before he reached it, was the principal cause of this fatal collision, for which I hold driver Hopkins chiefly responsible.

Guard Hamer who was paying no attention to the signals, nor to the speed of the train, nor, until the driver whistled, to his hand-brake, must in consequence of his negligence be regarded as nearly as much to blame as Hopkins.

If, as these men stated, in their desire to excuse themselves, there was a deficiency of vacuum registered on the brake gauge either before leaving Builth or at any time during the journey, their offences would be aggravated rather than mitigated thereby, inasmuch as they totally disregarded all the precautionary measures for the safety of the train which are enumerated in the rules. Had they done their duty, the failure of the brake to act either would not have occurred, or if it occurred would not have mattered, as the train should have been travelling at such a rate of speed as to be entirely controllable by the hand-brakes.

It was a very unfortunate circumstance that the loop points at the south end of the place were set for the down line, and stationmaster Davies committed a most serious mistake in placing them in that position. He says that he thought it was necessary for him to do so before he could lower the down home signal; which shows that he had taken little pains to make himself acquainted with the signalling of the place. It may, however, be stated on his behalf that in former days it was very usual to interlock the points and signals at passing loops on single line in the manner suggested by Davies. The arrangement had obvious disadvantages which are vividly exemplified in this case. The modern and far preferable practice is for the home signal at either end of a passing loop to be altogether independent of the position of the points at the other end of the loop, as was the case at Tylwch, which was only re-signalled and interlocked a few months ago.

Stationmaster Davies committed another error which, though unconnected with the collision, was in itself a source of much danger. There is an important rule in single line working, "that when trains which have to cross each other are approaching a tablet station in opposite directions, the signals in both directions are to be kept at danger, and when the train, which was to be first admitted into the station, has been brought to a stand, the home signal applicable to such train may be lowered to allow it to draw forward into the station, &c."; the object being to ensure that neither train shall over-run the starting signal, and foul the single line on which the other train is approaching.

Davies' evidence makes it clear that he did not bring the mail train to a stand before he admitted it to the station, and in thus breaking the rules, he exposed both trains to unnecessary danger.

It rarely happens that the down mail train has to pass another train at Tylwch, and it is therefore not necessary, as a general rule, to have a second man on duty at this place during the early hours of the morning, as the stationmaster can very well attend to the mail.   But when two passenger trains have to cross each other, it is hardly possible for one man to attend to the tablet instruments, signals, issue and collection of tickets, and platform duties for both trains at one and the same time, and, under those circumstances, a second man should be present, a relief man, if necessary, being employed for the purpose.

I have, &c.,

The Assistant Secretary,   H. A. YORKE,
Railway Department, Board of Trade.   *Lt.-Col., R.E. (Retired).*

APPENDIX.

DAMAGE TO ROLLING STOCK.

Stock forming Down Mail, Moat Lane to Brecon.

Engine No. 65.—Steel buffer beam badly bent, and angle irons broken ; frames and life-guards badly bent and splashers damaged ; footplate and fall-plates damaged ; flexible vacuum pipe destroyed, and wrought-iron vacuum pipes damaged ; bogie slightly damaged.

Cambrian third-class, No. 158.—One headstock, two buffer castings and one stay-rod broken ; two buffer-rods bent.

Cambrian Composite, No. 149.—One headstock, two headstock caps, three buffer castings, two buffer-blocks, one footboard and two step-irons broken.

Cambrian third-class, No. 241.—One headstock, one buffer casting, and one step-stay broken ; and mouldings at ends and sides damaged.

Cambrian passenger van, No. 104.—No damage.

Stock forming 5.10 a.m. Excursion from Builth, September 16th, 1899.

Engine No. 49.—Oak buffer-beam destroyed ; buffer-beam plates and angle irons bent ; and life-guards damaged.

Cambrian passenger van, No. 6.—Two solebars, two headstocks, one longitudinal, four diagonals, and two middle-bearers smashed ; and nearly half the body of van completely smashed ; four axle-boxes broken.

Cambrian bogie composite, No. 266.—First three compartments completely smashed, viz., first, second and third-class ; one headstock smashed ; solebars damaged ; one buffer casting, one axle-box, lamp irons, gas fittings, and alarm communication fittings broken ; buffer-spring and rods, and floor damaged.

Cambrian third-class, No. 204.—One headstock broken ; buffer-rods and step-irons bent.

Cambrian third-class, Nos. 206, 40, 163, 186, 174 and 38.—No damage.

Cambrian third - class, No. 39.—Hose pipe damaged.

Cambrian van, No. 105.—No damage.

Printed copies of the above Report were sent to the Company on the 30th October.

PRO: RAIL 1053/8

Since 1840 the Board of Trade has been responsible for inspecting railways and approving the safety of their plant and procedures before permitting them to carry passengers. The Vale of Towy Railway from Llandeilo to Llandovery was a case in 1858 where the inspector twice refused to pass the line for passenger trains before it was satisfactory. Once a line was open, inspectors had a duty to report on accidents, but railway companies were not obliged to heed their recommendations. The inspector's detachment increased his authority and enabled him to

comment not only on the actions of employees but also on the conditions under which they were employed. We see both these elements in the case of the report on the Tylwch accident.

In the following year, 1900, the position was altered by Parliament in the Railway Employment (Prevention of Accidents) Act whereby the Board of Trade was now authorised to impose rules on the companies for the protection of railway employees from dangerous practices. By 2000 the position has been further shifted to the point where, under the Health and Safety at Work Act, the Health and Safety Executive can issue detailed mandatory instructions aimed at increasing safety. These measures, and a much greater interest in safety generally, have improved safety standards but, in a more litigious age,

criminal prosecutions are now being raised with the result that investigations of accidents for the purpose of learning how to improve matters are delayed while the law takes its course.

CHESTER & HOLYHEAD LINE WASHED AWAY

Just to the east of Bangor there are two high rocky headlands, Penmaen-bach to the east and Penmaen-mawr to the west. Between them was a small village called Dwygyfylchi. Perhaps because the management of the Chester & Holyhead Railway felt this was a bit of a mouthful, the station they opened in 1849 was called Penmaenmawr. Around it grew up a

small and select town where a number of noteable Victorians came for relaxation. Gladstone, Tennyson, Elgar and Darwin all found the place agreeable. When the quarries on the headland were developed they proved a good source of setts for Victorian streets. Later they became a major source of railway ballast.

A general view of Penmaen-mawr looking to the west, *ca.* 1900. The accident occurred to the right of the picture.

LNWR Soc.

A view of the Penmaen-mawr viaduct, published in 1905, which demon-strates how the railway was squeezed between the sea and the cliffs.

DD Coll.

A former R.O.D. 2-8-0 locomotive as LNWR No. 2108 moves a train of ballast eastward towards Penmaenmawr station, probably in the early 1920s.   *F. Moore/S. Reid Coll.*

On 12 January 1899 a severe gale forced a breach in the sea wall just west of the Penmaen-bach tunnel. For 70 yards the railway track and sleepers were left suspended in mid-air. The LNWR had had the foresight to mount watchmen and they saw that the sea wall had collapsed. One of the men ran to Penmaenmawr where he was able to stop an eastbound goods train. The other man ran to the mouth of the tunnel, where he heard the sound of an express goods train from Manchester to Holyhead approaching. He placed detonators on the line and waved his lamp; the driver saw him and tried to pull up but, although the train was only travelling at 35 m.p.h., he was unable to avoid running onto the unsupported rails. The locomotive and first eighteen waggons were toppled into the raging sea. Both enginemen

A close-up of the locomotive after the 1900 accident.
F. Moore/S. Reid Coll.

were lost and the locomotive ended up on its side in the water. Surprisingly, some casks of stout in one of the shattered waggons remained intact.

PORTHKERRY VIADUCT

This is a story not so much about an accident as about poor construction standards, leading to what might have been a major disaster. As it was, an accident occurred during the repair works when an unfortunate workman fell from the viaduct, broke his skull and died.

On the Vale of Glamorgan line between Barry and Rhoose, a valley is crossed by an elegant 16-arch viaduct. During its construction in 1896, the contractors had problems with the stability of two of the piers. One had to be dismantled so that its foundations could be deepened; the other was underpinned. Within a fortnight of opening the line in December 1897, the embankment at the Barry end began to slip. On 10 January 1898 a more serious slip was found in the embankment with evidence of subsidence under pier No. 13. After the first 'down' train had passed, trains were stopped at the Rhoose end and passengers had to walk across the viaduct to a waiting train at the Barry end. Next day, it was decided that this practice

Train services were restored in only 30 hours by building a temporary diversion. On 22 January the badly damaged locomotive was lifted out of the sea and taken to Crewe.

was unsafe and passengers were taken by brake from Rhoose to Barry. More importantly, this meant that the coal traffic had to cease altogether.

The general manager of the Barry Railway who worked the line wrote to the directors of the Vale of Glamorgan Railway on 13 January to draw their attention to the cost of this temporary solution. He assessed it at £4,500 a year against receipts which he believed were unlikely to exceed £3,500, since the carriage of coal would be out of the question.

In order to recover the coal traffic as quickly as possible, the engineers, Forster, Brown Rees and Szlumper were asked to suggest how this could be done. They came up with three solutions. The first would cost £8,000 and would involve building a temporary wooden structure parallel to the viaduct for its whole length so that work on the viaduct could continue without disrupting train services. Secondly, they considered a short wooden

A photograph taken during the repair of the Porthkerry viaduct which illustrates the severity of the construction defects; 1898.   *PRO: RAIL 253/441*

structure to bypass the viaduct from pier 9 to the Barry end, costing £4,000. Thirdly, for £2,500 they could build a diversion round the head of the valley, curving away some distance from the viaduct. This they strongly recommended provided the land could be obtained.

On 19 January, Mr Strain of Glasgow recommended that the arch between piers 13 and 14 be supported at once and piers 9 to 15 be supported with timber. He wanted three concrete stays 10 ft thick by 4 ft to be inserted beneath the arches between piers 9, 10 and 11. Finally, he wanted earth to be filled at the Rhoose end in order to cover the arches with an extended embankment.

The board clearly found this indigestible and decided to build a temporary diversion in order to recover the coal trade. This single track of some 2.5 miles was completed with quite remarkable speed by 19 April.

They then turned their attention to a permanent solution. James Bell, engineer of the Barry wrote to the board on 14 April. He had two solutions. The more expensive would be a three-quarter mile permanent diversionary loop, which would entail excavating deep cuttings and building two long bridges. Instead, he

preferred to repair and extend the viaduct. His solution was less far-reaching than that put forward by Mr Strain and depended more on patching than replacing. As such it was accepted. Bell proceeded quickly and by 3 August was reporting that the work was nearly complete. Pier 12 had been underpinned, and piers 10 and 11 were nearly finished. However, there had been further settlement of piers 8 and 9 due to bad original workmanship. In a report which he wrote on 8 September but which he did not show to the board, perhaps because it painted such a dismal picture, Bell said that if he had known how bad the construction had been, he would not have recommended patching. He listed the problems. The foundations of piers 4 to 13 were being widened and underpinned as the old concrete was of very poor quality, in many cases no more than clay, and pier 8 had actually sunk through its foundations. The arch at piers 3 and 4 was replaced entirely. But there were cracks throughout in the arches and the parapet, and some of the piers were leaning as much as 17 inches towards Barry. He must have written the report on a particularly bad day as he concluded by stating that the whole thing needed pulling

Porthkerry viaduct from the north, *ca.* 1960.

A. Jarvis

A Barry-bound freight in the early 1960s proves the efficacy of the repairs.   *A. Jarvis*

down and starting again, for £40,000. A compromise seems to have been reached as some of the arches were replaced and the viaduct was extended at either end to overcome weakness in the original embankments. On 8 January 1900 it was reopened and has survived for 100 years. Bell's pessimism seems to have been excessive.

It formed part of the Vale of Glamorgan Railway which had been built at the instigation of coal owners in the Llynfi valley area seeking improved connections with the new port at Barry. From the outset in 1889, the Barry Railway agreed to work the railway and, when in 1893 it had to guarantee the shareholders 4% in order to obtain sufficient finance, it acquired the right to appoint four directors and thus became virtual owner.

The new railway was just over 20 miles in length, linking Bridgend with Barry, and was built by the then well-known engineer, Sir James Szlumper. Oddly, he acted as arbitrator in the subsequent dispute over the viaduct between the company and the contractor in which the contractor claimed £148,700 from the company; Szlumper found that the company should only pay £29,700.

Although a latecomer, the Vale of Glamorgan line survives in 2000, partially as a means of providing rail access to the coal-fired power station at Aberthaw, and partially as an alternate to the south Wales main line. Its name is perpetuated in the preserved railway between Barry and Barry Island, which is an interesting example of cooperation between local government and enthusiasts. It might have had a more glorious role if a project called the London & South Wales Railway had made progress beyond a parliamentary bill prepared in 1895. This amazing project envisaged a railway of over 150 miles between the Barry Railway line at Cogan, just west of Cardiff, and the Metropolitan Railway near Great Missenden with a link to the Midland near Hendon. A westward extension from the Vale of Glamorgan Railway near Bridgend would have made a connection with the Port Talbot and Rhondda & Swansea Bay Railways at Port Talbot. The whole was nullified by the GWR obtaining powers to build its South Wales Direct Railway, which shortened the distance between Swindon and the Severn tunnel by nine miles and, more importantly, bypassed the congestion around Bristol.

Llanberis Station. A LNWR 0-6-0 arrives with a train of six-wheeled passenger coaches, c. 1910.

St. Ffagan's Level Crossing *c.* 1950. This scene has been transformed; only the minor road and a plain double-track survive – even the course of the river has changed.

Private Collection

CHAPTER 9

A JOURNEY FROM NORTH TO SOUTH

Amlwch is a small town on the north coast of Anglesey which had grown as a port for the export of copper. In 1899 it had the most northerly railway station in Wales. Conveniently located just off the main street, it was a small brick building on the single platform with a generous canopy. Access to the booking-office was from the platform. The booking-clerk at Amlwch could have been forgiven for scratching his head and taking a deep intake of breath if, towards the end of 1899, he had been asked for a ticket to Barry Island. Most of his clients were interested in travelling to one of the stations down the line, such as Llangefni, at that time the county town of Anglesey, or to Bangor or Caernarfon. He had had visitors from the Manchester and Liverpool areas, but it was somewhat unusual for anyone to wish to travel to the south. As a result, the route was not clearly established in his mind; however the journey was made, he had a suspicion that it would require several changes of train. He also had an uncomfortable feeling that it would involve making some of those changes at places where the railway companies had made no particular effort to optimise the connection.

The problem was exacerbated by the passenger's insistence on avoiding the need for a cab or minibus between stations, and on remaining within the Principality, and the booking-clerk realised fairly quickly that one route stood out as being less indirect than others. In fact, it was relatively straightforward, if circuitous, as it followed the west coast through Caernarfon, Barmouth and Aberystwyth, to Carmarthen and Bridgend. With luck it should only involve eight changes of train and five railway companies.

A page from the 1899 Bradshaw showing the train services to Amlwch. The larger table both starts and finishes at Euston, demonstrating the pitfalls for the unwary user of timetables.   *PRO: RAIL 903/113*

A double-headed train at Amlwch hauled by 0-6-2Ts Nos. 7596 and 7680; 21 July 1934.   *H.C. Casserley*

Although he suspected that it would take much longer, he was tempted to examine the possibility of using what he had heard were the very picturesque lines through the centre of Wales, by way of Llandudno Junction, Blaenau Ffestiniog, Bala, Barmouth, Moat Lane Junction, Talyllyn Junction, Merthyr and Pontypridd. This would entail a short walk between the LNWR and GWR stations at Blaenau Ffestiniog. As he had been told there was a rather stiff climb up the hill between the Taff Vale and Barry Railway stations at Pontypridd, he decided to have a look at the possibility of changing trains in Cardiff. He felt he had to reject an ingenious plan that he rather fancied of finishing the journey through Brecon, Neath and Bridgend, as that would entail a cab ride between the stations at Neath; for the same reason he rejected a change at Builth Road for a train on the Central Wales line, as that would require a cab across Swansea.

A fifth route, which occurred to him as he studied the Railway Clearing House map hanging on the wall, had probably the fastest journey time of all but, as it was via Chester and Shrewsbury, he temporarily put it out of his mind. As he started to look at the possibilities wholly within Wales, he realised that he had better ask the passenger whether he was under any time constraint.

The staff at Amlwch had some cause to feel comfortable about the service of trains provided from this fairly small and remote place. Five a day in each direction covered the 17.5 miles between Amlwch and Gaerwen, the junction on the main line. It took three-quarters of an hour as there were five intermediate stops, but there were connections from each train in the direction of both Bangor and Holyhead. However, our booking-clerk began to feel uncomfortable about the Barry Island passenger's journey as soon as he remembered that the first train out of Amlwch did not leave until 7.40 a.m. This had always struck him as odd as there was an arrival as early as 6.05 a.m. which connected with the Irish Mail from Euston. However, there was a good connection at Gaerwen, as the train from Amlwch arrived there at 8.35 a.m., in time to pick up a train from Holyhead at 8.38 a.m. Transfer simply required the passenger to cross from the bay, through the substantial station building to the 'up' platform.

The station staff at Gaerwen in 1897. *LNWR Soc.*

At Menai Bridge there was another neat connection, for arrival at 8.51 a.m. would connect with a westbound train from Chester for Afon Wen at 8.56 a.m., arriving there at 10.40 a.m. As he started to work on the job, he felt reassured that at least on the LNWR someone had organised the timetable with passengers in mind. He was pleasantly surprised, therefore, that there was a good connection at Afon Wen with the Cambrian train

Cambrian 2-4-0 No 28 *Mazeppa*, an LNWR 18 in. 0-6-2T and station staff meet at Afon Wen in the early years of the century. *Ifor Higgon Coll.*

A Pwllheli to Porthmadog train at Afon Wen, headed by 4-4-0 No. 9018; 3 August 1953.   *H C. Casserley*

The inhospitable location of Afon Wen is emphasised in this view of an LMS train at the eastern end of the station; 18 July 1941.   *H.C. Casserley*

from Pwllheli, leaving at 10.45 a.m. No one would wish to spend long at that particular spot, perched on the edge of a bleak and windswept quarter of Cardigan Bay.

The Cambrian train then made its way south from the Lleyn peninsula, through the picturesque seaside town of Criccieth, to Porthmadog. There was an interchange station with the Ffestiniog Railway at Minffordd and

the line then crossed the Dwyryd and continued south past Harlech castle. Here was the straightest part of the route for miles, before it ran along the edge of the sea to Barmouth. This had been developed as an important tourist centre and holiday resort, with the train creeping through it, partly in a tunnel, to cross over the long Barmouth bridge across the Mawddach estuary. It traversed the Friog cliffs

A Machynlleth to Pwllheli train between Porthmadog and Criccieth, hauled by No. 9016; August 1954.

J.B. Snell

4 MT 4-6-0 No. 75009 approaching Morfa Mawddach, as Barmouth Junction became in 1960. The train is from Pwllheli to Machynlleth; September 1964.

J.B. Snell

Cambrian Railways 'Small Bogie' No 17 pulls away from Aberdyfi during the early part of the century.

Ifor Higgon Coll.

Dovey Junction (*sic*) with coast train arriving, hauled by No. 4599 with the 9.30 a.m. from Barmouth; 25 August 1948.

H.C. Casserley

The view eastward at Dovey Junction with two Cambrian trains around 1910.

W.G. Rear Coll.

Dovey Junction and a train from the coast seen from the Aberystwyth line at Glandyfi; August 1954.

J.B. Snell

at some height above the sea, then passed Tywyn and the Talyllyn Railway interchange, and after burrowing through and round Aberdyfi it followed the northern edge of the Dyfi estuary and was due at Glandovey Junction at 1.10 p.m.

Set out in the marshes of the Dyfi estuary, this could, under certain circumstances be a pleasant place to spend half an hour. Only if high tides combined with heavy rain was there a need for waterproof footware. The name of this junction which had no road connection was changed to Dovey Junction in 1904. It had originally been intended to build a long viaduct across the Dyfi estuary but the cost, together with resistance from up-river shipping interests, effectively killed the project. Nevertheless, the connection for Aberystwyth was not a bad one, with a train scheduled at 1.45 p.m., arriving at its destination at 2.30 p.m.

Between Aberystwyth and Carmarthen the railway penetrates the picturesque Cynwyl gorge, here seen from the verandah of a northbound goods brake van; late 1950s.

Ian L. Wright

A fascinating scene at Bridgend, *ca.* 1905. On the left is a Barry Railway 'J' Class 2-4-2T No. 87 on a Vale of Glamorgan line train. In the centre is a double-headed GW London-bound express piloted by 'Bulldog' Class No. 3422 *Sir John Llewelyn* leading an unidentified 'Duke'. On the right stands a saddle tank with a local train from the Tondu direction.

GBJ Coll.

Unfortunately, when the Amlwch booking-clerk looked up the Manchester & Milford timetable he was disappointed to find that, although the 2.40 p.m. departure from Aberystwyth covered the 42 miles to the junction at Pencader in two hours, the GWR required over one hour to reach Carmarthen Junction, only 15 miles away. The 6.08 p.m. train from there would not reach Bridgend until 8.45 p.m., too late for the Vale of Glamorgan line, but if the passenger went on to Cardiff, he would arrive at 9.30 p.m., in time for a connection at 10.00 p.m. with a Barry Railway train as far as Barry Town. The rest of the trip out to Barry Island would either have to be by cab or by train the following morning. The last train out to Barry Island left Barry Town as early as 7.41 p.m., so he did not have a loyal LNWR man's satisfaction of being able to blame the GWR for failing to make it.

He then wrote out the instructions:

QUICKEST ROUTE WITHIN WALES

7.40 a.m.	Dep. Amlwch	LNWR
8.35 a.m.	Arr. Gaerwen	LNWR
8.38 a.m.	Dep. Gaerwen	LNWR
8.51 a.m.	Arr. Menai Bridge	LNWR
8.56 a.m.	Dep. Menai Bridge	LNWR
10.40 a.m.	Arr. Afon Wen	LNWR
10.45 a.m.	Dep. Afon Wen	Cambrian
1.10 p.m.	Arr. Glandovey Junction	Cambrian
1.45 p.m.	Dep. Glandovey Junction	Cambrian
2.10 p.m.	Arr. Aberystwyth	Cambrian
2.40 p.m.	Dep. Aberystwyth	Manchester & Milford
4.40 p.m.	Arr. Pencader	Manchester & Milford
4.53 p.m.	Dep. Pencader	GWR
5.54 p.m.	Arr. Carmarthen Junction	GWR
6.08 p.m.	Dep. Carmarthen Junction	GWR
9.30 p.m.	Arr. Cardiff	GWR
10.00 p.m.	Dep. Cardiff	Barry
10.26 p.m.	Arr. Barry Town	Barry

He then had a look at the inland route. It was frustrating to have to repeat part of the coastal route between Barmouth Junction and Glandovey Junction but there was no way across the mountains. He quickly realised that there would have to be an overnight stop. The only question was where it should be.

From Amlwch there was no alternative to the 7.40 a.m. and picking up the train from Holyhead at Gaerwen at 8.38 a.m. However,

A view looking west towards the old Llandudno Junction station which was closed in 1897. The location of its replacement, the present station, is just behind the photographer.
Courtesy J.W.P. Arrowsmith/ W.G. Rear Coll.

Heading towards Betws-y-coed up the Conwy valley behind LMS No. 8392 on the 10.35 a.m. from Llandudno Junction; 3 June 1932.

H.C. Casserley

The same train calling at Pont-y-pant, viewed down the valley; 3 June 1932.

H.C. Casserley

this time the passenger would stay on the train as far as Llandudno Junction, arriving there at 9.51 a.m. Here, there was a frustrating wait until 11.55 a.m. for a train to Blaenau Ffestiniog, but at least the facilities should have been in good order as the station in its new location had only been open for two years. The journey up the Conwy valley would be pleasant and increasingly interesting as the country became more wild. In 1900 photographic evidence suggests that the upper stretches of the line ran through rather wilder, rocky scenery than in 2000; as elsewhere in Wales, the tree cover is now much higher and thicker.

The same train approaches
Roman Bridge.
H.C. Casserley

Betws-y-coed station in 1903, looking down the valley.

LNWR Soc.

With an air of expectation the train would enter the final tunnel, and roll through the damp darkness of the single bore for over two miles before bursting out into daylight at Blaenau Ffestiniog, to be surrounded by towering grey slate mountains. Arrival here at 1.10 p.m. would allow time for a quick lunch at the Queen's Hotel, even with the change of stations, as the GWR train for Bala left at 2.30 p.m.

The LNWR's station at Blaenau Ffestiniog with 'Cauliflower' 0-6-0 No. 8405 standing with the 4.30 p.m. train for Llandudno Junction; 3 June 1932.
H.C. Casserley

The LNWR station at Blaenau seen from the south with the Ffestiniog Railway exchange station prominent in the centre of the picture; early 1900s.

NLW

A nice display of roses enhances the platform serving the Ffestiniog and GW at Blaenau Ffestiniog. A train for Bala waits at the GW platform. The idle carriage stock on the sidings of both companies is typical of the Edwardian period. Also in the picture are two signal-boxes, a fine array of Ffestiniog signals and the Queen's Hotel.

WIMM

The next stage of the journey took just over one hour and was most spectacular. Crossing the bare mountains and traversing the side of a steep and wide valley, it would definitely be desirable to see this in daylight. According to the timetable, the train would arrive at Bala at 3.35 p.m. Here there was a change with a departure for Dolgellau at 4.05 p.m. It appeared from the timetable that this train would reach Dolgellau at 5.00 p.m.

Bala train in the former GWR station, headed by No. 5774 in August 1955.

J.B. Snell

The public platform at Trawsfynydd, looking towards Bala, soon after 1900.

GBJ Coll.

The view from the footplate of a Bala-bound train as it negotiates the high shelf above Cwm Prysor; *ca.* 1960.

A. Jarvis

However, as he looked more closely at the timetable he found an aspect of it confusing. It looked as though there was a mistake, for the 4.05 p.m. departure from Bala for Dolgellau was shown to be leaving Bala 22 minutes before its own arrival from Ruabon and Llangollen. When he looked at other times of the day, it seemed as though the same mistake had been perpetrated throughout, and in both directions. He was mystified by it and raised the point with the stationmaster. This older and more experienced officer had previously worked at Blaenau Ffestiniog and was therefore more familiar with the arrangements in that part of Wales. It transpired that there was a station called Bala Junction on the main line and that Bala itself was a mile up the Blaenau Ffestiniog branch. Bala Junction appeared in no timetable as it was inaccessible to the public, yet every train stopped there. Bala itself was served by a branch train. As the branch was single track, the departing trains

from Bala had to leave for Bala Junction before the incoming trains. The booking-clerk decided to try to clarify the position for his passenger, who might otherwise be confused. Despite the timetable, what was actually going to happen was that the train from Blaenau would arrive at Bala at 3.35 p.m. The passenger would disembark and wait until 4.05 p.m. for a shuttle service to Bala Junction. This only took a few minutes. There he would get out of that train and wait for a 4.15 p.m. departure to Dolgellau. He thought it would be prudent to alert the passenger to the fact that he could elect to wait at Bala Junction, rather than at Bala, by staying on his train from Blaenau and leaving Bala at 3.40 p.m. This was intended to make a connection at Bala Junction with a train heading east for Ruabon at 3.57 p.m. It boiled down to a question of which station offered the best facilities for waiting. He was advised that Bala was preferable unless the passenger was a railway enthusiast.

A 'Metro' tank arrives at Bala from the Ffestiniog direction with a substantial mixed train in the early part of the twentieth century.
Gwynedd Archives/ John Roberts Coll.

The 1.45 p.m. train to Barmouth stands alongside the former Cambrian station building at Dolgellau with 0-4-2T No. 1465; 5 August 1948.
H.B. Priestley

Having clarified that point, the booking-clerk reverted to Dolgellau. Here an end-on connection was made with the Cambrian which now provided the locomotive, but the train continued and was due to arrive at Barmouth Junction at 5.20 p.m. Here connection was made with a train on the coastal route from Pwllheli at 6.05 p.m.; this then followed the first route along the coast through Aberdyfi to Glandovey Junction and then headed eastward inland to Machynlleth. From here it climbed over the watershed at Talerddig to Moat Lane Junction, where it was due to arrive at 8.06 p.m. At that point the Mid-Wales line, now part of

Cambrian Railways 2-4-0 No. 41 waits on the wrong road at Dolgellau before working a GW train from Ruabon forward to the coast; *ca.* 1910. *Ifor Higgon Coll.*

An elevated panoramic view of Barmouth Junction with, in the distance, the bridge and town of Barmouth; *ca.* 1925. The branch from Dolgellau enters on the right and a coastal freight approaches from Machynlleth on the left. The connecting (goods only) side of the triangle may be discerned with the help of a brake-van and some parked waggons. *D.S. George & Son/Ifor Higgon Coll.*

A rural period piece at Penmaenpool with one of Aston's attractive 0-4-4T engines No. 23 (built in 1899) in the background.

Ifor Higgon Coll.

A Cambrian Railways locomotive (Sharp Stewart No. 45 as GW 900) working a GWR through train into Barmouth Junction from the Dolgellau direction; probably late 1920s.

Ifor Higgon Coll.

the Cambrian, branched south towards Brecon. The big question here was where to spend the night. As it turned out, the options offered by the timetable made the choice easy. The 8.25 p.m. from Moat Lane Junction terminated at Llanidloes at 8.45 p.m. That looked a distinctly more prospective place in which to find a comfortable bed than a remote and isolated railway junction. Furthermore, the stationmaster was able to inform him that the Trewythen Arms Hotel was reasonably close to the station.

The 'up' York Mail, photographed immediately east of Machynlleth, behind an unidentified BR Class 4 2-6-4T; August 1964.
J.B. Snell

The last 'up' Cambrian Coast Express storms its way towards Cemmes Road behind a shiny BR Class 4 No. 75033; 4 March 1967.
J.B. Snell

A double-headed train approaches Chapel Crossing *en route* to Talerddig, hauled by 4-4-0 No. 9024 and an unidentified '2200' Class; August 1954.

J.B. Snell

The view down the Talerddig cutting with an unidentified 2-6-0; 7 August 1954.

J.B. Snell

There was an opportunity to make an early start at 5.30 a.m., but the booking-clerk felt that, provided there was still time to reach Barry Island on the second day, it might be more prudent to choose the 10.30 a.m. Besides allowing time for a decent breakfast, it would ensure that a picturesque part of the journey was seen in daylight. The line climbed out of the Severn valley south of Llanidloes, and having crossed the watershed, entered the beautiful Wye valley. On its way the train would stop at Tylwch, where the booking-clerk remembered there had been a recent fatal accident arising from a collision between two trains. Then for much of the way the train followed the river Wye before heading south-west to Talyllyn Junction, where it was due to arrive at 1.21 p.m. There was then time for a comfortable change onto the Brecon & Merthyr Railway train from Brecon at 1.35 p.m.

Moat Lane Junction station showing the line from Llanidloes towards Newtown; the line from Dyfi Junction approached from the left behind the station building and joined the earlier line beyond the signal-box; 16 October 1962.

D. Keith Jones

A late Victorian photograph of Llanidloes station, looking south.

GBJ Coll.

The picturesque route of the Mid Wales line in the upper Wye valley.

J.E. Martin

Builth Road station with the LNWR Central Wales line on the left and the Cambrian line below and to the right.

H.C. Casserley

The Mid Wales line skirted the Wye for much of the route and here, just north of Builth Wells, a southbound train is headed by a Cambrian 'Small Bogie' 4-4-0 early in the 1900s.

Ifor Higgon Coll.

Talyllyn Junction with, on the left, a train from Newport to Brecon and, on the right, another from Brecon to Moat Lane Junction; 18 August 1956.   *Ian L. Wright*

Possibly, the route from here to Merthyr was the most spectacular part of the journey, at one stage heading for an impossibly high and steep mountainside before crossing the summit in the Torpantau tunnel at some 1,350 ft. The descent over the southern slopes of the Brecon Beacons was no less exciting. After a change of train at Pontsticill, Merthyr would be reached by 2.33 p.m. Here, in the depth of industrial south Wales, there was a delay of one hour before the Taff Vale train at 3.35 p.m.

A double-headed goods train at Talybont, hauled by Nos 3676 and 4690 preparing to attack the stiffening gradient towards Torpantau; 29 August 1963.   *B.J. Ashworth*

The ascent of the Brecon Beacons at Pentir Rhiw (*sic*); 12 June 1962.

H.B. Priestley

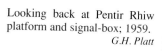

Looking back at Pentir Rhiw platform and signal-box; 1959.
G.H. Platt

Torpantau station looking north, 2 November 1962.
B.J. Ashworth

Dolygaer station, facing towards Merthyr; 1950s.
GBJ Coll.

This long interchange caused the clerk to look at the possibility of staying on the Brecon & Merthyr train at Pontsticill, travelling as far as Bargoed, and there catching a Rhymney Railway train to Cardiff. Unfortunately, the sevice he had just been looking at terminated at Pant, a short distance down the line on the outskirts of Dowlais, and the next B & M train through towards Newport would entail a further hour waiting at Talyllyn Junction. This did not appear to be worth doing.

Pontsticill Junction looking back towards Torpantau, from a train bound for Newport; 1950s. The line from Merthyr came in on the left.
R.E. Toop

The view south from the platform at Pontsticill with, on the left, the line ascending to Pant and Dowlais, and, on the right, the line descending towards Merthyr; 1954.
G.H. Platt

The interior of Pontypridd (Graig) station looking south towards Barry, *ca.* 1921. The capacity of the station appears to have exceeded the demands of the modest passenger traffic.   *E.T. Miller*

The exterior of the Barry Railway's station at Pontypridd (Graig) at the beginning of the twentieth century.
DD Coll.

Reverting to the Taff Vale train from Merthyr, at Pontypridd there was an option of changing for a Barry train rather than going all the way down to Cardiff. The train reached Pontypridd at 4.13 p.m., and a Barry train left for Barry from the Barry Railway station at 6.33 p.m. leaving a generous amount of time to change stations. It terminated at Barry Town at 7.11 p.m., in good time to catch the last train of the day to Barry Island at 7.41 p.m., arriving at 7.45 p.m. This involved 14 trains altogether, operated by six different railway companies.

Barry Island station exterior in 1959 and little changed between 1900 and 2000.   *G.H. Platt*

However, the alternative of going via Cardiff looked more attractive as it saved the two hours lost at Pontypridd. Arrival at Cardiff GW at 4.53 p.m. enabled connection to be made at nearby Riverside with the Barry Railway 5.10 p.m.

departure for Barry Island and arrival at 5.40 p.m. This route therefore achieved an earlier arrival at the destination, and required one less change of train. He accordingly wrote it out for the passenger:

SCENIC ROUTE

7.40 a.m.	dep. Amlwch	LNWR
8.35 a.m.	arr. Gaerwen	LNWR
8.38 a.m.	dep. Gaerwen	LNWR
9.51 a.m.	arr. Llandudno Junction	LNWR
11.55 a.m.	dep. Llandudno Junction	LNWR
1.10 p.m.	arr. Blaenau Ffestiniog	LNWR
2.30 p.m.	dep. Blaenau Ffestiniog	GWR
3.35 p.m.	arr. Bala	GWR
4.05 p.m.	dep. Bala	GWR
4.15 p.m.	dep. Bala Jc.	GWR
5.20 p.m.	arr. Barmouth Junction	Cambrian
6.05 p.m.	dep. Barmouth Junction	Cambrian
8.06 p.m.	arr. Moat Lane Junction	Cambrian
8.25 p.m.	dep. Moat Lane Junction	Cambrian
8.45 p.m.	arr. Llanidloes.	Cambrian
10.30 a.m.	dep. Llanidloes	Cambrian
1.21 p.m.	arr. Talyllyn Junction	Cambrian
1.35 p.m.	dep. Talyllyn Junction	Brecon & Merthyr
2.11 p.m.	arr. Pontsticill	Brecon & Merthyr
2.13 p.m.	dep. Pontsticill	Brecon & Merthyr
2.33 p.m.	arr. Merthyr	Brecon & Merthyr
3.35 p.m.	dep. Merthyr	Taff Vale
4.53 p.m.	arr. Cardiff General	Taff Vale
5.10 p.m.	dep. Cardiff Riverside	Barry
5.40 p.m.	arr. Barry Island	Barry

He was disappointed that he could not do better, especially in the LNWR area and, as he looked again at the map, it occurred to him that greater use of trunk lines rather than branch lines, however picturesque, might offer some savings in time. If, for example, the passenger remained on the 8.38 a.m. from Gaerwen all the way to Rhyl, he would arrive there at 10.23 a.m. in time to catch the 10.55 a.m. to Denbigh. Arrival at Denbigh at 11.31 a.m. would enable transfer to the 11.40 a.m. Corwen train and

arrival on the GWR's Ruabon to Dolgellau line at Corwen at 12.31 p.m. So far so good, and definitely better than the route through Blaenau Ffestiniog, as at this time the passenger would just be settling down to his lunch at Blaenau. But, sadly, the GWR had no train westbound from Corwen between 10.30 a.m. and 3.53 p.m. and the latter was precisely the train with which he had already planned to connect, down the line at Bala Junction.

A LNWR train heading north from Denbigh, probably 1923.
W.G. Rear Coll.

Llanrhaeadr station, looking south towards Ruthin and Corwen, *ca.* 1910.
GBJ Coll.

The booking-clerk still had a feeling that provided he could persuade the passenger to travel through England, it might be possible to achieve the whole of the journey from Amlwch to Barry Island in a single day. He therefore decided to examine the possibilities opened up by staying on the 8.38 a.m. from Gaerwen as far as Chester. This major interchange was reached at 11.12 a.m., and there was a convenient connection with the 11.22 a.m. LNWR train to Shrewsbury, one of the few not requiring a change at Whitchurch. At Shrewsbury it would be possible to make a connection with the North and West and South Wales Express which arrived from Manchester and Crewe at 12.26 p.m. and departed for Hereford at 12.33 p.m., arriving at 1.41 p.m. It left at 1.47 p.m. and ran non-stop to Pontypool Road where it split, the leading portion heading for Bristol at 2.43 p.m., and the Newport and Cardiff portion leaving at 2.48 p.m. and reaching Cardiff GWR station at 3.23 p.m. From there the 3.42 p.m. Barry Railway train would reach Barry Island at 4.12 p.m. The booking-clerk decided to recommend this journey, involving only five trains and three railway companies. It would also ensure maximum use of the LNWR, diluted only by the unavoidable use of the Barry.

The 10.15 a.m. train from Chester to Whitchurch, hauled by one of the former LNWR 2-cylinder simple 2-4-0s; 10 August 1932.   *S. Reid Coll.*

QUICKEST ROUTE

7.40 a.m.	dep. Amlwch	LNWR
8.35 a.m.	arr. Gaerwen	LNWR
8.38 a.m.	dep. Gaerwen	LNWR
11.12 a.m.	arr. Chester	LNWR
11.22 a.m.	dep. Chester	LNWR
12.15 p.m.	arr. Shrewsbury	LNWR/GWR
12.33 p.m.	dep. Shrewsbury	LNWR/GWR
3.23 p.m.	arr. Cardiff General	GWR
3.42 p.m.	dep. Cardiff Riverside	Barry
4.12 p.m.	arr. Barry Island	Barry

He was tempted to examine the possibility of maximising the use of pure LNWR trains by checking on the timing of trains from Abergavenny Junction over the LNWR and Rhymney Railway to Cardiff. However, this would entail waiting at Hereford until 4.00 p.m. and arrival at Cardiff RR at 6.16 p.m., taking about twice the time of the more direct route through Pontypool Road. Arrival would, however, still be in good time to catch the last train to Barry Island.

He was frustrated to find that there was only one purely LNWR train a day from Shrewsbury to Abergavenny Junction on which GW tickets were not valid. This would have reduced the use of the joint GW/LNW service south of Shrewsbury operated by the GWR, but it left Shrewsbury at the unattractive time of 3.30 a.m.

He was about to put all this together in a neat folder when another thought occurred to him. He was tempted to ignore it as it involved using the GWR route between Chester and

An LNWR cross-country express leaving Shrewsbury in the direction of Hereford and Abergavenny with a 'Jumbo' piloting a 'Dreadnought'; undated. *F. Moore/S. Reid Coll.*

A GWR express hauled by a 'Duke' approaches Shrewsbury at the same location, probably in the 1930s.
Rev. A.W.V. Mace

Shrewsbury. This was one of the few cases in Britain where there was direct competition between the GWR and the LNWR. It had other disadvantages, such as a change of train at Gobowen and at Oswestry, but thereafter it ran through the centre of Wales. It was, however, dependent on reaching the last train from Merthyr to Cardiff. This was a Rhymney train operating over the GW/Rhymney joint line by way of Quakers Yard. It was due to leave Merthyr at 8.00 p.m. and would at least enable him to get as far as Barry Town. But to reach Merthyr in time for the connection he would need to be at Talyllyn Junction in time for the 5.10 p.m. B & M train from Brecon due at 5.30 p.m. He was pleased to find there was a train arriving at Talyllyn Junction from Moat Lane Junction at 5.23 p.m., having left there at 3.10 p.m. But at this point his heart sank as the only

connection from Oswestry arrived at Moat Lane Junction at 12.24 p.m., having left Oswestry at 10.57 a.m. There was no hope of reaching Oswestry in time as the earliest he could get to Chester was on the LNWR train at 11.22 a.m. To pursue this route any further was going to involve both breaking the journey and crossing the border, so he decided it could reasonably be ignored after all.

A hundred years later, although the track is still in place, Amlwch no longer has a train service; Holyhead is now the northernmost destination in Wales while Barry Island remains the southernmost. It is now possible to make the journey in five hours with only one change of train, in Cardiff. It is no longer possible to avoid slipping into England, between Saltney and Wrexham and between Chirk and Abergavenny, but the service appears to have a future.

The recently restored LMS barrier at Llandudno; October 1999.   *DD*

APPENDIX I

The following assumptions of train capacity have been made:

LONG DISTANCE

Two brake thirds with three eight-seater compartments each	48
Four seconds or thirds with seven compartments each	224
One first with six compartments seating six each	36
Two first/third composites seating 36 each	72
Add balance	20
	say 400

GENERAL

Two six-wheelers with five third class compartments, each with 10 seats	100
Two brake/thirds	60
Third/ first composite with 20 thirds and 18 firsts	38
	say 200

LOCAL

Two or three four- or six-wheelers	say 100

LINE	MILES RUN	TRAINS UP & DOWN	SEATS PER TRAIN	DAY SEAT MILES 000's
LNWR				
Holyhead – Chester	84	20	400	672
Afon Wen – Bangor	27	8	200	43
Blaenau Ffestiniog – Llandudno	31	14	200	87
Llandudno – Chester	48	8	200	77
Caernarfon – Bangor	8	10	200	16
Gaerwen – Amlwch	17	12	100	20
Mold – Brymbo	8	8	100	6
Denbigh – Rhyl	10	16	200	32
Denbigh – Corwen	18	8	100	14
Denbigh – Rhuthin	8	6	100	5
Denbigh – Chester	20	16	200	64
Swansea – Knighton	90	10	200	180
Newport – Nantybwch	20	8	200	32
Merthyr – Abergavenny	25	12	200	60
Brynmawr – Ebbw Vale	3	12	100	4
				say 1,312
GWR				
Wrexham – Brymbo	5	10	100	5
Ruabon – Dolgellau	45	10	200	90
Blaenau Ffestiniog – Bala	25	10	200	50
Pontypool Road – Neath	41	10	200	82
Pontypool Road – Newport	10	34	200	68
Abergavenny – Pontypool Road	11	22	200	48

Brynmawr – Pontypool Road	9	10	100	9
Newport – Blaenavon	13	24	100	31
Newport – Nantyglo	14	18	100	25
Aberbeeg – Ebbw Vale	6	20	100	12
New Milford – Severn Tunnel Junction	120	8	400	384
Cardiff – Severn Tunnel Junction	20	20	400	160
Carmarthen – Swansea	32	8	200	51
Swansea – Cardiff	47	12	400	226
Carmarthen – Newcastle Emlyn	25	8	100	20
Whitland – Cardigan	27	8	100	22
Whitland – Pembroke Dock	27	12	200	65
Llanelly – Llandovery	31	8	200	50
Llanelly – Llandeilo	19	6	200	23
Bridgend – Abergwynfi	13	10	100	13
Bridgend – Nantymoel	10	10	200	20
Tondu – Porthcawl	9	8	200	14
Pyle – Porthcawl	3	14	200	8
				say 1,476

MIDLAND

Hay – Brecon	17	8	200	27
Brecon – Swansea	41	4	200	33
Swansea – Brynamman	19	10	200	38
				say 98

ALEXANDRA DOCKS

Pontypridd – Newport	15	8	100	12

MANCHESTER & MILFORD

Pencader – Aberystwyth	42	6	100	25

BARRY

Cardiff – Barry Island	9	50	200	90
Bridgend – Barry	20	10	100	20
Barry – Porth	20	6	100	12
Cardiff – Pontypridd	15	18	100	27
				say 149

WREXHAM, MOLD & CONNAHS QUAY

	13	20	100	say 26

TAFF VALE RAILWAY

Merthyr – Cardiff	24	20	200	96
Treherbert – Cardiff	23	20	200	92
Maerdy – Pontypridd	9	20	200	36
Pontypridd – Aberthaw	15	12	100	18
Cardiff – Cadoxton	6	16	200	19
Cardiff – Penarth	4	30	200	24
Aberdare – Abercynon	7	18	100	13
				say 298

BRECON & MERTHYR

Brecon – Newport	46	6	200	56
Pontsticill – Merthyr	5	12	100	6
Pant – Dowlais	2	8	100	2
Brecon – Pant	19	4	100	8
Rhymney – Newport	22	6	100	13
				say 85

CAMBRIAN

Moat Lane – Brecon	60	8	200	96
Builth Road – Brecon	28	4	100	11
Welshpool – Machynlleth	40	12	200	96
Machynlleth – Aberystwyth	20	12	200	48
Machynlleth – Pwllheli	57	12	200	137
				say 388

RHYMNEY

Rhymney Bridge – Cardiff	25	16	200	80
Cardiff – Merthyr	24	10	200	48
Cardiff – Senghennydd	10	10	200	20
Ystrad Mynach – Cardiff	8	8	200	13
Llancaiach – Dowlais	5	10	100	5
				say 166

PORT TALBOT RAILWAY

Port Talbot – Pontycymmer	16	10	200	32
TOTAL				say 4,067

NOTE: The sum of passenger train miles for the Welsh railways above is just over 6,000. This bears comparison with the 1903 figure of 8,000 derived from the table in Chapter 3. Allowance has to be made for an uncertain number of excursion trains not included in the timetables and for the growth in travel over four years.

APPENDIX II

PRINCIPAL TRAINS FOR THE YEAR 1999

It has been assumed that seating capacity is:

HST	480
'Pacer' '143'	122
'142'	105
'Sprinter' '150'	149
'153'	70
'156'	160
'158'	138
DMU.	130
Mk II 2nd	64
Mk II 1st	42

	PASS. TRAIN MILES	SEATS PER TRAIN		DAY SEAT MILES 000's
Valleys	4,394	average	120	527
West Wales / Cardiff	1,942	HST	480	932
	5,414	158	138	747
	616	average	120	74
Cardiff / Severn Tunnel Jc. & Newport	968	HST	480	465
	2,712	158	138	374
Newport / Abergavenny	1,040	158	138	144
Swansea / Knighton	712	153	70	50
Aberystwyth / Welshpool	1,200	158	138	166
Pwllheli / Machynlleth.	912	average	150	137
Holyhead / Llandudno / Shotton	760	HST	480	365
	1,264	158	138	174
	2,032	MK II	300	610
Llandudno / Blaenau Ffestiniog	434	DMU	130	56
Chirk / Chester	420	158	138	58
Wrexham / Shotton	336	143	122	41
TOTAL				say 4,920

FOR COMPARISON, THE 1999 CAPACITY OFFERED BETWEEN LONDON AND SOUTHEND

FENHURCH ST - CENTRAL	7,144	average say 400	2,857
LIVERPOOL ST - VICTORIA	5,248	average say 400	2,099
TOTAL			
			4,956

BIBLIOGRAPHY AND SOURCES

Most of the primary material is derived from the files in the Public Record Office and contemporary newspapers. The following have also been consulted and offer opportunities for further reading:

All England Law Reports.

Barry, D.S.M. *The Regional History of the Railways of South Wales.* David & Charles, 1980

Baughan, P.E. *Regional History of the Railways of Mid- and North Wales.* David & Charles, 1980

Briwnant Jones, G. *Talerddig in GW Days.* Gomer, 1999

Briwnant Jones, G. & Dunstone, D. *The Vale of Neath Line,* 2nd ed. Gomer, 1999

Briwnant Jones, G. & Dunstone, D. *The Origins of the LMS in South Wales.* Gomer, 1999.

Butt, R.V.J. *The Directory of Railway Stations.* PSL, 1995

Chapman, C. *The Vale of Glamorgan Railway.* Oakwood, 1998

Dyos, H.J. & Aldcroft, D.H. *British Transport, An Economic Survey from the 17th century to the 20th.* Penguin, 1974

Elwyn Jones, G. *Modern Wales.* Cambridge University Press, 1984

Ellis, C. Hamilton, *Railway Carriages in the British Isles 1830-1914.* Allen & Unwin, 1965

Ellis, C. Hamilton, *British Railway History,* 2 vols. Allen & Unwin, 1954

Great Britain, Passenger Railway Timetable. Winter 1998/9.

Gale, J. *The Maenclochog Railway.* John Gale, 1992

Jackson, G.G. *British Locomotives.* Sampson Low, ca.1930

Jenkinson, D. *History of British Railway Carriages.* Pendragon, 1996

Jones, A. *Welsh Chapels.* Sutton, 1996

Journal of Transport History, vol. 3. David & Charles, 1971

Morris, J.P. *The North Pembroke & Fishguard Railway.* Oakwood, 1969

Morton, H.V. *In Search of Wales.* Methuen, 1947

Norman Smith, D. *The Railway and its Passengers.* David & Charles, 1988

Parry Jones, D. *Welsh Country Up-bringing.* Batsford, 1932

Pollins, H. *Britain's Railways, An Industrial History.* David & Charles, 1971

Simmons, J. *The Victorian Railway.* Thames & Hudson, 1991

Simmons, J. *Railways of Britain.* Routledge & Kegan Paul, 1961

Simmons, J. *The Railway in Town and Country.* David & Charles, 1956

Simmons, J. *The Railway in England & Wales.* Leicester Univ., 1988

Tuplin, W. A. *North Western Steam.* Allen & Unwin, 1963

Tuplin, W. A. *Great Western Steam.* Allen & Unwin, 1958

Tuplin, W. A. *Great Western Saints & Sinners.* Allen & Unwin, 1971

Tuplin, W. A. *Midland Steam.* David & Charles, 1973

Turnock, D. *A Historical Geography of the Railways of Great Britain & Ireland.* Ashgate, 1998

Turnock, D. *Railways in the British isles: Landscape, Land Use, and Society.* David & Charles, 1982

Welsh Office. *Digest of Welsh Statistics.* 1997

Welsh Office. *Welsh Transport Statistics.* 1998

Williams, John. *Digest of Welsh Historical Statistics.* Welsh Office

Wren, W.J. *The Tanat Valley Light Railway.* Oakwood, 1979

INDEX